THE PROTECTORS

THE PROTECTORS

*Harry J. Anslinger
and the Federal Bureau of Narcotics,
1930–1962*

John C. McWilliams

DELAWARE
Newark: University of Delaware Press
London and Toronto: Associated University Presses

Associated University Presses
440 Forsgate Drive
Cranbury, NJ 08512

Associated University Presses
25 Sicilian Avenue
London WC1A 2QH, England

Associated University Presses
P.O. Box 488, Port Credit
Mississauga, Ontario
Canada L5G 4M2

The paper used in this publication meets the requirements
of the American National Standard for Permanence of Paper
for Printed Library Materials Z39.48-1984.

Library of Congress Cataloging-in-Publication Data

McWilliams, John C., 1949–
    The protectors : Harry J. Anslinger and the Federal
Bureau of Narcotics, 1930–1962.

    Bibliography : p.
    Includes index.
    1. Anslinger, Harry Jacob, 1892– . 2. United
States. Bureau of Narcotics—Officials and employees—
Biography. 3. United States. Bureau of Narcotics—
History. 4. Narcotics, Control of—United States—
Biography. 5. Narcotics, Control of—United States—
History—20th century. I. Title.
HV5805.A57M35 1990   353.0076'5'0924[B]   88-40328
ISBN 0-87413-352-1 (alk. paper)

PRINTED IN THE UNITED STATES OF AMERICA

For My Wife

Polly D. K. McWilliams

Contents

Preface

The successful completion of this story, which originated as a dissertation, was made possible by the encouragement, guidance, and advice of several individuals whose contributions facilitated a better finished product.

I shall never forget a Monday night after a seminar in October 1982, when Dan Katkin first suggested federal drug enforcement as a topic worthy of serious, scholarly study. Although I had little more than a passing interest in narcotics-related issues at the time, I quickly became intrigued with the life of Harry J. Anslinger.

It is my view that the life of Commissioner Anslinger has been misinterpreted. Too few scholars and journalists have bothered to examine this man's life beyond the surface, satisfying themselves that Anslinger and the Federal Bureau of Narcotics were regressive and lacked innovative approaches to solving the nation's narcotics problems. Anslinger was not an anachronism in federal law enforcement in the manner of J. Edgar Hoover, as described by Richard Gid Powers. On the contrary, the commissioner and several of his agents made important contributions that have been largely ignored. It is my intention to portray Anslinger and the FBN in a revisionist light, believing that too much of his career has been left in the shadows.

In this book I have tried to shed new light on the activities of Anslinger and the Federal Bureau of Narcotics. Much has been written about his drug enforcement policies, but of the numerous scholars and journalists who researched his career, none has paid serious attention to either Anslinger's peripheral interests or to his extraordinarily versatile agents. Consequently, this book is intended to provide a more accurate and comprehensive examination of a small and relatively obscure law enforcement agency that has been frequently overlooked.

The best source of primary material on Anslinger, covering his youth and pre-FBN drug enforcement activities as well as his public career, is a collection of thirteen boxes of papers he donated to Pattee Library at Pennsylvania State University. (He earned a two-year degree there in 1915.) At least five people have examined these papers for the purpose of writing their own books. Their interest likely was on drug policies, but it is difficult to comprehend how they could have missed or ignored the numerous hints Anslinger left in these hundreds of papers and the three books he co-authored. These sources contain obvious clues that he was involved in much more than simply the strict enforcement of anti-marijuana laws, which has been the common perception. I've perused the collection on two different occasions, three years apart, and it almost seems as though he deliberately left behind a mystery.

For additional insight into his unofficial life, I interviewed several former agents who worked for him or knew him personally. All but one were extremely cooperative and willing to contribute to my research. Only Henry L. Giordano, Commissioner from 1962 to 1968, refused to discuss his activities, abruptly terminating our interview when I asked about the Marijuana Tax Act, a subject I thought rather innocuous. Otherwise I came to respect the many agents I talked with for their professionalism and integrity. Though we sometimes encountered philosophical differences, I never sensed that they were responding out of a defensive or confrontational attitude. In the course of my research I had the good fortune to have talked with several agents who enhanced this study with first-hand accounts of FBN activities over the past fifty years. George Belk, Howard Chappell, John Cusack, Mike Picini, Tom Tripodi, and Garland Williams made contributions in varying degrees that enabled me to produce more accurate research. I thank them for their cooperation.

Any project of this scope is as much the sum result of many contributions as opposed to an individual effort. At Penn State I own a debt of gratitude to Professors Alan A. Block, Ira V. Brown, and Philip Jenkins, whose efforts helped smooth many rough edges. The staff of Pattee Library, particularly in the Government Documents section, deserves special recognition for their proficiency and patience with so many questions.

For Anslinger's personal life I interviewed several of his friends and acquaintances in the Altoona/Hollidaysburg area, including his attorney and social companion (she has requested anonymity), who spent a great deal of time with Anslinger after his wife died in 1962. Their recollections of Anslinger provided me with a very different perspective and convinced me that there was a sharp contrast between the public Anslinger who mixed with important Washington figures and the private citizen who derived much pleasure from the two-block walk to pick up his mail at the Hollidaysburg post office and a stag night with old friends at the Blair Country Club.

I also owe many thanks to other support personnel. In Cathy Thompson I was blessed with the most efficient and competent "word processor" imaginable. Glen Cooper and John Wilder, agents in charge of the Bangkok and Washington, D.C., offices respectively, were especially encouraging. Maury Devine is one of the most congenial and helpful people I encountered during this project. Len "Rip" Rzepczynski quite literally "opened the door" and put me in touch with the "real" people in drug enforcement; my "network" expands continually because of his early support. I am tremendously indebted to Rebecca Carroll whose contributions to this book were expert and invaluable.

Above all, I thank my wife, Polly, who squeezed time from her demanding Advanced Placement English classes to painstakingly read each draft of this thesis several times. The most important supporter, she is to be commended for being dutifully tolerant of my constant preoccupation with Commissioner Anslinger and anything associated with the FBN.

Shannon made the down periods tolerable and always provided welcomed, unconditional support.

Introduction

Since the beginning of this century, the adoption and enforcement of federal drug legislation has been both controversial and inconsistent. Never has a widely supported narcotics-related law been passed by Congress. From the adoption of the Harrison Act (a revenue measure to help control the international opium trade) in 1914 to the early 1980s, drug legislation has been subjected to numerous modifications, ranging from conservative to radical.

One individual who has attracted attention for his influence and direction in the formulation of narcotics laws is Harry J. Anslinger (1892–1975). Appointed commissioner of the Federal Bureau of Narcotics at its inception in 1930, Anslinger survived five presidential administrations while guiding the bureau though the Depression, a global conflict, and the Cold War era. He was still at the helm halfway through the Kennedy presidency as the nation entered the turbulent drug culture in the 1960s.

Though the Harrison Act was the first federal law enacted as a measure regulating narcotics, Harry Anslinger would become a controversial subject of notoriety and derision in relation to the adoption of international treaties and subsequent legislation—in particular the Marijuana Tax Act of 1937. Respected by those who believed that the solution to the drug abuse problem lay in stringent inflexible laws and lengthy prison sentences, and scorned by others who saw the "narcotics czars'" policies as insensitive, repressive, and self-serving; Harry Anslinger nevertheless managed to conduct bureau affairs uninterrupted for more than three decades.

Anslinger's tenure as narcotics commissioner for thirty-two years is virtually unparalleled—only the FBI's J. Edgar Hoover could boast of a longer reign—and this achievement alone merits a full-scale investigation of his career. Yet his longevity as an administrator becomes even more significant when one considers the intricacies of Washington politics. Institutional changes, social conditions, and philosophical shifts are commonplace. But Anslinger survived at the head of a small agency, whose average number of field agents from 1930 to 1962 was only 242, bringing stability and organization to a bureau that previously had been handicapped by ineffective and incompetent leadership. As vulnerable as he was to the whims of congressional and party politics, Anslinger almost always managed to obtain a budget increase over the preceding year, which he accomplished largely by cultivating congressmen who were members of appropriations committees.[1] Even during the worst years of the Depression, the bureau suffered no severe appropriations cuts, losing no more than other federal agencies between 1931 and 1939, as stipulated in the Economy Program that mandated drastic cuts for government personnel.

Narcotics legislation in the United States has also at various times come under attack from diverse sources such as the American Medical Association, the American Bar Association, sociologists, legal scholars, criminologists, politicians, psychiatrists, and scores of "revisionist" observers in the 1960s and 1970s. Harry Anslinger has been the focus of much of the criticism. Because he had such an impact on the bureau and personally molded antinarcotics policies, he commonly has been associated with the present-day laws that govern the prohibition of certain controlled substances.

In its annual report for 1932, *Traffic in Opium and Other Dangerous Drugs,* Federal Bureau of Narcotics officials considered marijuana to be nothing more than an inconsequential nuisance.[2] Curiously, and for reasons still open to vigorous debate, by 1935 Anslinger regarded marijuana as a menace to society and declared an all-out war against this "killer weed." By the end of the decade he had succeeded in convincing most states to adopt the Uniform Narcotics Act to control intrastate traffic in the drug. He was the major lobbyist for the adoption of the federal Marijuana Tax Act of 1937 that placed marijuana in substantially the same category as other contraband narcotic drugs whose effects were far more debilitating. On the surface, the Tax Act appeared merely to be another revenue-raising piece of legislation, since it imposed only a token transfer tax of one dollar an ounce for registered buyers, sellers, importers, growers, physicians, and veterinarians who paid a yearly tax. The concept of a "prohibitive" tax was not new, but the act was monumentally significant in that it was a prelude to the adoption of Draconian anti-marijuana laws over the next thirty years.

Anslinger's role in the Marijuana Tax Act (and later his support for the Boggs Act in 1951 and the Narcotic Control Act in 1956 that dramatically stiffened the penalties for drug offenses) has attracted numerous studies of the development of federal narcotics legislation. Sociologists; legal scholars; free-lance journalists; and, to a lesser extent, historians have analyzed the "Anslinger phenomenon" from diverse perspectives. The one characteristic these authors have in common, regardless of their particular disciplines, is that they have limited themselves to focusing their attention on Anslinger's narcotics policies and have produced research connected with their fields of specialization. Other aspects of his career, however, were equally controversial, though not directly related to narcotics enforcement.

For example, indisputable evidence links Anslinger and several of his senior agents to the intelligence community in the formative years of the Office of Strategic Services (OSS) during World War II and into the 1950s after the OSS was re-born as the Central Intelligence Agency in 1947. Anslinger had a long-standing relationship with General "Wild Bill" Donovan that dated back to the 1920s; when President Franklin Roosevelt appointed Donavan director of the OSS, the general continued to rely on Anslinger as a source for personnel trained and experienced in investigative work. Moreover, Anslinger's wife was connected to the Andrew Mellon family, of which some members served in the OSS during World War II, including Mellon's son-in-law David Bruce, the well-known Chief of Station (COS) in London.[3] At least three of the FBN's top agents were on loan to the OSS in the 1940s and continued to perform classified chores for the CIA, yet they remain relatively unknown and obscure. They were involved for years in international activities with the full knowledge and approval of their boss. Consequently, the relationship among the FBN, the CIA, and the OSS is critical in ascertaining the role of Harry Anslinger as intelligence gatherer. Unfortunately, the details of those projects may remain buried in the files of their respective agencies; they are not immediately available, but the existing evidence is worth investigating.

Anslinger also was among the first to recognize the existence of the Mafia and organized drug rings in the United States. Convinced that there was a secret Sicilian society, he promulgated a scare about the Mafia in much the same way J. Edgar Hoover convinced many Americans that communists were the most serious threat to American security. While Hoover steadfastly refused to recognize the existence of the mafia until the early 1960s, Anslinger, through the enforcement of narcotics laws, fiercely fought to wipe out organized gangsters as early as 1931. The extent of his involvement in the battle against underworld figures is another phase of his career that has usually been overlooked. Under Anslinger's direction, the Federal Narcotics Bureau played a key role in the deportation of Lucky Luciano (1946), provided testimony at the Kefauver hearings on organized crime for which the commissioner supplied a secret list of eight hundred underworld figures (1951), and was directly involved in the Apalachin raid (1957). Despite the demands put upon him as the nation's number one narcotics enforcer, Anslinger exhibited a curious fascination—obsession would not be too extreme—with the history, organization, and personalities associated with the Mafia.[4]

Several times his ascent up the bureaucratic ladder has been recounted, but for all the attention given to Anslinger's narcotics policies, no one has explained in detail how this man advanced from the Consular Service in the State Department to the commissioner of the Federal Bureau of Narcotics. His diverse background requires a more in-depth examination as well as his qualifications for this newly created position. Anslinger's rather unique background would enable him to extend his tentacles into many corners of political Washington that touched on issues not directly related to the responsibilities of the Federal Narcotics Bureau.

The commissioner, it seems, was as proficient in counterespionage activities as he was in implementing drug policies. This little known facet of his career further justifies a comprehensive study of his tenure in the Federal Bureau of Narcotics. An awareness of Anslinger's "secret side" will help explain his role in clandestine activities and his sometimes close relationship with the intelligence community.

It is also important to identify his political allies and investigate how they helped secure his appointment. Anslinger was a Republican appointed by a Republican president (Hoover) in 1930. That he survived the Roosevelt landslide in 1932 and managed to hold on for the next thirty years is a minor phenomenon. Even more significant was how he prevented his bureau from being swallowed up by several attempts to reorganize federal investigative agencies within the enforcement branch of the Treasury Department.

Also significant is Anslinger's role in the crusade against marijuana in the 1930s. That the commissioner vigorously supported the Marijuana Tax Act in 1937 is fairly well known, but the reason is not so clear. Sociologist Howard Becker argues that Anslinger manufactured a marijuana epidemic in the media for the purpose of creating a law—and concomitantly a new class of criminals—that would justify the existence of the bureau and enhance the prestige of Anslinger as its commissioner. Becker suggests that Anslinger was a "moral entrepeneur," but that does not fully account for why Anslinger chose to launch his campaign in 1935.[5]

The drug problem and legislative attempts to alleviate it are not unprecedented. In his analysis of the American temperance movement, Joseph Gusfield comments that "the significance of Prohibition is in the fact that it happened."[6] Albeit terse, it is also descriptive of the Marijuana Tax Act of 1937 as the Federal government's culminating action in the increasingly heated, ten-year controversy associated with the drug prior to its enactment. The fact that it happened was proof (for the second time in two decades) that the government was subject to the influences of temperance. Prior to the Harrison Act, an opium addict could legally be administered a physician's dosage of narcotics to alleviate his misery. By the early 1920s, however, because legislation had created such a negative effect on the people's image of addicts, they were no longer perceived as helpless, downtrodden souls, but as despicable, evil deviants who were no good to themselves or to the society in which they lived.

The Marijuana Tax Act accomplished essentially the same thing only with a different twist. Instead of regulating opium, cannabis (which was omitted from the Harrison Act) was the targeted substance. In 1914 people already dependent on narcotics—addicts—were subjected to criminal sanctions; in 1937 users again were the primary concern. As with the Harrison Act, a law was passed in the guise of a revenue measure to bring a "new" drug under federal control. Instantaneously, an already large class of criminals was expanded, and with it the need for enforcement.

The central character in this scenario was Harry Anslinger. At once admired and besmirched, loved and loathed, Anslinger and his actions have inspired numerous interpretations and analyses of the role and the responsibility he assumed as the formulator and moving force behind the Tax Act of 1937 and the excessively austere anti-drug laws that followed during the next quarter century. Generally those who championed the cause, as Anslinger did, jealously defended their actions and ingenuously pleaded for other concerned citizens to heed the potential dangers manifested in marijuana—the "killer weed."

Marijuana was not the only drug Anslinger fought. He frequently referred to opium and its derivatives as he garnered support for a more generalized war on drugs. To do this, Anslinger appealed to many organizations whose members were predominantly white Protestants, sharing a basically conservative ideology and a tough "law and order" attitude. Sensing that middle-class Americans would willingly help in the battle to preserve society and civilization as they knew it, Anslinger was not above mixing religion with politics. Often he exhorted audiences with a metaphoric reminder that even narcotics were in the domain of the Almighty: "Opium is the finger of God. It smites and it heals. It is the gift of heaven when it stills the agonies of death caused by cancer."[7] On occasion, Anslinger resembled more a combination of William Jennings Bryan and Jerry Falwell than a narcotics bureaucrat.

Actually, Anslinger's crusade against marijuana contained more than a hint of present-day evangelism. He engendered passionate enthusiasm among his backers and a large measure of skepticism and derision among his many ardent opponents. Immovable in his belief that he was on the side of right and in a spirit of militant resistance to the opposition, he marshaled his narcotics agents as an army to disseminate the bureau's policies to millions of loyal, God-fearing Americans.

Guided by what he believed were eternal truths rather than time-bound opinions, Anslinger embarked on a mission in the mid-1930s that required him to delicately appease the concerns of his following while reassuring

supporters in pharmaceutical firms, the print media, and state level enforcement agencies that he was unwavering in the battle against the evils
of marijuana. At the same time he also had to appear congenial and
unmenacing to congressional leaders on whom he depended for needed
financial and political support.

Anslinger's real contribution can be seen in the evolution of federal
narcotics legislation, and more particularly in an understanding of the
Marijuana Tax Act. Over a half century after its passage in 1937, no
tactic yet exists to cope with marijuana smoking, indeed with drug use in
general. In August 1985, this again became clear when Attorney General
Edwin Meese sounded an all too familiar refrain:

> All the enforcement efforts that we can try in this country, all the police
> agencies both in this nation and world wide will never be able to stem
> the supply of drugs in this nation until we have first decreased the
> number of users and have decreased the demand for these drugs.
>
> Already, this week alone, we have confiscated and eradicated over
> 200,000 marijuana plants, . . . confiscated numerous weapons, taken
> over greenhouses where marijuana was being grown, [and] taken apart
> booby traps that were used to prevent the law enforcement agents from
> getting into the fields.
>
> Although many states have been involved for some time in efforts to
> destroy cultivated marijuana cannabis plants, approximately 2,200
> federal, state and local law enforcement officers joined in a coordinated
> campaign to uproot the plants beginning Monday.[8]

Fifty years of organized campaigns against the use of marijuana failed to
produce any significant results. What this effort has shown, however, is
that the problem cannot be solved simply through tough anti-drug legislation. Though authorities have applied more than rhetoric to solving the
problem—vigorous and innovative approaches have been taken—federal
drug enforcement agents are overwhelmed in their effort to stop the
tremendous flow of narcotics through illegal trafficking. As an indication
of the Justice Department's level of frustration, the problem of combating
drug use has been viewed in military terms. Only two weeks after Attorney
General Meese announced his department's strategy, a survey revealed
that 89 percent of city officials in communities with populations of 30,000
or more strongly favored the use of the military to combat trafficking.[9]

During his long tenure, Anslinger became the architect of federal narcotics policies, his tremendous influence enabling him to construct international agreements such as the Geneva Convention in 1931 and the Single
Convention in 1961 that unified all the many agreements from previous
conventions. Equally influential was his input in domestic legislation
including the Marijuana Tax Act of 1937, the Boggs Act of 1951, and the

Narcotic Control Act of 1956. In addition, he served as the American representative to the United Nations Commission on Narcotic Drugs until 1970. For four decades Commissioner Anslinger *was* the Federal Bureau of Narcotics, and he left a legacy of tough enforcement that is admired today by agents and supervisory personnel in the reorganized Drug Enforcement Administration (DEA). Without question, Anslinger was the guiding force in drug legislation, enjoying a sphere of influence that has not yet been fully appreciated by historians or criminologists.

In Washington, Harry J. Anslinger enjoyed the support of many politicians who capitalized on the narcotics problem as a nonpartisan issue. Few elected officials could afford not to cast their votes for narcotics laws in the 1940s and 1950s as the Bureau reported that drug addiction among America's adolescents was on the rise. Democrat or Republican, they praised the bureau's effectiveness and efficiency, and deferred to Anslinger as a model public servant. Republican Congressman Gordon C. Canfield of New Jersey lauded Anslinger as "not only one of America's great administrators, but one of the finest administrators in the world."[10] The commissioner was also commended for his foresight in the late 1930s when Republican Congressman John J. Cochran of Missouri suggested that his actions merited "a medal of honor for his advanced thought that resulted in the U.S. having a supply of narcotic drugs throughout the World War II period sufficient for civilian needs, for the Armed Service, and for the needs of our Allies."[11] The "supply for sufficient civilian needs" consisted of a 300-ton stockpile. How Anslinger managed this and what effects it had on the world market are discussed in chapter 5.

Anslinger also won admirers in the upper house as Democratic Senator Estes Kefauver from Tennessee paid homage to him as "a great public official who is doing a remarkable job."[12] Kefauver, of course, had a new and vested interest in organized crime, chairing the Special Committee to Investigate Organized Crime in Interstate Commerce. No doubt Kefauver was expressing his gratitude to the commissioner for the contributions his top agents made to the committee in their capacity as investigators. In the July 1951 issue of *American Magazine,* Democratic Senator Paul H. Douglas of Illinois recommended "public praise for Commissioner Anslinger for the fine, devoted and tireless job he is performing quietly."[13]

This was typical of the adulation bestowed on Anslinger, and it was echoed by literally dozens of other politicans who, reflecting their constituents' anxieties over the evils of a resurging drug menace, were quite pleased to have their names associated with the narcotics Bureau's fight against the illicit drug traffic. As might be expected, Anslinger also drew continued praise from the more conservative magazines, pamphlets, and newspaper chains. Whether it was *The Voice* (published by The Board of Temperance, Prohibition, and Morals of the Methodist Church), *The*

Union Signal (also a temperance publication), *The National Sheriff,* or the Hearst syndicated newspapers, they were dependable and consistent in their support of bureau policies.[14]

Anslinger's prestige was felt far beyond Washington circles and nationally circulated periodicals. As a regular annual participant in international conferences since the Geneva Convention, he established a worldwide reputation as a no-nonsense administrator whose knowledge and expertise in narcotics were unmatched. Recognized by his peers as one who distinguished himself time and again with his performance and record of efficiency, Harry J. Anslinger was regarded as *the* expert in his field—the consummate law enforcement bureaucrat. When in 1952, Sir Leonard Lyall, former President of the League of Nations Opium Board, called Anslinger "the greatest living authority on the world narcotic traffic," he voiced the collective sentiments of many others.[15]

In the past two decades, however, Anslinger has been treated far less kindly by academic observers. In fact, critics of the Federal Bureau of Narcotics heavily outnumber its defenders. True, he could rely on politicians, sensational publications, and international personages for their loyalty, but they supported him. They did not defend him in the scholarly arena where his policies were subjected to critical examination and scientific challenge, especially after the 1937 passage of the Marijuana Tax Act.

Probably the classic exposition of this antagonism is Larry Sloman's quasi-biography of Anslinger, *Reefer Madness: Marijuana in America.* Sloman makes no pretense of offering the reader a balanced account of either Anslinger or the bureau. Rather, it is an account of the perceived failures, foibles, and foolishness of the commissioner.

The onslaught begins with the opening sentence of the preface: "Harry J. Anslinger becomes comprehensible only as part of a conspiracy." Other than briefly citing, "the fear that ugly troll occasioned when no one was safe smoking a joint in his own home," the "conspiracy" is never explained. On the following page, the attack continues. In a discussion centering around Anslinger, Richard Nixon, and J. Edgar Hoover; the writer of the preface, William S. Burroughs, cynically concludes that there was "not a man among them who could have pulled off a successful coup in a banana republic. They bungled and failed, right down the line." Later, Anslinger is labeled a "Neanderthal right-winger." But Sloman, as editor-in-chief of the drug-oriented *High Times* magazine, was an extremist in his opposition to anti-marijuana laws. Perhaps the most biting and insensitive passage in Sloman's discussion of Anslinger's death, "Throughout the country among the cannabis 'degenscenti,' thousands of small flames were fired up to mark the occasion."[16] The author may have been intentionally hyperbolizing, but this assessment is nevertheless faulty. Although it is possible that a few fanatics might have reveled in the passing of Harry

Anslinger, it is unlikely that "thousands" across the nation simultaneously participated in any kind of joyous ceremony, especially since the press gave his death minimal attention. His funeral was a small, private ceremony attended only by family members and a few close friends. There were no dignitaries from foreign countries, no politicians, not even official representatives from the Drug Enforcement Administration. According to Reverend John Martin, the Presbyterian minister who conducted the funeral rites, it was Anslinger's wish that there be no fanfare or publicity.[17]

Reefer Madness is a depiction of Harry Anslinger as the stereotypic dull, one-dimensional bureaucrat, lacking in initiative and direction, whose only reason for existence was to make life miserable for marijuana smokers. Anslinger did play a pivotal role in anti-marijuana legislation, and he did actively campaign for increasingly stiffer penalties, penalties that by present-day standards would be unconscionable and perhaps a constitutional violation of the "cruel and unusual punishment" clause of the Eighth Amendment. But whatever his obsession with marijuana—and this is only what Sloman focused on—Harry Anslinger came to the Federal Bureau of Narcotics in 1930 already experienced in diplomatic relations through his work in the State Department.[18] He was knowledgeable in the clandestine operations of organized smuggling rings he encountered while in the Bahamas, and he demonstrated his cunning and resourcefulness by his participation in intelligence operations in Western Europe during World War I. His ability to speak fluent Dutch, German, and French (he was also conversant in Spanish) combined with his diplomatic skills and law school training to make Anslinger well qualified for his appointment. His policies might be challenged, but not his competence.

Regardless of his position on narcotics enforcement policies, Anslinger brought with him qualifications rarely found in other Washington bureaucrats. Sloman's assessment of Anslinger as a "Neanderthal right-winger" who "bungled and failed," is blatantly unfair and without basis. His philosophy on drug enforcement might have been perceived by his critics as regressive, but the commissioner was enlightened in matters of bureaucratic survival and intelligence gathering. Unfortunately, because most of the interest in Anslinger has centered on his war on drugs, an enormous area of his professional career has been left virtually untouched.

THE PROTECTORS

1
Getting Started: From Consul to Commissioner, 1915–1930

Not much is known about Harry Anslinger's parents.[1] His father Robert was trained and worked as a barber in Switzerland. Rather than serve two years in the Swiss army, as was required of every adult male, he decided to leave Switzerland and emigrated to America.[2] Undoubtedly Robert Anslinger shared with millions of other European immigrants the dream of a better life in a new world as he and his wife Christiana landed on Ellis Island in 1881. He was more fortunate than most of his fellow passengers in that he had a ready skill he could convert into income to support his family.

Beginnings: Impressions and Imitations

For two years Robert Anslinger was employed as a barber in New York, but was unable to adapt to an urban lifestyle, and decided to venture westward, eventually settling in central Pennsylvania. He had barely established himself in the small town of Houtzdale when in 1888 he uprooted his family again. This time, though, they traveled just 30 miles southwest to Altoona, where he continued to barber in several local shops. But work was intermittent, and he found it difficult to meet the monthly expenses without the benefit of a fixed income. With a large family to support he was forced to abandon his trade and look for steadier employment. In 1892 he took a job with the Pennsylvania Railroad. The twentieth of May that year also brought the birth of a son, Harry Jacob, the eighth of Robert and Christina's nine children.

The Altoona in which Harry Anslinger grew up was a bustling, prospering town where the opportunity to work in the local industries was often more enticing to school-aged boys than was earning a high school diploma. Like many young men at that time, Harry wanted to quit school to earn money, and at the end of the eighth grade he followed his father and went to work for the railroad. Although he did not attend classes in the traditional sense, neither did he drop out of school. Beginning in the ninth grade, at the age of fourteen, he completed his course requirements as a part-time student in the morning session. In the afternoons and evenings he maintained his job with the railroad.

Although he never received a high school diploma, Anslinger enrolled at the Altoona Business College in 1909 and was privately tutored at nights during the next two years. In 1913 he requested and was granted a furlough from the Pennsylvania Railroad so he could enroll at the Pennsylvania State College where he entered a two-year associate degree program consisting of engineering and business management courses. On weekends and during vacations he continued to work for the railroad as a utility employee.[3] While in State College he indulged a passion to one day become a concert pianist and earned tuition money as a substitute piano player for silent movies in a downtown theater.

"WORKIN' ON THE 'PENNSY'"

By the time he graduated from the two-year program, he had performed in several capacities for the railroad company either routing cars in the Transportation Department, requisitioning engine parts as a master's mechanic, or constructing telephone and telegraph lines. His most important assignment, however, was within the Intelligence Department where he learned the value of collecting and analyzing information acquired by subtle techniques.

In the role of detective, he demonstrated his flair for sleuthing when he was summoned to investigate a tragic accident in which a woman was killed at a grade crossing by the "Broadway Limited." The victim's husband claimed that her death was the result of her shoe getting wedged in the track and that she made little effort to dislodge it because she could neither see nor hear the oncoming train due to a curved right-of-way. Within a month the bereaved husband filed a $50,000 suit against the Pennsylvania Railroad for negligence. After a thorough survey of the crossing site, company lawyers ruled out the possibility of foul play and prepared to settle the claim. Detective Anslinger was unconvinced that it was an open-and-shut case.

Suspicious about the accident occurring at a remote crossing intersection so infrequently used by pedestrians, Anslinger conducted his own search and discovered the victim's basket of groceries in a wooded area in close proximity to the tracks. Since the items in the basket were undisturbed—not strewn about as they would have been after colliding with a train—he immediately eliminated accidental death. On questioning the couple's neighbors, he learned that the husband and his wife had quarreled violently on the morning of her death. Once a subsequent interrogation with the husband revealed that she had threatened suicide, the trumped-up suit was dropped. Anslinger saved the railroad $50,000 and was promoted to captain of the railroad police.[4] This impressive display of perseverance and attention to details was the beginning of his ascent to the Bureau of Narcotics.[5]

Anslinger claimed that two incidents during his youth were tremendously influential in his career as narcotics commissioner. The first was a traumatic experience he had with the agony of addiction. In *The Murderers: The Story of the Narcotics Gangs,* he vividly recounted how as a twelve-year-old he visited a neighboring farmhouse and heard the screams of a woman on the second floor. Later he learned that the woman, like many others of that period who relied on the painkiller, was addicted to morphine, a drug whose dangers most medical authorities did not yet recognize. Soon her husband ran down the stairs and sent him to town to pick up a package at the drug store. Within minutes after the husband administered the drug, the woman's screams stopped and she was again at ease.[6] Harry Anslinger never forgot those screams or the anguish of the woman suffering the pains of addiction. Nor did he forget that the morphine she required was sold to a twelve-year-old boy—no questions asked. In 1906, in the absence of any federal anti-drug laws, this indiscriminate sale of narcotics was not unusual. This experience, he later observed, was an ugly memory that convinced him of the need for strict regulation and control over the use of narcotics. It also strengthened his belief that enforcement and a punitive approach to narcotics—even though "post hoc justification"—was necessary to eradicate the problem of drug addiction.

Anslinger's exposure to the kind of men he worked with on the railroad also affected his behavior as narcotics commissioner. Working his summer vacations away from Penn State on a "Pennsy" construction crew landscaping flower beds, he often came into contact with Italian immigrants. Occasionally he would overhear them, in broken English, talk of a "Black Hand."[7] Though he did not know precisely the nature of the Black Hand, he could sense from the context that it was a kind of extra-legal society brought from the old country. The Italians did not discuss it openly or in a casual manner but spoke of it in awe. They referred to it as an invisible government that effected a mutual protection for its members and enforced it with violence and brutality. Anslinger's story of the Black Hand may have been apocryphal and later exploited for political benefit, but he frequently made reference to it as the basis for his all-out war on the Mafia in the 1940s and 1950s.[8]

Despite a natural inclination to avoid any contact with this terrorist organization, he inadvertently became involved. One day while working along the track bed, he was startled by the sight of an apparently unconscious man lying in a ditch. He recognized the badly beaten man as Giovanni, one of the Italians on his work crew. Though the victim was unable to furnish any clues as to who was responsible for this horrible act,

Anslinger suspected immediately the involvement of the Black Hand or "Mano Nero" as it was known in Italy.

Giovanni, a humble, hard-working immigrant, who was the victim of an underworld shakedown, refused to be intimidated. Miraculously he survived. While Giovanni was recuperating in the hospital, Anslinger questioned him to learn the identity of his assailant. Only after Anslinger reassured Giovanni of the safety of his family did the Italian reluctantly reveal the name of "Big Mouth Sam." Anslinger sought out the extortionist and threatened to kill him if he ever harassed anyone else on the railroad.[9]

Thus, as early as 1915 the budding detective was exposed to an organized criminal syndicate. It was a conviction he held thirty-five years later when he testified before the Kefauver Senate Crime Investigating Committee that the "Black Hand" was what the Italian immigrants referred to as "Mafia" in Italy. As an impressionable young man, Anslinger heard and witnessed first-hand the nefarious activities of this secret society. Though his story about the Black Hand may well have been apocryphal, as Commissioner of Narcotics he became obsessed with fear and loathing of the Mafia and the evil it represented. Anslinger hated the Mafia, but in a sense he needed it, just as he would need other enemies throughout his career.

"WHAT DID YOU DO DURING THE WAR, HARRY?"

Anslinger's detective work on the Pennsylvania Railroad so impressed the division superintendent, G. Charles Port, that when the latter was called to Harrisburg by Governor Martin G. Brumbaugh to head the state police, he asked Anslinger to accompany him. In September 1916 Anslinger went to the state capital, where he was responsible for reorganizing a department and a field force of 2,500 personnel. Eventually he was appointed deputy fire commissioner in charge of arson investigations. He remained in Harrisburg a year until the United States entered the war in Europe to "make the world safe for democracy."[10]

At five feet, eleven inches and 190 pounds, Anslinger was a vigorous, healthy twenty-five year-old, physically in the prime of his life. His railroad experience made him a highly desirable inductee in the armed forces. Initially he applied for admission to the Officers' Training Camp program, but when he was not accepted, he volunteered as an enlisted man. Both times he was rejected because he could not pass the physical examination as a result of an eye injury he had sustained as a boy.[11] Anslinger contributed his talents in a different capacity: he served his country during wartime in the Ordnance Department where, as assistant to the Chief of Inspection of Equipment, he was in charge of recruiting civilian personnel and checking the honesty of manufacturers and other personnel. Again he had ample opportunity to exhibit initiative and tact in proving himself capable of handling intricate military transactions.

Early in 1918 he was recommended for commission as a second lieutenant in the Ordnance Reserve Corps, and he continued a rapid progression up the ranks. In May he was offered a position with the American Car & Foundry Company "at a very high salary." However, wanting to remain with the federal government, he applied for a position with the diplomatic corps in the State Department.[12] With his qualifications as an investigator and his ability to speak fluent German, no doubt learned from his parents, Anslinger was assigned as an attaché in the American Legation at The Hague where he quickly mastered Dutch as well. During his three years in Holland, he performed consular-related work and participated in behind-the-scene intelligence reporting and investigations.

Tension peaked in the latter months of 1918, particularly in Holland, a neutral country wedged between Germany and the German army in Belgium. Virtually every government—including the United States—was eager to obtain and evaluate every scrap of information possible, especially as the end of the war appeared imminent. In his capacity as an intelligence gatherer, Anslinger was required to attend social affairs, dinners, and garden parties where he mingled with nobility and heads of state who might willingly or inadvertently reveal bits of information.

When Kaiser Wilhelm II prepared to abdicate, the Netherlands granted him asylum. Anslinger was immediately ordered to Count Bentinck's castle in Amerongen where the Kaiser would live in exile. According to Anslinger, the American government did not want the Kaiser to abdicate, because "the Social Democrats will bring on revolution, strikes, and chaos."[13] It was therefore vital that this information be relayed to the right people. Because Anslinger's mission in this quiet Dutch town potentially could have influenced the course of events in the post-war era, Secretary of State Robert Lansing ordered him "not to divulge to any person by word of mouth, or in writing, either by letter or telegram, or by any other means of communication, your point of destination in Europe."[14]

As an accomplished linguist, his services to the American minister were invaluable, and he was sent on several undercover assignments. In the months preceding the armistice, Anslinger was instructed to establish personal communication with the Kaiser in order to verify Germany's plans, which had been reported from a neutral country. By assuming the identity of a harsh-speaking German, Anslinger bluffed his way past Dutch security guards and gained clearance to travel with the Kaiser's entourage without interference. Passing himself off as a member of the Dutch intelligence corps, he relayed information to one of the Kaiser's court counselors that abdication was entirely useless and unnecessary. Anslinger carried out his assignment and conveyed the message to the proper authorities, but, of course, the Kaiser did not remain on the throne. Anslinger continued to travel with the Kaiser's entourage, acting as an intermediary for the exchange of views between himself, his government, and the Kaiser's staff.[15]

CONSUL ANSLINGER

In August 1921, Anslinger was offered the position of clerk attached to the American commissioner at Berlin, who was actually stationed in Hamburg. Because of an urgent need for assistance to re-patriate American seamen, he boarded the SS *Mongolia* three weeks later for Germany.[16] There he was first exposed to international narcotics problems; Hamburg, according to Anslinger, was a worldwide distribution center for illicit drugs. He was in the German city only two years before he was reassigned to La Guaria, Venezuela, in 1923.[17]

Anslinger loved Germany and was sorry to leave the many friends and acquaintances he made in embassies throughout Europe. Germany also offered all the social and cultural amenities he required, and he felt comfortable with his work and the duties he performed as the American representative. In contrast, La Guaira at that time was a remote post with little appeal. Anslinger was even less enthusiastic about the move after he had contacted a friend in the Venezuelan embassy who reported to him that "there are nothing but the poorest of schools in La Guaira, either public or private, and only the Spanish language is used," that "streets are so narrow that most are impassible for motor cars," and that "the hotel in La Guaira is very poor and charges $40 a month per person."[18] Recently married to the former Martha Denniston, a relative of Secretary of the Treasury Andrew W. Mellon, Anslinger was discouraged by the expensive housing and particularly by the substandard educational facilities available to his wife's twelve-year-old son, Joseph.[19] He wondered what the future held for him at La Guaira and began to question the wisdom of a State Department career.

Anslinger sailed for Venezuela with few expectations, convinced that La Guaira was as bleak as he had imagined. Stories from various sources about the city being "one of the worst ports" only reaffirmed his fears. Despite the fact that it compared "favorably with any tropical country where negro blood predominates," nothing he encountered there changed his thinking. The city and its environs were as dismal as he had envisioned. He hated it and wanted out; a transfer anywhere was better than La Guaira.

If the tone of his letter to a State Department official was any indication, Anslinger complained about nearly everything in La Guaira from health and housing to heat and hurricanes. A State Department official acknowledged that the coastal city was not a desirable post and tried to placate

Anslinger by explaining that it was not always possible to assign consular personnel to the most attractive locations. He then offered encouragement and tried to be positive by telling Anslinger that he was "confident that you are too good an officer to admit bitter defeat this early after only five months at your post."[20] This was little consolation for a disgruntled consul who likened this assignment to a form of banishment.

La Guaira was a beautiful town that lay at the foot of a sheer and tropical mountain and along a cresent-shaped beach dotted with palms, mangos, and banana trees. But with a population of only 6000, it was not sufficiently enlivening to suit the young and ambitious Anslinger. Except from observations on revolutionary movements and occasional reports on pearl smuggling, Anslinger's job was uneventful, and he lamented constantly the monotony and tedious paper work of the American consulate in La Guaira. "Down here," he grumbled, "my activities are smothered as there is absolutely nothing of interest. I cannot even find a little Communist about."[21] To one of his closest friends in Hamburg he complained, "Turtles are slow but life and work here [are] slower."[22] The high cost of living, particularly on a Vice-Consul's salary, and the lack of adequate schools forced his wife and her son to take up residence in Caracas so Joseph could be tutored by a Harvard graduate. Because of the distance and traveling expenses, the Anslingers spent time together only on weekends. Anslinger may not have been overstating his discontent by complaining that "the spirit must be stronger than the flesh to endure."[23] But Anslinger did endure, and in 1926 he was finally granted his request for transfer and was sent to Nassau in the Bahamas. His stay on the small Caribbean island would prove no less influential on his career than "the morphine-addicted woman in Altoona" or the "Black Hand" incident on the Pennsylvania Railroad.

CHASING RUM-RUNNERS AND BOOTLEGGERS

The Bahamas in the 1920s were an important way station for American rum-runners who were transporting illicit supplies of liquor to American bootleggers. Native Bahamians, who were not encumbered by prohibition laws, were getting rich fast. American Treasury agents, already overwhelmed by domestic smuggling, were powerless to act against the flow of contraband liquor from the Bahamas. Brigadier General Lincoln C. Andrews, former chief of the Prohibition Bureau, complained bitterly that the problem was further aggravated by Great Britain's lackadaisical attitude and refusal to cooperate with the United States. Only after months of badgering by the American government did the British accede to demands for a conference on cooperation against smuggling.

The meeting took place during an exceptionally hot London July. Representing the United States was General Andrews and the youthful, unassuming Consul Anslinger, who told of ships that passed, not in the night but in broad daylight, loaded with choice liquors for American shores. He testified at the hearing how he had observed whiskey ships clearing Nassau for the high seas and returning empty in a few days, obviously transferring their cargo at sea or slipping into some hidden cove in the Florida Keys. Contributing to this illegal trafficking, he claimed, was the benevolent attitude of colonial officials toward the smuggling rings.

Confidently and dispassionately, Anslinger convinced British officials to accept greater responsibility and take a more vigorous role in the enforcement of Prohibition laws. Through diplomatic negotiations, the Consul won an agreement with the British that ships leaving Nassau had to specify where they were going and have in their possession on return a landing certificate to prove where they had been. The "Anslinger Accord" was effective. The Treasury Department was so impressed with Anslinger's diplomatic coup that Secretary Mellon borrowed Anslinger from the State Department to obtain similar agreements with Canada, France, and Cuba. Anslinger was assigned to the Treasury for a month. He never left.[24]

When General Andrews returned to Washington, he remembered Anslinger's extraordinary administrative abilities and took the consul with him to organize and work as chief of the newly created Division of Foreign Control in the Prohibition Unit. His new job description was consistent with his background as an investigator for the Pennsylvania Railroad and intelligence gatherer during the war years. Responsible for collecting information and damaging evidence to be applied to diplomatic channels to "embarrass, handicap, and render unprofitable the business of liquor smuggling abroad," Anslinger established his capability in covert operations.[25]

As chief his primary duty was to carry out the provisions of the London arrangement. In what was a job tailor-made for the former consul, Anslinger applied his diplomatic approach as a solution to smuggling of illegal liquor into the United States and secured additional treaties affecting smuggling from Newfoundland, Nova Scotia, Vancouver, Cuba, and Antwerp. In 1926 and 1927 he dealt with the control of smuggling through international agreements and exchanges of information as a delegate to conferences in London and Paris. In 1929 he was rewarded for his work: he was promoted effective October 30 to the post of Assistant Commissioner of Prohibition to oversee the Narcotics Control Board at an annual salary of $6,500.

Anslinger was a loyal prohibitionist. In spite of the mismanagement, incompetence, and corruption within the Prohibition Bureau, he believed Prohibition could work if it were more properly administered and enforced. His experience in railroad investigations and war-related intelligence work as well as his exposure to international affairs convinced him that the Volstead Act was more in need of a repair shop than a salvage yard. In 1928 he put his "better ideas" on paper and submitted them to a national competition in New York City.

Anslinger's plan to enforce the Eighteenth Amendment included ways to prevent smuggling, eliminate illegal manufacture, and more effectively coordinate government agencies. He suggested that Congress "give power to the President to employ the Navy to cooperate with the Coast Guard in the suppression of liquor smuggling" and that the Department of Justice "be authorized to investigate and report on such penalties issued by Treasury Department officials." In proposing his plan for coordinating Justice and Treasury investigations, he exhibited managerial acumen and insight. With Justice more directly involved, investigations and prosecutions would be centralized, criminal records would be more efficiently compiled, and the plan would encourage inter-agency cooperation by "eliminating friction, rivalry and jealousy between departments."[26]

Perhaps most revealing in his plan were his recommendations for more stringent penalties. As originally written, the Volstead Act stipulated that it was an offense for anyone to manufacture, sell, or transport liquor. Anslinger wanted to amend the Act to ban the purchase of alcohol for non-medical purposes. According to his proposed revision, the penalty for the first illegal purchase would be a fine not less than $1000 and imprisonment not less than six months. For a second or subsequent offense the penalty would be a fine no less than $5,000 nor more than $50,000 and imprisonment for not less than two years nor more than five years. This is early evidence of Anslinger's universal solution for problems of enforcement—heavy fines and long jail sentences. He advocated extreme punishment for Volstead violators in 1928 just as he would for marijuana offenders a decade later. Throughout his life he consistently relied on severe sanctions to deter or at least "remind" violators of their transgression.

Prohibition and Narcotics

Anslinger's responsibilities in the Division of Foreign Control were not limited to the enforcement of prohibition. He was also assigned to study the international aspects of the fight against narcotics smuggling, which had increasingly become a matter of concern to governments around the world. Since the passage of the Harrison Narcotic Act in 1914, laws had been enacted which further defined and restricted the use of narcotics in the United States. Prompted by international treaty obligations to control the flow of opium and aided by the efforts of Dr. Hamilton Wright, who believed in the total elimination of narcotics except for medical purposes, the act was intended primarily as a revenue measure.[27]

ENFORCEMENT

The act was not without flaws. Because it mandated federal intervention, it alienated the American Medical Association (AMA), which aimed to be self-governing and wanted to maintain its own medical standards.[28] Addicts, who formerly were treated as patients, were now regarded as criminals and jailed. Even the legality of the act was open to question as the Supreme Court wrestled with its perplexities on several occasions before the 1928 *Nigro v. U.S.* ruling declared that the Harrison Act was indeed constitutional.[29]

Enforcement of the Harrison Act was assigned to the Bureau of Internal Revenue in the Treasury Department and would remain there until October 1918, when the Volstead Act was passed over President Wilson's veto. With the added burden of enforcing prohibition, Treasury officials realized that the existing bureaucratic apparatus was inadequate for prosecuting both narcotics and liquor law violations. A special committee appointed by Secretary of the Treasury William McAdoo recommended the creation of separate agencies, one to handle the enforcement of the Harrison Act, the other to enforce prohibition.[30] It was anticipated that these agencies would solve administrative problems while providing the Treasury Department with efficient and effective enforcement.

The plan might have worked had it not been for a political deal. Partly in a concession to "wet" opposition, civil service requirements were waived for prohibition agents. Consequently agents were hired not on merit or ability but according to political patronage. It may have been politically convenient, but it was disastrous for Prohibition enforcement, and it was a significant factor in the failure of the Eighteenth Amendment.[31]

Between January 1920 and February 1929, 187 agents were fired or forced to resign for "intoxication and misconduct," 121 for "extortion, bribery, or soliciting money," and 118 for "unsatisfactory service and insubordination." A total of 752 agents, or 28 percent of the agents employed, were dismissed for collusion, dereliction of duty, submitting false reports, perjury, illegal disposition of liquor, and embezzlement, and other charges.[32] When the new Narcotics Division, headed by Colonel Levi G. Nutt, a former official of the Alcohol Tax Division, was placed in the Prohibition Unit, its agents, unlike those in Prohibition, were subject to civil service examinations.[33] Corruption was not immediately halted, nor was it unknown among narcotics agents, but it became considerably less frequent.

END OF THE CLINICS

The biggest problem confronting Chief Nutt in the early 1920s was what to do about the many maintenance clinics where doctors sold narcotics openly and legally. Before taking any action, Nutt first sent questionnaires to members of the AMA asking for their advice and opinions on the legitimacy of narcotics treatment and the benefits of ambulatory treatment (allowing addicts to be dispensed dosages of narcotics by licensed physicians as opposed to confining them involuntarily to an institution or sentencing them to prison terms). In what was historically the beginning of a series of philosophical inconsistencies, most doctors and scientists registered their opposition to ambulatory treatment and supported institutionalization.

In 1919 Chief Nutt ordered his agents to investigate all known maintenance clinics to assess the conditions and determine their effectiveness in curing addicted patients. In reality this was akin to a jury's deciding a defendant's guilt before hearing the evidence; there was little doubt that the clinics would be ordered to stop treating addicts. The only question was when the Narcotics Division would make its move.

By early 1920 Nutt began to shut down the clinics. In less than three years not one operated legally in the United States. Prior to 1920 addicts could receive treatment under trained supervision. They may not have been cured—few were—but it was possible to keep records of who they were and to monitor their activities since they reported regularly to the clinic. When the clinics were closed and doctors were no longer permitted to treat them, the addicts were literally forced into the street where they resorted to illicit means to obtain illicit drugs.

DOWN ON THE FARM

Closing the clinics did not ease the affliction for people dependent on narcotics. If the government denied them the benefits of ambulatory treatment, an alternative was a must. Addicts became a particularly nettlesome issue for Congress in the mid-1920s. Since addiction per se was not a crime, it would have been unconstitutional to jail them en masse. Confining addicts to institutions for psychiatric care was one possibility, but the mental hospitals were already seriously overcrowded, as were the federal penitentiaries.[34]

Even if Congress could have circumvented legal procedures, it could not have found cell space for addicts in the federal prisons. By 1 April 1928, the three federal penitentiaries had a cell capacity of 3,738 but a population of 7,598, more than double the capacity they were equipped to hold. There were also administrative problems. Wardens did not want to be bothered with addicts, prisons were not capable of handling them, and the addicts' association with the general inmate population was viewed as detrimental for both groups.[35]

After several congressional recommendations were advanced in 1927 and 1928 to address the addict problem, Representative Stephen G. Porter, a Pennsylvania Republican and chairman of the House Ways and Means

Committee, introduced H.R. 12781. Intended to alleviate the strain on the federal penitentiaries, Porter's bill provided for the establishment of two prison-hospitals that he referred to as "farms." The purpose of the farms (one east and one west of the Mississippi River) was to act as a clearing house for addicts already in penitentiaries or state and county jails as well as addicts still at large. That was the pragmatic reasoning behind the bill. But the congressman also seemed sympathetic to the plight of the addict and progressive in his thinking on rehabilitating them:

> I am thankful that we have gotten away from the old idea that they are "drug fiends"—nine out of ten of these unfortunate people acquire the habit through accident, through no fault of their own, and as we shall show you, they are anxious to be cured.

In his next sentence, however, Porter cautioned that the government should not adopt a paternalistic approach to the addicts because they were not the only victims:

> Paradoxical as it may seem, they are a great menace to society because they are constantly attempting to make those around them, those that are near and dear to them, addicted to the drug.[36]

The need for the farms was obvious to Congress, and their potential for easing a critical situation was not lost on Representative John C. Cochran, who concluded his testimony in the farm bill hearings with a plea that the bill should be reported favorably without delay and passed before adjournment.

> The establishment of proper hospitals or farms for the treatment of Federal and State prisoners should no longer be delayed. Your prisons are overcrowded, thousands of men now confined never being placed in cells because there is no room. . . . Since it is a case of building either additional penitentiaries or prison hospitals, I am sure you will see the wisdom of constructing the prison hospitals.[37]

Prison wardens, physicians, and Chief Nutt of the Narcotics Division, who testified at the hearings, joined with congressional committee members in their support of the farms. In addition to congressional support, the Porter farm bill also had the backing of newspaper magnate William Randolph Hearst, who had been publishing stories on the horrors of narcotics addiction for many years. According to Dr. Walter L. Treadway, Assistant Surgeon General of the U.S. Public Health Service, who ran the farms:

The unflagging efforts of Mr. Hearst and his newspapers have been chiefly responsible for the establishment of these farms and the arousing of the people to combat the narcotic evil. He deserves the gratitude and thanks of his fellowmen.[38]

On 19 January 1929, a law was passed unanimously for the farms to be built in Lexington, Kentucky, and Ft. Worth, Texas. Spread over 1,054 acres, the Lexington farm was the first to open, in 1935, and included facilities for 1,000 addicts who received medical treatment and psychiatric counseling as well as vocational training. Neither of the farms was limited exclusively to addicts in federal prisons, as any addict could apply voluntarily for treatment.[39]

Establishing the Bureau of Narcotics

Once the drug farms had been approved, Congressman Porter wasted no time proposing legislation for the creation of an independent Bureau of Narcotics, which he saw as a logical next step. He wanted the new agency to be separated from the Prohibition Bureau so that it could function more effectively in domestic and international affairs. It would also be more efficient since both enforcement and policy-making personnel would be contained in the same bureau.

CONGRESSMAN PORTER AND H. R. 11143

Ardent supporters of the Harrison Act who wanted narcotics and prohibition laws divorced from the beginning welcomed the Porter bill. Treasury Secretary Mellon, however, was less enthusiastic. In a letter read at the opening of the hearings, he announced that after he had given the plan consideration, the "Treasury Department is entirely sympathetic to any move that would aid in the elimination of narcotic addiction." He may have been supportive of legislation pertaining to narcotic addiction, but he was ambivalent about the need for such a bill and conditional in offering his support because:

There is some doubt in my mind as to the necessity of creating a separate bureau to accomplish what is sought for in this bill. However, realizing the good sought to be accomplished by the bill, the Treasury Department will support the bill.[40]

Porter's justification for creating a new narcotics bureau rested essentially on three premises. First, disassociation of the Prohibition Unit and Narcotics Department would facilitate efficiency and centralization. Second, foreign governments doubted the credibility of the existing Federal Narcotics Board because it was controlled by three lay members of the

Cabinet. Third, the congressman stated vaguely that "it might assist in an international way in the future."[41] Though at least one committee member, Congressman John N. Garner, thought it peculiar that representatives in other countries would take more seriously the opinions of three medical men on the narcotics board as opposed to three Cabinet members, the bill was never seriously challenged.

On the matter of facilitating enforcement and efficiency, the Assistant Commissioner of Prohibition, who headed the Narcotics Division, expressed some misgivings. When asked by Representative Issac Bacharach if he thought the new bill would prevent smuggling to any greater extent than under the present law, Harry Anslinger replied, "I do not know if it would improve it or not."[42] When the question was repeated for further clarification, Anslinger's answer was still non-commital. Congressman Garner then asked Anslinger how beneficial legislation would be if no assurances could be given that smuggling would be reduced. Before the assistant commissioner had time to respond, Congressman Porter quickly interjected that the bill would mean better administration, which would reduce smuggling. This was not the last time the Bureau would have to answer charges that its ability to stop smuggling was something less than it should be.

Another issue that caused concern during the hearings was the extension of civil service requirements to officers of the bureau. Remembering the ineptitude that plagued the Prohibition Unit, Congressman Garner was surprised to learn from Anslinger that in some departments the Secretary of the Treasury was permitted to appoint some deputy commissioners without reference to civil service requirements.[43]

The general lack of enthusiastic support for the bill also became clear throughout the hearings. Not once did any witness attempt to impress upon the committee the seriousness of the smuggling problem or the necessity for the establishment of a new narcotics bureau. The Treasury Department may have sponsored H.R. 11143, but it did nothing to get it passed. It seems that it was not so much active support but rather lack of opposition that enabled the bill to be reported out of committee.

Porter introduced the first of his two anti-narcotic bills, H.R. 9054, on 23 January 1930, designed to "authorize the Government to deny licenses to any registrants under the Harrison Act who are habitually addicted to narcotic drugs or who have pleaded guilty or have been convicted of violating the narcotic laws."[44]

The second bill, H.R. 11143, which he introduced two months later on 26 March, was intended "to create a separate and independent bureau of narcotics in the Treasury Department."[45] Except for the AMA objecting to what it considered cumbersome regulations and complex licensing procedures for physicians handling narcotics, the bill encountered no resistance. After extended hearings by the House Ways and Means Committee, H.R. 11143 was reported unanimously to the full House where it passed without dissent.[46] The bill also now had the full support of Secretary of the Treasury Mellon. In a letter to Senator Royal S. Copeland on 6 April, Mellon was much more enthusiastic about H.R. 11143 than he had been when it was first introduced:

> In order to remove any possible misunderstanding as to the position of the Treasury with respect to the bill creating the bureau of narcotics, introduced by Congressman Porter and reported by your committee (H.R. 11143), I assure you that the bill has my approval, and I believe that its enactment will be a substantial step forward in the control of narcotics.[47]

With only three inconsequential amendments pertaining to exact language, H.R. 11143 was passed by the Senate in early June. Three days later, on 9 June 1930, President Hoover signed the bill into law. After sixteen years of co-existing in the same agency, narcotic and liquor law enforcement finally were separated into distinct bureaus. As stipulated in the Act, a Bureau of Narcotics headed by a commissioner appointed by the president with the consent of the Senate was created within the Treasury Department. The duties of the new commissioner were primarily to enforce the Harrison Act, with powers conferred upon him as provided in the Narcotic Drugs Import-Export Act pertinent to the regulation of narcotic drugs. The new act also created a Division of Mental Hygiene in the Office of the Surgeon General. Congressman Porter did not live to see his Bureau of Narcotics function. After a prolonged illness, he died at the age of sixty-one on 27 June, just three days before the law went into effect.

SCANDAL

The year 1929 brought havoc to the country and to the Narcotics Bureau. The stock market crashed in the fall, and an ensuing ten-year economic depression shook the public's faith in American institutions. While the Porter bills were proceeding through Congress, a federal grand jury investigated charges of misconduct against narcotics agents in New York City. Its findings included several instances of incompetence or dereliction of duty on the part of some agents. One example involved eight agents who had physically surrounded a pusher selling $500 worth of narcotics but had allowed him to escape without arrest. The agents did not even enter or search the building where he made the deal. The jury lacked any concrete proof of corruption but was of the opinion that circumstances suggested collusion between the agents and drug dealers.

Other suggestions of this kind of unethical behavior also surfaced. On one occasion agents in the New York City office failed to inform the United States Attorney of evidence important to a prosecution. In another, two agents padded their expense accounts and went unpunished save for a reprimand from Prohibition Commissioner James M. Doran.[48] One of the agents later testified confidentially that subsequent to the reprimand, he was given a salary increase and promoted to a higher position. There was also a charge of fiscal irresponsibility concerning the appropriation of $80,000 in the Narcotics Division of the Prohibition Department for prohibition enforcement. As a result of this transfer of narcotics money, the division was severely hindered in making arrests for nearly six months, since these funds were earmarked as advance money for agents to make buys from suspected pushers.

A grand jury also found several pieces of evidence that a recently appointed Prohibition agent, who had left the Narcotics Division under suspicious circumstances, was associated with a known drug peddler. Worse, the jury found that at least one agent was himself a user of drugs. In addition, Federal authorities were told that collusion was suspected between a subordinate authority in Washington who had supervision over the destruction of seized drugs and a narcotics agent in charge of an office covering several large states.

The deeper the jury probed, the more corruption and incompetence it uncovered; there seemed to be no bottom. It learned that beginning in April 1929 the federal narcotics office in New York City was padding the records. The forging was done by the agent in charge who directed two agents of the local office to copy the records of cases made by the New York police department which did not represent violations of the federal narcotics laws and with which federal agents were not at all involved. Each of the cases was then given a file number in the local narcotics office and separately reported to the narcotics office in Washington.

The falsifying of arrest reports continued for four months during the middle of 1929 and resulted in padding the records of the New York office of 354 cases. The names of the agents attached to these cases were chosen arbitrarily without the knowledge of the agents themselves. The figures in these monthly reports were forwarded to Washington and ultimately were entered into the annual report of the federal narcotics office presented to Congress and made public. The agents may have been incompetent and dishonest, but they realized that if they released the actual—lower—numbers they would jeopardize their job security.

The New York agents did not act on their own initiative in padding the figures. The grand jury learned through the testimony of the Assistant Deputy of Prohibition in Charge of Narcotics, William C. Blanchard, that the Washington office ordered the padding over the telephone. According to Blanchard, he did not approve of the practice but was acting under orders from the Deputy Commissioner, Colonel Levi G. Nutt. When confronted with allegations of ordering agents to pad arrest reports, Nutt denied ever giving any such orders. Curiously, though, the padding continued well into the summer of 1929—with the knowledge of the Washington office and without protest.[49]

The reputation and the integrity of the Narcotics Division had been seriously impaired. Any one of the charges of misconduct or impropriety was damaging enough but might have been attributed to a lack of discretion or sound judgment. The padding of arrest reports, however, was too blatant to pass off as an honest mistake. For Levi Nutt, the central figure in this scandal, the story was just beginning to unfold.

Added to his official problems as Narcotics Chief, Nutt was also embarrassed by the grand jury investigation of his son, Rolland, and his son-in-law, L. P. Mattingly, who operated a law and accounting firm in New York City. Rolland Nutt, in return for a fixed monthly payment, handled tax matters and represented various clients of L. P. Mattingly & Co. before the Tax Unit of the Treasury Department and Federal Board of Tax Appeals. In January 1926 he and Mattingly handled the account of a client who had been penalized an additional income tax assessment by the Internal Revenue Department for the years 1919, 1920, and 1921. Normally this would not have aroused the attention of a grand jury, but Arnold Rothstein was in no sense an average client.

Referred to by social historian Lloyd Morris in *Postscript to Yesterday* as the "J. P. Morgan of the underworld," Rothstein was unquestionably one of the most powerful and influential racketeers of his day. Suspected of fixing the 1919 World Series (the infamous "Black Sox" scandal), Rothstein had extensive control of gambling activities, liquor distribution, and international narcotics traffic. In 1928, two days before Herbert Hoover was elected president, Rothstein was murdered on New York's Fifth Avenue. He lingered for two days but never identified any of his associates. Volumes of his records, letters, and other documents might have implicated several prominent businessmen and politicians, but most were lost or destroyed.[50]

The grand jury was satisfied that Rolland Nutt did not meet personally with Rothstein, but it was interested in how the L. P. Mattingly firm came to represent the racketeer. As it turned out, Rothstein had assigned his power of attorney to Nutt and Mattingly in 1926 to represent him before the Treasury Department in connection with securing a reduction of the assessment, which was subsequently resolved in 1927. Correspondence between Rothstein and L. P. Mattingly & Co. revealed that Mattingly borrowed from Rothstein a total of $6,200.

Colonel Nutt testified that he did not know that either his son or his son-in-law had ever represented Arnold Rothstein in any matter until the proceedings began. Both Rolland Nutt and Mattingly testified that they had never represented anyone in a narcotics case. The grand jury concluded that "though their aforesaid acts may be thought indiscreet, we find no evidence that the enforcement of the narcotic laws was affected thereby." Colonel Nutt may have been unaware of the Rothstein connection, but his son's involvement with the world's foremost organizer of narcotics traffic together with his own personal problems in the Narcotics Division made it impossible for him to survive in his Washington position.[51]

The findings of the federal grand jury in February 1930 resulted in a full-scale reorganization of the federal narcotics force. On 28 February Levi Nutt was removed and demoted to field supervisor of Prohibition agents, later to head the Alcohol Tax Unit in Syracuse. Even under normal circumstances, Nutt's removal would not have been totally unexpected. Several attempts to oust him or drop him to a minor position failed only because of his strong ties with Congressman Joseph G. Cannon and Senator Medill McCormick. By the time the shake-up in the Narcotics Division was completed, seventeen agents of the New York narcotic squad had been ordered transferred to distant cities.

APPOINTMENT

Before the grand jury findings were released and scandal rocked the Narcotics Bureau, Levi Nutt was virtually assured appointment as the new Commissioner of the Federal Bureau of Narcotics. But the padding charges and personal problems made him a liability, and the Treasury Department found it awkward to keep him on. To bring stability to a demoralized agency, Secretary Andrew Mellon appointed his relative by marriage, Harry Anslinger as acting Commissioner on 1 July 1930, at the Bureau's inception.[52] The selection of Anslinger did not come as a complete surprise, as he had been under consideration since late spring. His hometown newspaper praised his informal candidacy but noted that Anslinger was low-key about his chances and "was not actively seeking the part."[53] Actually the only reason he was not appointed until July was Congressman Porter's preference for Rear Admiral Mark Bristol as commissioner, and President Hoover did not wish to unnecessarily affront the dying congressman.[54]

During the summer of 1930, the White House received dozens of letters commending the work of Acting Commissioner Anslinger and recommending that Hoover keep him on as commissioner. In the first two weeks of July, for example, California state Senator Sanborn Young wrote twice to the president to "express my appreciation of your appointment of Harry J. Anslinger as Acting Commissioner" and to convey to him "the gratitude of all of us who are interested in this cause [narcotics enforcement] and I greatly hope it will be made permanent."[55] Many letters of support arrived from other state politicians, United States senators, Republican party workers, and private citizens.

Harry Anslinger may not have been actively seeking the appointment, but he had loyal friends working on his behalf to pressure Hoover. His old boss from Prohibition days in the Bahamas, General Lincoln Andrews, offered his assistance, expressing his view that "New York politics will go further than anything else," suggesting that "Bill Donovan could be of help."[56] Harry Smith, a San Francisco supporter, secured the endorsement of the Stanley Dollar Steamship Company by promising "a system of foreign espionage and cooperation we hoped to perfect which would materially aid the companies in the problem which confronts them."[57] The "problem" Smith was referring to was the heavy fine assessed against the company when 300 cans of smoking opium were found by searchers. Smith's effort, obviously, was not totally altruistic. Since he "delivered more than I thought possible, in view of certain opposition," he wondered in a letter to Anslinger if he "might be designated 'Deputy' if you are appointed."[58]

More beneficial to Anslinger than Harry Smith, however, was Sanborn Young. Satisfied that Anslinger was the best possible candidate for narcotics commissioner, Young secured endorsements from Paul Shoup, president of the Southern Pacific Railway; J. O. Hays, John W. McNabb, and Mark Requa (close personal California friends of the president); and congressmen and newspaper editors in western states. Young also reported the endorsements of United States Senators James Watson of Indiana and Reed Smoot of Utah, who was tracked down honeymooning in Hawaii at the time.

Anslinger was not the only candidate for the $9,000-a-year appointment. Admiral Bristol, Congressman Porter's choice, possessed impressive credentials from his former positions as American High Commander to Turkey and Commander of the Pacific Fleet of the Navy.[59] Another military man, Captain Richmond P. Hobson, a hero of the Spanish-American War, was a Progressive-era congressman from Alabama. Hobson had long been a potent force against drugs, whether speaking on a temperance platform or on the radio. He helped organize the International Narcotic Education Association in 1923 and the World Narcotic Defense Association in 1927. Senator David A. Reed of Pennsylvania suggested Elmer S. Irey of the Intelligence Unit in the Treasury Department. Criminologist Dr. Carleton Simon, who headed the New York City Police Department's narcotic squad; and Elizabeth Wright, widow of Dr. Hamilton Wright, the leading force behind the Harrison Act, were also under consideration.

More than a dozen applicants contended for the position of commissioner, including Dr. Emelyn Jones, another Pennsylvanian, from Johnstown. Jones' candidacy posed the dilemma of having two applicants from the same state. He was appointed by Governor John S. Fisher to a position in the State Department of Vital Statistics and had the support of Senator Reed after Irey withdrew his candidacy. But Jones' reputation as a physician was shoddy, and Anslinger's strong support from Pennsylvania's senior Senator Joseph R. Grundy and Congressman J. Banks Kurtz enabled him to survive an early scare. Anslinger's familial connection—no matter how far removed—with Secretary of the Treasury Mellon, who heartily endorsed him, was of obvious benefit.

The lobbying paid off. On 23 September 1930, President Hoover officially appointed Anslinger Chief of the Bureau of Narcotics in the Treasury Department.[60] By this time Anslinger had the support of the National Association of Retail Druggists (NARD), the AMA, and the Hearst publishing empire. Congressional allies consisted of several key people including Fiorello H. LaGuardia who regarded Anslinger as a "most efficient commissioner who is building a real service of competent men."[61]

On 9 December the Committee on Finance voted favorably to report the nomination of Anslinger. Confirmation appeared to be all but guaranteed until one week later, when New York Sen. Royal S. Copeland asked that the nomination be postponed until the next executive session. For two days Senator Copeland delayed Anslinger's nomination until he was satisfied that the candidate was deserving. Speaking on the Senate floor just before Congress adjourned for Christmas recess, he explained that he requested the delay in order to convince himself of Anslinger's qualifications. As a physician and Health Commissioner of New York prior to his election, the senator held some concerns over a person with no medical background being named narcotics commissioner. On 18 December Senator Copeland ended the delay when he stated in his address that

> I have had a visit with Mr. Anslinger and made investigation of certain criticisms which had been brought to my attention. I am satisfied after due consideration, that the appointment is a worthy and proper one, and I move that the nomination be confirmed.

It is not certain whether Anslinger was able to reassure the senator that his lack of medical expertise would not be a limitation nor hinder his ability to perform as commissioner, or if Senator Copeland was impressed with the Bureau's seizure of a million dollar's worth of narcotic drugs the day before. If Anslinger was grandstanding with a timely seizure, it was effective. In fact, it made such an impact on Senator Copeland that he had an account of the raid in the *Washington Herald* inserted in the *Congressional Record,* commenting that "this commendable act is evidence that Mr. Anslinger is going to make an effective and useful commissioner."[62]

It had taken Anslinger only a decade to rise from a clerk in the Consular

Service at The Hague to Commissioner of the Federal Bureau of Narcotics. By the time he was appointed, he had done intelligence work for the State Department in Europe and enforced Prohibition for the Treasury in the Bahamas. At thirty-eight he was a youthful but experienced bureaucrat with definite ideas on the nature of narcotics policies and law enforcement. Neither Senator Copeland nor anyone could have known in 1930 that Harry Anslinger, more than any other individual, would control federal drug policy and extend his influence beyond narcotics enforcement over the next three decades.

2

Anslinger at the Helm, 1930–1937

When the Federal Bureau of Narcotics was created on 1 July 1930, it effected an extensive change in the organization of federal narcotics law enforcement activities. The investigation and detection of illicit narcotics traffic, which generally had been functions of an enforcement unit in the Bureau of Prohibition under the supervision of the Commissioner of Prohibition, were transferred to the new bureau. The Federal Narcotics Control Board (composed of the secretaries of State, Treasury, and Commerce), which administered the permissive work pertaining to import and export duties for narcotic drugs, was abolished.

Anatomy of the FBN

Under the Act of 1930, a separate and independent Narcotics Bureau in the Department of the Treasury was assigned both the powers requisite for the enforcement of federal narcotics laws as well as the permissive features of the narcotics drug import and export act. A Division of Mental Hygiene (formerly the Narcotics Division) was also established in the office of the Surgeon General of the United States Public Health Service. The primary duty of this new agency was to conduct investigations and research that would aid the Commissioner of Narcotics and augment the treatment of addicts in the two new federal narcotics farms.

At its inception, the organization of the bureau provided for an Office of Narcotic Control, a Division of Foreign Control, an Administration Division, a Legal Division, a Returns Division, a Drugs Disposal Committee, and Offices of Field Supervision and Special Investigation. Within its first two years, however, eleven more offices or divisions were added to facilitate departmental activities.

For the purposes of enforcement work in the field, the forty-eight states, Hawaii, Puerto Rico, and the Canal Zone were divided into fifteen districts bounded according to the Circuit Court of Appeals districts. In compliance with the Porter Act, personnel in the Narcotics Division of the Bureau of Prohibition were transferred to the Bureau of Narcotics. At the close of the fiscal year 1931, there were 426 office employees and 271

agents. Appropriations for its first full year of operation were $1,712, 998.[1]
With the organizational structure in place, the Commissioner had only to
uphold his duty to enforce existing narcotics laws. But since this was a
newly created orphaned bureau, he also had to demonstrate that it was not
an agency in name only, without power and effect.

The first major task confronting the new commissioner was the complete reorganization of the old Narcotics Unit in the Prohibition Bureau.
This bureaucratic realignment resulted in a change-over from enforcement
on a strictly local basis by a little-known unit of the government to the
formulation of broad national and international policies.

Prior to 1930 and the creation of the Federal Bureau of Narcotics,
enforcement efforts had comparatively little effect in curbing illicit traffic.
Commissioner Anslinger realized that the major enforcement problems
consisted of detecting and preventing unlawful importation into the United
States. He reasoned correctly that foreign overproduction and low prices
were the main factors that created an abunndant supply for most of the
addicts in the United States.

In a "Crime and Narcotics" lecture delivered at Dickinson College in
1932, Anslinger briefly outlined his concept of the proper policy to be
followed by the Bureau of Narcotics if it was to achieve a high level of
proficiency in controlling drug syndicates and smuggling activities. Rather
than concentrate on individual peddlers and addicts, Anslinger felt that
the federal government should break up international rings of narcotics
runners, and stop interstate narcotics traffic rather than clean up the
numerous dens that fell under local police jurisdiction.[2]

From his office five flights above Fourteenth and K Streets (headquar-
ters are now at Fourteenth and I Streets), the commissioner waged the
federal government's war on international smuggling and meticulously
formulated its strategies to combat drug traffic. In theory his ideas were
sound; realistically they were impractical. With less than 250 agents to
guard 4,000 miles of border and 20,000 miles of coastline, the Bureau
could not prevent illegal drugs from entering the country. To achieve full
enforcement, one agent would have had to maintain the security of 100
miles of the United States border, a high expectation.

Of the three decades Harry Anslinger was Commissioner of Narcotics,
none was more eventful or significant than the first. During the 1930s
Anslinger cultivated and sustained solid political ties with key members of
both parties and gained the support of dozens of interest groups and
lobbies, making himself virtually immune to opposition within or outside
the federal government. In a short period Anslinger developed a keen
understanding of Washington politics and the importance of establishing
influential connections. He demonstrated his mettle and ability to survive
crisis situations on several occasions because of this support system. The

combination of politics, existing social conditions, and Anslinger's personality resulted in the enactment of the Marijuana Tax Act in 1937, the federal legislation that ultimately opened the door for the government's (and Anslinger's) policy of exceedingly severe penalties for drug violations over the next fifty years. By the end of the decade, both Anslinger and his bureau had become embroiled in a controversy that began with the rise and spread of a "killer weed," as it had been labeled by the press.

The Menace of Marijuana

Until the early 1930s marijuana was known primarily in the southwestern states where its use was most commonly associated with indolent Mexican laborers who were perceived by most Americans as "criminal types." They were noted for brandishing knives and were said to have a proclivity for drunkenness and disorderly conduct. Though erroneous, the generalization fostered the stereotype of marijuana-smoking Mexicans committing violent acts. When they ventured north across the Rio Grande looking for low-paying jobs in the fields from Texas to California, they brought marijuana with them. The drug was yet a relatively isolated problem; the rest of the nation knew of its existence but was generally indifferent to it. Anslinger later recalled that outside of the law enforcement people in the Southwest, bureau officials in Washington did not know anything about it. They had only heard that Mexicans were reported to have caused a lot of trouble after smoking marijuana. They became irrational and maniacal, often requiring "four policemen to take care of them because when they were violent they had superhuman strength."[3]

EMERGENCE OF THE "KILLER WEED"

About the same time, demands for federal legislation began to emanate from city officials in New Orleans, who linked an increase in their crime rate during the 1920s to the use of marijuana. The crime increase might well have been attributed more to prohibition violations, but since there was popular support to legalize alcohol, marijuana drew the attention as a crime-producing drug. One of several individuals who played an active role in promoting the city's campaign for anti-marijuana legislation was a local physician, Dr. A. E. Fossier, who delivered a paper before the Louisiana State Medical Society in 1931, titled "The Marijuana Menace." In his opening paragraph he related the myth (since discredited) of the military and religious sect of the Assassins in Persia that in 1090 A.D. "committed secret murders in blind obedience to the chief after [becoming] intoxicated with hashish."[4] Later in his speech, Dr. Fossier claimed that marijuana in large doses produces "excitement, delusions, hallucinations, . . . with a tendency to willfull damage and violence." One of the discussants, Dr. Frank R. Gomilla, Commissioner of Public Safety, was so alarmed about the dangers of marijuana that he assured the audience that the New Orleans Police Department would be especially vigilant for locations of the drug which he felt "should be put in the same class as heroin."

In the same year that Dr. Fossier exhorted government officials to take legislative action against marijuana, the district attorney of New Orleans, Eugene Stanley, published his article "Marijuana As A Developer of Criminals." Stanley's article differed little from Dr. Fossier's speech. Like the doctor, he cited the Assassins story, even with the same date, 1090 A.D. Anxious to generate publicity for legislation against a drug so vicious, Stanley felt that it was absolutely vital that the federal government recognize the magnitude of the problem and intervene before it got out of hand:

> Inasmuch as the harmful effects of the use of marihuana are daily becoming more widely known, and since it has been classed as a narcotic by the statutory laws of seventeen American states, England, and Mexico, and since persons addicted to its use have been made eligible for treatment in the United States Narcotics Farms, the United States will unquestionably be compelled to adopt a consistent attitude toward it, and include it in the Harrison Anti-narcotic Law, so as to give Federal aid to the States in their effort to suppress a traffic so deadly and as destructive as that in the other forms of narcotics now prohibited by this Act.[5]

Fossier and Stanley were correct in anticipating the rapid spread of the Mexican weed. Like jazz, marijuana went up the Mississippi River from New Orleans to river ports in the Midwest and branched out into northeastern cities. Even the Wickersham Commission heard testimony "that the use of a new drug—Marihuana of the hashish family—is spreading over the United States."[6] By the mid-1930s, newspapers and popular magazines were headlining the "marijuana menace" in nearly every part of the country. No longer associated exclusively with migrant Mexicans, it was being grown in city backyards and vacant lots, along roadways, and even in the fields of federal prisons by ingenious inmates. By 1936 it was said to have replaced liquor in Harlem and was considered chic as a new diversion in affluent Westchester County, New York. It even found its way into New Deal work relief programs when narcotics agents discovered that men in the Civilian Conservation Corps in New Hampshire and Works Progress Administration employees in New York were smoking it.[7]

As long as marijuana was confined to Mexicans in the Southwest and to other illegal aliens, the bureau gave it little notice. But when it began to spread into midwestern and northern states, Anslinger mobilized his

narcotics force into a nationwide crusade against a drug whose properties
and effects were more feared than understood. The biological effects of the
drug were fiercely debated throughout the decade by noted scientists and
physicians who were unable to form a clear consensus. When one of them
did express uncertainty as to its potency, Anslinger turned a deaf ear,
arguing that while some were inclined to minimize the harmfulness of the
drug, ample evidence provied that it had a disastrous effect upon many of
its users.

THE "ASSASSIN OF YOUTH" AND OTHER HORRORS

What caused perhaps the greatest concern was the ease and speed
which marijuana seemed to gain popularity among a totally new and
different group of users—young people. The media immediately picked up
on this latest trend, as did Harry Anslinger. In July 1937, he co-authored
with Courtney Riley Cooper "Marijuana: Assassin of Youth," which was
published in *American Magazine*. Theirs was not the only article on this
subject. Other highly sensationalistic pieces soon followed. "Youth Gone
Loco," "One More Peril for Youth," and "Danger" were typical accounts
exaggerating the threat to America's adolescent population.[8] Exploitative
literature focusing on the assault on youth by marijuana was effectively
debunked in the next decade by scholarly investigation. But until then,
Anslinger and the Bureau of Narcotics capitalized on the free and unexpected publicity.

More outlandish than the "assassin of youth" propaganda were the
fantastic reports of marijuana's horrible effects. There was no research at
the time to prove or disprove the influence marijuana had on the user's
personality or behavior, but it was easy to believe the worst. The editorial
outcry against the evil of cannabis blamed the weed as a cause of sex
crimes, murder and, indeed, almost anything for which there was no ready
explanation. Countless stories of heinous acts committed by users while
under its effects were reported on a regular basis by 1937. In the technical-
styled monthly *Popular Science,* William Wolf detailed an ugly picture of
marijuana's effects:

> Continued use of the drug, for example, will lead to a delirious rage in
> which the addicts are temporarily irresponsible and inclined to commit
> the most horrible and violent crimes. Any increase in crime in a com-
> munity usually is attributed by authorities to marijuana. Many murders
> are committed either by persons not responsible while under the influ-
> ence of the drug, or by persons who deliberately smoke it to gain a false
> courage for the commission of a planned slaying. Prolonged use is said
> to lead to mental deterioration and eventual insanity.[9]

Popular Science enjoys a reputation of straightforward and objective reporting. Sensationalistic and tabloid-type publications exercised less discretion in objectivity and were more concerned with increasing sales by providing the reader with more graphic accounts.

Regardless of who published them, stories about marijuana and its power to radically alter an individual's behavior had wide-spread appeal. This publicity was not lost on Anslinger, who also promoted the notion that the marijuana smoker was a serious threat and was responsible for an increasing number of criminal acts. To Anslinger marijuana was the most dangerous of drugs; it was more degenerating and debasing to a person's character than opium. Where opium's effects at least were predictable, marijuana's destructiveness lay in its propensity to transform one's rational thoughts into the commission of unspeakable, heinous acts. In this respect Anslinger saw the battle against marijuana as analogous to good versus evil, as illustrated by two of Robert Louis Stevenson's fictional characters in a speech the commissioner made at the Women's National Exposition of Arts and Industry:

Take all of the good in Dr. Jekyll and the worst in Mr. Hyde—the result is opium. This is not so with marihuana. Its importance in the Pharmacopoeia is not intrinscially indispensable. Marihuana may be considered more harmful in its potentialities for evil than its limited advantages for medical or commercial purposes. It is Mr. Hyde alone.[10]

Later in his speech he told, as he had so many times, of the effects of "cannabis," and how prolonged use of marijuana frequently caused a delirious rage which sometimes led the user to commit such violent crimes as assault and murder. That is why, he told his predominantly female audience, marijuana was justifiably called the "killer drug." If a person became a habitual user of this "narcotic poison," mental deterioration, if not insanity, would result. For that reason marijuana was often referred to as the "loco weed."

Once Anslinger realized he had captured his audience's attention, he told of how the marijuana habit caused "physical wreckage and mental decay." It was also devastating to an individual's character by rendering him so degenerate that he committed criminal acts and fell into the underworld. Anslinger was convinced that a significant majority of rape, assault, and murder cases were directly associated with the use of marijuana.

Anslinger never softened his views. Indefatigable in his effort to disseminate anti-marijuana propaganda, he made countless speeches before women's clubs, temperance groups, church organizations, parent-teacher associations; and congressional hearings. In testifying before a House

Committee on Appropriations, Anslinger seized the opportunity to create a pernicious image of marijuana as he engaged in a bit of sensationalizing himself:

MR. MCLEOD: Marihuana is as dangerous a drug as there is, it it not?

MR. ANSLINGER: I would say so; just as dangerous as the other drugs, if not more so, because it incites the user to crime.

THE CHAIRMAN: It is likely to produce a homicidal tendency in the man that uses it, a tendency to kill or inflict violence?

MR. ANSLINGER: We have many records of violence having been committed by users throughout the country.[11]

Many of the instances of marijuana-related violence Anslinger made reference to during his testimony were brief two- or three-sentence descriptions he recorded on half-sheets of paper with the word "Crime" handwritten in the upper right-hand corner. Obviously he had been accumulating them in a file anticipating that he might find them useful. Usually they were abbreviated versions of lengthier, more descriptive accounts:

Albuquerque, New Mexico February 1934
Although Mariguana [sic] offenses do not show up directly in many cases, it is estimated that probably fifty percent of our violent crimes in this district may be traced to mariguana addicts.

Arizona March 15, 1934
I am of the opinion that those addicted to the use of this drug (marihuana) are far more dangerous than those addicted to the other forms of narcotics in that it make[s] the user of it very brazen and fearless.

September 1934
George Derrigan, 25, beat his wife at 834 Jones Street, San Francisco. Neighbors called the police. Inspectors Frank Ahern and Barney Reznik found Derrigan "hopped up" with marihuana.[12]

Anslinger also had a collection of horror stories precisely detailed, in which offenders were usually racially identifiable, either black or Hispanic. These he repeated several times before congressional hearings where he would supplement his testimony with explicit photographs of the victims' mangled bodies. Many of them often found their way into the trade periodicals. The more popular ones included descriptive accounts of violence, or they moralized against the use of marijuana:

In New Jersey in 1936, a particularly brutal murder occurred, in which case one young man killed another, literally smashing his face and head to a pulp. One of the defenses was that the defendant's intellect was so prostrated from his smoking Marihuana cigarettes that he did not know what he was doing.

Colored students at the Univ. of Minn. partying with female students (white) smoking and getting their sympathy with stories of racial persecution. Result pregnancy.

West Va.—Negro raped a girl eight years of age. Two Negroes took a girl fourteen years old and kept her for two days in a hut under the influence of marihuana. Upon recovery she was found to be "suffering from" syphilis.[13]

One of the bureau's raids must have provided for some anxious moments for the arresting inspector and comic relief for the smokers, despite probable conviction:

Undercover agent invited to marihuana party. Suggestion that everyone take off their pants, both male and female. Agent dropped blackjack while disrobing and had to arrest immediately.

Floyd Baskette, editor of the *Daily Courier* in Alamos, Colorado, was convinced that the marijuana problem was an ethnic one:

I wish I could show you what a small marihuana cigarette does to one of our degenerate Spanish speaking residents. That's why our problem is so great; the greatest percentage of our population is composed of Spanish speaking persons, most of whom are low mentally, because of social and racial conditions.[14]

Commissioner Anslinger wrote numerous position papers overstating the influence of marijuana and distributed them to agents in the Narcotics Division throughout the country. Not surprisingly, most of the agents shared their supervisor's feelings. William C. Crawford, who headed the State Bureau of Narcotics in California, believed that marijuana had a worse effect than heroin because it gave men "the lust to kill without motive." To substantiate his claim, Agent Crawford cited the case of a man in Eureka who decapitated his friend with an ax but was unable to recall the incident a few hours later.[15]

By far the marijuana-induced homicide incident most often cited by Anslinger was the multiple murder case of Victor Licata, a young Mexican charged with slaughtering his family:

A twenty-one-year-old boy in FLORIDA killed his parents, two brothers and a sister while under the influence of a Marihuana "dream" which he later described to law enforcement officials. He told rambling stories of being attacked in his bedroom by his "uncle, a strange woman and two men and two women," whom he said hacked off his arms and otherwise mutilated him; later in the dream he saw "real blood" dripping from an axe.[16]

This was Anslinger's favorite graphic tale of marijuana and murder which he included in Congressional testimony and relied on as unconditional proof of the drug's direct relationship to criminal behavior in his "Assassin of Youth" article.

UNIFORMITY THROUGHOUT

Because marijuana had been excluded from the Harrison Act, the strategy adopted by the federal government to control the weed was to encourage the individual states to handle related problems and pass appropriate legislation. They were expected to adopt a Uniform Narcotics Drug Act which included anti-marijuana laws. But most state legislators thought that the "problem of preventing the abuse of narcotic drugs was one exclusively cognizable by the Federal Government."[17]

The states were reluctant to pass the Uniform Narcotics Drug Act for several reasons. First, in the Depression years the added economic burden of enforcement would have been a tremendous strain on already limited financial resources. Second, the special licensing of doctors, dentists, and other professional groups who dispensed narcotic drugs would require more administrative time and endless red tape. Third, affected professional associations voiced wide-spread objection to the power given to the courts to revoke or suspend the licenses of those who practiced medicine or dispensed pharmaceuticals. Finally, the public was generally apathetic to the problem of marijuana in states outside the Southwest. Generally, people in northern and eastern states did not perceive marijuana as a pressing problem and therefore were not receptive to passing unnecessary legislation.[18]

When Anslinger was appointed in 1930, only sixteen states had enacted a uniform law, and that had taken seven years. Anxious to promote cooperation with the states to attain the maximum efficiency in intrastate enforcement, the commissioner sent letters to the governors of each state requesting statistical information relative to state narcotics law enforcement and announced that he wished to propose a fourth draft of a uniform law.[19] In 1931 Anslinger suggested that the National Conference of Commissioners on United States Laws meet in Washington, where on 12 October 1932 it finally accepted a fifth draft of a uniform state narcotics act. Under the terms of the act it was unlawful for anyone to "manufacture, possess, have under his control, sell, prescribe, administer, dispense, or compound any narcotic drug except as authorized."[20] Cocaine, opium and its derivatives (morphine, codeine, and heroin), and any narcotic drugs otherwise synthetically produced were specifically included in the act. Only incidentally was cannabis mentioned in the fine print of sub-section fourteen.

Anticipating resistance from the states, Anslinger emphasized that the facilities of the bureau were not designed to provide for the police work of narcotics law enforcement throughout the country. The federal role in this problem, he maintained, should be limited to the detection and elimination of the larger wholesale source of illicit supply within the states. Matters of prevention, care and treatment of addicts, and the regulation of licenses were also within the jurisdiction of the individual states.

Clearly, Anslinger wanted only a limited role for the FBN in the intra-state narcotics enforcement. But he knew that existing state legislation was either incomplete or ineffective and that if he was to be successful in attacking the problem on the federal level, he would need cooperation at the state level. For that reason he personally lobbied for the adoption of the uniform law, meeting with state legislatures as they convened. Initially adoption went slowly, with only four states enacting it in 1933. Anslinger faced a difficult task in convincing the states of the need for such an act. In a memorandum to a Treasury official, he reported that he had testified on behalf of the Uniform State Narcotics Act before a committee meeting of the New Jersey legislature. Initially the committee, composed of doctors and druggists, was "exceedingly hostile but after several hours of explanation, they finally agreed to re-draft the bill."[21]

Appearing before the Appropriations Committee in 1934, Anslinger testified that it was impossible to predict how individual states would respond to the proposed legislation. At that time only two additional states, Nevada and New York, had adopted the act. Even when some states, such as Indiana, did consider it for enactment, the legislature "mutilated it to the point where it [was] entirely useless." In other states, like Georgia, it never made it through both houses.[22]

Despite growing concern over the spread of marijuana in the early 1930s, Anslinger repeatedly stressed that the problem could be brought under control without federal intervention if all the states adopted the Uniform Narcotics Act. Even when the weed began to make its way north, causing alarm and publicity, Anslinger still regarded marijuana as an intrastate problem. In testimony before the same appropriations committee he explained why:

MR. MCLEOD: Would you recommend that marihuana be included, as far as possible, under the Federal Drug Act?

MR. ANSLINGER: Not at this time.

MR. MCLEOD: Is your opposition due to the fact that it would take a larger force to enforce it?

MR. ANSLINGER: Oh, no sir; not that. It is a question of having the States say, "All right, Uncle Sam is doing it."

I am putting a marihuana provision, included in the proposed Uniform State narcotic drug law before every legislature next month, to enact. If the States will go along with that, then the Federal Government ought to step in and coordinate the work, but until the States become conscious of their own problems I think it is a mistake for the Federal Government to take on the whole job.[23]

Through 1934 and most of 1935 Anslinger continued to oppose a federal anti-marijuana law and tried to persuade the states to pass the Uniform Act. He also enlisted the help of President Roosevelt who called upon the states to adopt the law as a "powerful weapon against the dope menace" in a national radio broadcast. In addition to the states accepting their "imperative duty"—adopting this reform—Roosevelt asserted that "the legislatures will give to their own people far better protection than they now have against the ravages of the narcotic drug evil."[24] Anslinger's renewed campaign for nationwide uniform laws was moderately effective; by the end of 1935 a total of twenty-seven states had passed the act.

Anslinger was less successful in arousing public opinion in favor of the Uniform State law which would relieve the FBN of local enforcement responsibilities. Since it was obvious that many states were not supportive of the law, he altered his tactics to secure its passage. Instead of minimizing the illicit use of and traffic in marijuana as he had done for nearly three years, he dramatized the rapid spread of the drug as "causing much concern by the Bureau of Narcotics." Because he had been receiving daily reports on the abuse of marijuana, Anslinger contended that the situation with regard to its use was "so alarming that all states and communities should act IMMEDIATELY to provide vigorous measures for the extinction of this lethal weed."[25]

To shape public opinion and inform the citizenry about the "killer weed," Anslinger manipulated the media. He also enlisted the help of organizations sympathetic to his revitalized crusade against the drug. In addition to the Hearst newspaper chain, moralist groups such as the General Federation of Women's Clubs, the Woman's Christian Temperance Union, and the World Narcotics Defense Association led by Admiral Hobson were particularly helpful. Anslinger's intention was to fire the marijuana controversy, and in 1936 he categorized it in a speech before the Hobson organization as "one of the most troublesome problems which confronts us today in the United States."[26] During appropriations hearings in December 1936, he went so far as to confirm Congressman Louis Ludlow's supposition that marijuana was "about as hellish as heroin," even though Anslinger had admitted only a year earlier that it was not even addictive.

If Anslinger expected the "marijuana myth" to arouse public opinion in support of the Uniform Law, he was not disappointed, for 1935 proved to be a turning point when an additional eighteen states adopted the law. Whether the public really believed that the use of marijuana was reaching epidemic proportions or that it did represent a national threat, "Anslinger's Army" effectually influenced legislative opinion and created the need for laws. The anti-marijuana campaign, however, may have been too successful. Anslinger had long wanted legislation for the states, but the heightened public awareness of marijuana as a result of the FBN's propaganda blitz stimulated demand for federal legislation. When identical bills were introduced in 1935 by Senator Carl Hatch and Congressman John Dempsey of New Mexico to prohibit the shipment and transportation of marijuana in interstate and foreign commerce, Anslinger was forced to reassess his opposition to federal legislation.[27] Although neither of the bills reached the floor, their introduction signaled a growing sensitivity to such a law among members of Congress. Still, Anslinger was not enthusiastic about a federal anti-marijuana statute at this time.

ALIENS AND ADDICTS

Anslinger was supportive of politicians who sought to pass drastic counter-measures against what they perceived as an increasing volume of drug trafficking. One way to at least reduce the demand for illicit narcotics was to reduce the number of drug addicts. But because the federal prisons were already overcrowded and the narcotics farms had not yet opened, confining addicts in institutions was not a practical solution. More realistically, argued Congressman Hamilton Fish, drug users should be removed from the general population. In May of 1930 he had offered H.R. 3394, providing for the deportation of aliens convicted in violation of the Harrison Act.

While the deportation of alien peddlers might seem to be a radical approach to the contemporary observer, it was not preposterous in 1930. (The post-World War mindset of disillusionment, intolerance, and apprehension over volatile international affairs produced a mood of xenophobia that resulted in two major pieces of restrictive immigration legislation passed by Congress with scant opposition in the 1920s.) Fish's bill, in fact, was actually an amendment to Section 19 of the Immigration Act of 1917 which included the Harrision provision that aliens who peddled narcotics be deported. Since "narcotics are one of the worst evils in this country" and "one-third of the prisoners in federal penitentiaries are convicted for offenses against narcotics laws," the congressman reasoned that American taxpayers were not obligated to maintain them and that they ought to be deported.[28]

When Fish introduced his bill, however, it met with opposition from Congressman William H. Stafford of Wisconsin, who vigorously objected to the deportation of what he felt were helpless addicts: "It outrages my sense of justice to an unfortunate user of opium when he chances to be an alien."[29] It may have been genuine concern about the welfare of addicts or Stafford's realization that many war veterans who had become addicted to morphine—an opium derivative used as a painkiller—would be deportable. In any event, Fish immediately offered to add an amendment that specified "dealer" and "peddler" and excluded "addict."

Representative John C. Schafer, also of Wisconsin, had some questions about the wording of the bill and asked for confirmation that

> the provisions of this bill would not apply to one who sells a drink nationally advertised and consumed, manufactured in Atlanta, Ga., by a company which had done more than any other institution or anybody to bring about the sumptuary prohibition law, whose product has been found, upon examination to contain derivatives of cocaine, would it?[30]

He was assured that employees of the Coca-Cola Company or consumers of its product, which contained a cocaine extract until 1906, would not be subject to deportation under the bill.

Congressman Fish was conciliatory to those who raised these and other objections to the bill, but the proposed legislation still failed to come to a vote. Congressman Stafford suggested that further action be delayed until the next day. On July 3 the bill was voted on and passed in the House of Representatives despite the protests of Congressmen LaGuardia and John Cochran that it was unnecessary to enforce the narcotics law.

When the Senate Committee on Immigration held hearings on H.R. 3394 in January 1931, Commissioner Anslinger testified that there were approximately 500 deportations a year and that aliens were, indeed, at the root of the narcotics problem. Anslinger's "expert" opinion as well as his statistics contributed significantly to the passage of the deportation bill which the bureau frequently used to disrupt the traffic in narcotics.

Because of the deportation provision of the Alien Act, the Bureau maintained records of known addicts gathered from doctor's reports, local law enforcement agencies, and rough approximations based on the surveillance of traffic. Throughout the 1930s Anslinger reported that between 50,000 and 60,000 Americans were drug addicts. Compared to the 250,000 to 300,000 commonly reported at the turn of the century, this represented a considerable reduction. Despite having no way of confirming the accuracy of these figures, Anslinger took credit for his role in reducing the number of addicts.

Generally in the 1930s there was a cohesive anti-drug consensus. Most were in agreement that, while opium and its derivatives could be used productively, the drugs' potential to debilitate the user necessitated that they be rigidly controlled. This belief and the concern for economic survival during the Depression precluded any heated debate on federal narcotics policies except for marijuana. Through the period of the marijuana scare, 1934–37, Anslinger continued to describe the harmful effects of marijuana without being held accountable. The cases of violence he cited—no matter that they were exaggerated—could be documented; if necessary Ansligner could prove that the crimes did occur. The only details of the incident known to the public, though, were those released to the media by the Bureau of Narcotics. If Anslinger said that the offender was a known user of marijuana, few people were likely to question his authority, and it was largely accepted that the drug was a contributing factor to the crime.

The exact circumstances of a murder, rape, or assault incident were not always easily identified. Surely it was possible that the marijuana smoker was prone to violent behavior without smoking the drug. Perhaps he committed the act of violence while he was under the influence of a mixture of marijuana and a more potent drug such as heroin or opium. It might also have been possible, as later established in the infamous Victor Licata case—Anslinger's favorite—that the slayer was known to have been emotionally unstable long before he murdered his family. Anslinger never made any reference to Licata's medical history when he testified about the tragedy in the congressional hearings, nor was he ever requested to.

Because Anslinger was more concerned with manipulating the "marijuana menace" to his own advantage, the public and Congress had been misinformed and inadequately educated about the drug's physiological effects. Scientific research to determine the effects of the drug and its relationship to violent criminal behavior was desperately needed. Only then could there be a better understanding of how to deal with it effectively and intelligently.

No solid evidence was gathered in the mid-1930s proving that marijuana had the capability to turn sane and otherwise law-abiding citizens into criminals who wantonly committed horrible, violent crimes. Most of the Bureau's assumptions about the drug, often inaccurate, were based on experiments conducted by scientists long ago (Dr. Moreau's "Du hachich et dealienation mentale," written in France in 1845, for example, was frequently cited by Anslinger) or by doctors who formed their conclusions based on the results of isolated tests (as opposed to performing precise, scrupulously monitored observations of human subjects under controlled laboratory conditions). More recently Dr. Pascal Brotteaux in "Le hachich, herbe de folle et de reve" (1934) declared that hashish "causes paralysis of the higher centers, especially of the will, . . . resulting, at all events when the drug is used to an excessive extent, in serious mental disorder, or even lunacy."[31] Dr. Brotteaux was joined by other members of his profession who attempted to analyze the chemical properties of marijuana and study its effects on human beings. Dr. Henri Bouquet, in his thesis "The Insane of Tunis" (1900), referred to "Indian hemp as an etiological factor in the greater part of mental disorders." A later experiment in 1930 by Dr. Dhunisboy of India showed that "prolonged use of Indian hemp usually leads to insanity." And in 1933 Dr. Gueche drew attention to the dangers of cannabis addiction "from the point of mental hygiene" and observed "that chronic intoxication led, in the end, to hallucinatory insanity."[32] Apparently a combination of three doctors dealing with extraordinary, isolated cases and a lack of scientific evidence convinced them of the extreme hazards associated with marijuana.

However, at least one member of the medical profession was not convinced that marijuana was the dangerous drug the Bureau of Narcotics was making it out to be or that it was solely responsible for many of the reported atrocities that resulted from smoking it. In 1937 Dr. Michael V. Ball of Warren, Pennsylvania, responded to a document published by the League of Nations and sanctioned by the FBN. Dr. Ball attested that marijuana alone was not responsible for producing the devastating effects attributed to it by the bureau. When a person was charged with committing violent acts while under the influence of drugs, Ball argued, it was most likely a combination of narcotics and alcohol which incited the user to brutality. In refuting the theories adhered to by the Narcotics Bureau, he described his own personal experience with the drug in a letter to an FBN official:

> Like every medical student, I experimented with the extract hemp and found a certain sedative action but as every scientific experiment ever recorded will show, the effect of the pure extract is very uncertain, large doses are required and seldom do the dreams take place that the writers talk about. I believe that unless the common hemp is mixed to make an alcoholic beverage, or used to smoke with henbane, belladonna and opium, it has very little if any psychological action.[33]

Great misconceptions abounded concerning narcotics, Dr. Ball maintained, that served only to confuse both the public and law enforcement agencies. He suggested that the current research only demonstrated that the user's reaction to marijuana was predicated on the individual's biological and personality characteristics. It was erroneous, therefore, to conclude that all users of the drug would exhibit identical behavior patterns. Before it could be scientifically confirmed that marijuana was a "killer drug," more testing under controlled conditions was required with people as the subjects. To achieve more definitive results, Ball wrote directly to Anslinger with the hope that laboratory studies could be performed with human subjects so that the symptoms could be properly observed. To persuade the commissioner at least to consider his suggestions, the doctor enclosed a pamphlet that outlined his research and the results which showed marijuana to be far less dangerous than the media (and the FBN) were reporting it to be.

Anslinger was not swayed by the doctor's findings and was in no way prepared to give serious consideration to the opinions of anyone he considered to be so out of touch with the accepted thinking on the subject. Anslinger replied to Dr. Ball that his findings surprised him since they contradicted most of the recognized authorities on the subject. Of the hundreds of letters he received, Anslinger avowed that only a handful entertained any doubt about marijuana's effects.[34] In his single-mindedness, Anslinger remained fixed in his determination to portray marijuana as an almost unbeatable foe—a "killer weed." He explicity conveyed his notion to Dr. Ball, insisting that "the marihuana evil can no longer be temporized with, and must be subjected to the same rigid method of control as traffic in other dangerous drugs."

In addition to the handful of physicians who questioned the popularized facts of marijuana, a small element of the press held misgivings about the government's national and international crusade against the supposed menace of marijuana. An editorial of 23 February 1932, in the *New York Sun* commented that "a great deal of nonsense is uttered about narcotics, the trade in them and addiction to them" and that the drug scare was most likely to "have been formed on the knowledge of too few cases to warrant popular alarm over the situation." The writer supported his argument by noting that since most Americans were so adversely affected by the Depression, they could not possibly afford to buy the drug. Furthermore, it defied logic for drug dealers to expect destitute users to sustain a profitable market for them.[35]

The above quotation was the exception to the rule. For every article or editorial that questioned the government's war on cannabis, dozens more were written which were decidedly pro-bureau and anti-marijuana. Perhaps the best example of anti-drug journalism of the latter category was written by the Commissioner himself in his *American Magazine* article. As noted earlier, Anslinger spared none of the gruesome details in depicting the Victor Licata tragedy. This kind of anti-marijuana rhetoric from the Commissioner of Narcotics, particularly as it was related to violent crimes, proved to be most effective in mobilizing favorable public opinion of the Bureau. But if the FBN was to put a stop to the illicit drug traffic in the country, it needed legislative assistance.

3

The Second Prohibition: Outlawing Marijuana, 1933–1937

Anslinger's ambivalent attitude throughout the debate for federal anti-marijuana legislation in the mid-1930s was not philosophically based. His bureau was already experiencing difficulty maintaining a sufficient level of personnel and appropriations for investigating violations of the Harrison Act and monitoring the importation of opiates. If Anslinger's manpower situation was less than adequate when he assumed office, it grew dramatically worse. As the nation braced itself for the worst years of the Depression, government cutbacks in spending were the rule across the board; the Federal Bureau of Narcotics was no exception.

Anslinger had no misgivings as to the wisdom of a federal anti-marijuana law but, realizing how limited his resources were, decided that 1933 was not a propitious time to involve the FBN in the federal regulation of another drug. Even nominal enforcement would require far more agents than he could possibly spare. Moreover, legal complexities merited consideration. The Harrison Act had been declared constitutional, but it had also been subjected to judicial review on five occasions, and Anslinger did not want to be saddled with legislation that had a history of inconsistent interpretation. Any law banning marijuana had to be written with very careful and precise language to insure its constitutionality. Also, the past experience of Prohibition served as a constant reminder of the difficulty Anslinger would have in trying to achieve total enforcement—not to mention prosecution—of an increasingly popular habit.

Hard Times, Soft Enforcement

For the Bureau's first year of operation, 1931–32, Congress was willing to appropriate $1.7 million. The annual appropriation for the fiscal years 1932 and 1933 was only $1.525 million a decrease of roughly 10 percent. From that level the budget allocation continued to shrink steadily. Initially the budget appropriation for the Bureau in 1934 was pared an additional 8 percent to $1.4 million. But President Roosevelt's Economy Bill went into effect before the funds were actually transferred to the Bureau, and Budget Director Lewis W. Douglas slashed another $400,000, representing an overall reduction of 34 percent from the previous year.[1] In a three-year period the Bureau of Narcotics lost $700,000 in operating funds.

Severe budgetary cuts meant that money the bureau had allocated for travel was reduced to almost nothing and that funds to pay informants for valuable information on drug rings and trafficking were too meager to buy much more than second-hand information. Not only was Commissioner Anslinger lacking in operating funds, he was also forced to "furlough" (lay off) eighty of his agents. The original force of 323 was faced with impossible task of policing importers, wholesalers, and retailers of narcotics; the drastic reduction in the number of agents to a skeleton crew enervated Anslinger's Narcotics Bureau.

Just to keep the bureau operating, Anslinger was forced to take extreme measures. The commissioner prohibited practically all but the most urgent local and long-distance telephone calls and other means of communication. Transportation allowances suffered similarly, as did per diem schedules, salaries, and administrative expenses. Even with a reduced staff, many of the FBN's local offices still had insufficient funds to cover the agents' salaries. Added to the problem of cutbacks in field personnel was the difficulty Anslinger experienced in recruiting new men. Most of those who attained eligibility under the civil service requirements shunned the Narcotics Bureau in favor of the Secret Service, which offered shorter hours and safer working conditions. Among those who did apply for positions as narcotics agents, many were leftovers from the old Prohibition Bureau. However badly the FBN needed men, it would not become, according to Assistant Deputy Commissioner of Narcotics Louis B. Ruppel, "the dumping ground for prohibition agents who now find themselves out of jobs or scheduled to be out of them very shortly."[2]

If any traffickers in narcotics had been present during Anslinger's testimony before the Appropriations Committee in 1934, they would have reveled in the commissioner's embarrassment when he related how his agents could not keep up with the criminals because "they use fast cars— Lincolns or Cadillac cars."[3] It was a humbling experience for Anslinger to have to go to local police authorities and ask to borrow an automobile for two or three weeks until the federal agents apprehended their suspects. To make the bureau more independent, Anslinger submitted a request for fifteen "new fast cars," one for each district which increased its fleet to 105 vehicles. Even with the increase, the ratio of agents to automobiles was nearly three to one.

Anslinger also testified that his agents were always at a serious, life-threatening disadvantage because of the weaponry they were issued. The Army .45-caliber firearms were inadequate for investigations because they were too cumbersome to be carried comfortably and indiscreetly. For field work Anslinger told the committee that the service revolvers were perfectly visible, easily detectable, and represented a real danger to the agents. As standard equipment, the commissioner recommended that a detective special—a smaller, less conspicuous firearm—be distributed to each agent at a total cost of $2,000.[4]

The decrease in operating expenses combined with the loss of manpower severely diminshed the Bureau's undercover activities. The situation grew so desperate that agents were forced to maintain their contacts and informants with money out of their own pockets and then often had to wait two months or longer for reimbursement. As a cost-cutting measure Anslinger tried to reduce the previous year's expenses for "buying" evidence by paying informants on a "reward basis" rather than pay them off "per diem." The policy saved money but was otherwise ineffective since there were fewer informants.

Cost-cutting had its limits, however. In 1935, the commissioner vociferously protested to Budget Director Douglas that the bureau was given woefully inadequate funding and even requested to appear before him for a reinstatement of $100,000. To convince Douglas that it would be a grave mistake to slash funds from the Bureau of Narcotics, Anslinger argued that the problem of illicit narcotics traffic was growing at incredibly wild proportions. As evidence he cited the area of southern California as a prime target for a "bumper crop" of marijuana.

Anslinger was not alone in his concern for the West Coast state. California Senator William G. McAdoo expressed his fear that bootleggers, who were put out of business when Prohibition ended, would presumably turn to selling drugs in the same way they sold contraband liquor. Senator McAdoo echoed Anslinger's anxiety that 1933 was not an appropriate time to cut back on the agency whose services were so essential in fighting the drug evil.

> Crippling the Narcotic Bureau's work is disastrous at this time. With the coming of repeal, prohibition racketeers are entering the dope traffic. Some of the country's most vicious criminals are participating.[5]

"Reefer Madness": The Marijuana Tax Act

The problem of enforcement and the lack of success of the Uniform Narcotic Law were two factors that prompted Anslinger to accept an invitation to attend a conference in New York City in January 1936 with representatives from Columbia University, the State Department, the League of Nations, and the Foreign Policy Association. The meeting, however, was unproductive, for they could not circumvent the problem of exercising legal control over interstate and foreign commerce. For that reason, a frustrated Anslinger advised Stephen B. Gibbons, Assistant Secretary of the Treasury in Charge of Customs, Coast Guard, and Narcotics, that although the conference discussed every conceivable possibility for the federal government to control the production and distribution of marijuana, under the existing taxing power of interstate commerce laws "it would be hopeless to expect any kind of adequate control."[6]

In anticipating a constitutional challenge to anti-marijuana legislation, Anslinger suggested that the Supreme Court case *Missouri v. Holland* (1920) might be a key to the problem of obtaining the necessary federal power. In this case the Court had to determine if, in protecting migratory birds in the United States and Canada by observing closed seasons, Congress was encroaching on local rule. The court allowed the regulatory statute because it had been enacted as required by international treaties with Canada to protect the birds from extinction. Invoking Article I, Section 8 of the Constitution, the Court decided that the federal law was "necessary and proper." Commissioner Anslinger recommended that a similarly constructed treaty should be adopted to provide for the control of marijuana. Since the marijuana treaty would be based on an earlier case, it was not expected to meet with constitutional problems. Otherwise, as Anslinger observed in his memorandum, the proposed legislation need only satisfy appropriate cabinet and commercial interests:

> The State Department has tentatively agreed to this proposition, but before action is taken we shall have to dispose of certain phases of legitimate traffic; for instance, the drug trade still has a small medical need for marijuana, but has agreed to eliminate it entirely. The only place it is used extensively is by the Veterinarian, and we can satisfy them by importing their medical needs.
>   We must also satisfy the canary bird seed trade, and the Sherwin-Williams Paint Company which uses hemp seed oil for drying purposes. We are now working with the Department of Commerce in finding substitutes for the legitimate trade, and after that is accomplished, the path will be cleared for the treaties and for a Federal law.[7]

Upon "discovering" the *Holland* case Anslinger was confident he had the legal means to place marijuana under federal control.

In the summer of 1936 Anslinger was one of four American delegates appointed by President Roosevelt to attend the Conference for the Suppression of Illicit Traffic in Dangerous Drugs in Geneva, Switzerland. Attempting to secure an international treaty, he urged members of twenty-six other nations to incorporate control of marijuana in any drug treaty that their respective governments might adopt. Anslinger failed to get the agreement he wanted in Geneva, but shortly after his return to Washington the Treasury Department began to prepare anti-marijuana legislation for Congress to consider. In January 1937 Anslinger met with the department's legal staff and medical experts to determine how they should present their case. Congressional hearings already had been scheduled for the spring.

While the Treasury Department was preparing its witnesses and organizing its data, the first session of the Seventy-Fifth Congress was presented with three bills dealing with the regulation of marijuana. Senator Carl Hatch re-introduced his bill prohibiting shipment and transportation of cannabis in interstate and foreign commerce, and Congressman Fish re-submitted a resolution prohibiting importation. On 28 January Congressman Thomas C. Hennings of Missouri introduced a third marijuana bill which would have prohibited "sale, possession, and transportation of cannabis except in compliance with regulations to be made by the commissioner on narcotics."[8]

In preparation for introducing a federal anti-marijuana bill, the Treasury Department invited fourteen government officials to participate in a conference for the purpose of identifying the physiological effects and legal definitions of marijuana.[9] As Commissioner of Narcotics, Anslinger was in attendance, but except for an occasional anecdote, his input in the discussion was limited, with most of the conversation dominated by scientists and lawyers. Alfred L. Tennyson, the bureau's legal counsel, stressed that in the hearings the department would have to justify why marijuana should be prohibited, and defend the proposed legislation to varnish (Sherwin-Williams) and birdseed industries that used various parts of the plant for commercial purposes.

Anslinger's most significant contribution during the conference was in the area of the drug's effects. When S. G. Tipton, a member of the legal staff, asked the commissioner if he could substantiate the horror stories about marijuana with factual incidents, Anslinger assured him that "we have a lot of cases showing that it certainly develops undesirable characteristics." Anslinger then inquired of Dr. Carl Voegtlin, Chief of the Division of Pharmocology of the National Institute of Health, if smoking marijuana caused insanity. The doctor replied less than authoritatively, "I think it is an established fact that prolonged use leads to insanity in certain cases, depending on the amount taken, of course." Voegtlin's observation was not based on any scientific research. The real purpose of the conference, it seemed, was primarily to allow Treasury officials to re-affirm their pre-determined position on federal anti-marijuana legislation.

On 14 April 1937, the Treasury Department's administrative proposal to control marijuana was finally presented in the House of Representatives. H.R. 6385 was introduced by Robert L. Doughton of North Carolina to

> impose an occupational excise tax upon certain dealers in marihuana to impose a transfer tax upon certain dealings in marihuana, and to safeguard the revenue therefrom by registry and recording.[10]

The provisions of the bill were three-fold. It required that all manufacturers, importers, dealers, and practitioners register and pay a special occupational tax. Next, it mandated that all transactions be accomplished through use of written order forms. Finally, it imposed a tax on all transfers in the amount of one dollar an ounce for transfer to unregistered persons. The most significant difference between the proposed Marijuana Tax Act and the Harrison Act was a prohibitive tax for transfer to registered (one dollar an ounce) and unregistered (one hundred dollars an ounce) persons.

Hearings conducted by the House Ways and Means Committee were opened by Congressman Doughton on 27 April and continued for five days through 4 May. The testimony given during the hearings merits a close examination, as it accurately reflects both the attitude and depth of understanding that contributed to this momentous piece of federal narcotics legislation.

Clinton Hester, Assistant General Counsel in the Treasury Department, was the first witness. Hester got to the point quickly. On the basis of an extensive two-year study conducted by the Treasury, he stated that "Indian hemp . . . is now being used by high school children in cigarettes. Its effect is deadly."[11] In providing a brief background for the bill, he concluded that the leading newspapers had advocated federal legislation to control traffic in marijuana, cited an AMA editorial supporting the bill, and presented statistics supplied by the Bureau of Narcotics, "proving" that the major criminal in the United States was the drug addict.

When Hester concluded his brief presentation, Congressman J. Hamilton Lewis asked whether the bill was necessary, since the marijuana tax could be added as an amendment to the Harrison Act. As one of the participants in the January treasury conference, Hester had anticipated the question and rapidly gave detailed reasons why, legislatively, that would not be wise. First, he replied, the Harrison Act included only production of narcotics outside the United States. Marijuana, for the most part, was grown within the American borders and would not be included in the Harrison Act. He also noted that opium and cocoa leaves, which were subject to the Harrison Act, had legitimate medicinal value; marijuana, on the other hand, had industrial uses, thus differentiating the two substances. Most significant, since the Harrison Act had been sustained by the Supreme Court, Hester and the Treasury Department did not want to subject it to further judicial scrutiny by adding an entirely new provision, preferring to leave its wording intact.

Rather than model the anti-marijuana bill entirely on the Harrison Act, under which no one could buy narcotics without registering and paying an occupation tax, the Treasury strategy had been to incorporate provisions of the recently enacted National Firearms Act. Under that law anyone was permitted to buy a machine gun or a submachine gun without registering, but he had to pay a $200 transfer tax and record the purchase on an official form. H.R. 6385 combined features of both statutes. Anyone who wanted to purchase marijuana had to register and pay a yearly fee. For these "legitimate transfers" the tax was one dollar an ounce. For non-registrants or "illegitimate transfers" the tax was $100 an ounce. At the time, marijuana could be bought legally for two dollars a pound. This prohibitive tax was borrowed from the Firearms Act.

That the Commissioner of Narcotics was the first witness to follow Hester's introductory remarks was not surprising, and Anslinger was consistent in his testimony. After identifying himself, he related the same tired story of marijuana as having originated with the Assassins of Persia a thousand years ago and how marijuana, more odious than opium, was the Jekyll and Hyde of narcotics.

The first question directed to Anslinger was from Congressman John D. Dingell who, apparently unfamiliar with the subject, tried to learn exactly what it was he and the committee were trying to prohibit:

MR. DINGELL: I want to be certain what this is. Is this the same weed that grows wild in some of our Western states which is sometimes called the loco weed?
MR. ANSLINGER: No, sir; that is another family.
MR. DINGELL: That is also a harmful drug-producing weed, is it not?
MR. ANSLINGER: Not to my knowledge; it is not used by humans.
THE CHAIRMAN: In what particular section does the weed grow wild?
MR. ANSLINGER: In almost every state in the Union today.
MR. REED: What you are describing has a very large flower?
MR. ANSLINGER: No, sir; a very small flower.[12]

The committee members obviously possessed little knowledge about marijuana, not only its physical appearance and habitat, but as it later became evident during the hearings, they knew no more about its properties and effects than what they read in the newspapers. Anslinger and the Treasury Department could not have asked for a more naive and gullible audience. Getting H.R. 6385 out of committee was little more than a matter of going through the motions.

What represented the most serious challenge to Anslinger's authority came from Congressman Fred Vinson, who was puzzled as to why the commissioner would wait until 1937 to recommend this kind of legislation. Anslinger responded that it was only in the last three years that marijuana had become a menace. Congressman Vinson chastised him for being so slow in getting to this legislation and expressed surprise that Anslinger had not urged passage in Congress before 1937.

Congressman John McCormack of Massachusetts inquired about marijuana's effects, and Anslinger must have found it difficult to restrain himself. He conceded that the weed affected people differently, but, wanting to make a good negative impression, he offered his expert opinion that "some people will fly into a delirious rage and many commit violent crimes." To a follow-up question pertaining to its use by the criminal class, Anslinger stated, "It is dangerous to the mind and body and particularly dangerous to the criminal type, because it releases all of the inhibitions."[13] After the first round of questioning the Commissioner referred to a prepared written summary of his favorite cases that had given him credibility with the media, appropriations committees, and Congressional hearings on bills that would increase the penalties for repeat offenders.

After graphically detailing a half-dozen incidents of marijuana-produced insanity, murder, sex crimes, and addiction, Anslinger reinforced his testimony citing the scholarly work of Eugene Stanley and A. E. Fossier. He was obviously well prepared for telling the committee what it needed to hear. Interestingly, for all the horrors he associated with marijuana, Anslinger did not subscribe to the stepping-stone theory that the drug led to harder narcotics:

MR. DINGELL: I am just wondering whether the marihuana addict graduates into a heroin, an opium, or a cocaine user.

MR. ANSLINGER: No, sir; I have not heard of a case of that kind. I think it is an entirely different class. The marihuana addict does not go in that direction.

MR. DINGELL: A hardened narcotic user does not fall back on marihuana?

MR. ANSLINGER: No, sir; he would not touch that.[14]

As supporting documents, Anslinger had inserted in the hearings transcript several Narcotics Bureau tables of statistics on seizures, the extent of traffic, and a state-by-state breakdown of marihuana laws. He also submitted the Floyd Baskette letter, Frank Gomila's research, and a report of his own titled "Marihuana Is the Mexican Term for Cannabis Indica."[15]

Anslinger had good cause to be satisfied with his performance during the first day of the hearings.

On Thursday and Friday, the third and fourth days of testimony, the Ways and Means Committee heard statements from representatives of various companies who used parts of the marijuana plant for industrial purposes. The William G. Scarlett & Co., the Philadelphia Seed Company, and the National Institute of Oilseed Products were concerned that new regulations would adversely affect their businesses. Generally they supported the bill but wanted exemptions for what they regarded as legitimate uses:

MR. SCARLETT: We handle a considerable quantity of hempseed annually for use in pigeon feeds. That is a necessary ingredient in pigeon feed because it contains an oil substance that is a valuable ingredient in pigeon feed, and we have not been able to find any seed that will take its place.

THE CHAIRMAN: Does the seed have the same effect on pigeons as the drug has on individuals?

MR. SCARLETT: I have never noticed it. It has a tendency to bring back the feather and improve the birds.

We are not interested in spreading marihuana, or anything like that. We do not want to be drug peddlers. But it has occurred to us that if we could sterilize the seed there would not be the possibility of the plant being produced from the seeds that the pigeons might throw on the ground.[16]

After Scarlett explained the process of sterilization to the satisfaction of the committee, it agreed that the seed industry would be permitted to continue using marijuana in its product.

The only serious critic of the bill who appeared before the committee was Dr. William C. Woodward, Legislative Counsel for the AMA. Dr. Woodward's testimony, on Tuesday, 4 May, the last day of the hearings, was anything but routine. It was obvious from his opening statement that his opinions were not well-received by either Treasury officials or committee members:

Mr. Chairman and gentlemen. It is with great regret that I find myself in opposition to any measure that is proposed by the Government, and particularly in opposition to any measure that has been proposed by the Secretary of the Treasury for the purpose of suppressing traffic in narcotics.[17]

To clarify his position that he was sympathetic to the narcotics problem, he stated how he had cooperated with Hamilton Wright in drafting the Harrison Act and that he had been a frequent visitor to the Narcotics Bureau during the past two years. As a physician and attorney Woodward possessed a unique perspective on the medical and legal ramifications of H.R. 6385, but he was not supportive of what he perceived as the ill-advised federal regulation of marijuana.

The doctor's opposition became evident when Woodward acknowledged that a drug problem existed but questioned the media coverage and chastised the Ways and Means Committee for not inviting more witnesses to appear, witnesses who had the expertise to confirm or deny the allegations made about marijuana. Woodward never denied that narcotics addiction was a problem. But he did express surprise that the committee had not been presented with more substantial evidence.

If the use of marijuana did cause crime, he asked, why did the committee not invite authorities in related fields to offer their opinions on the matter? Much of the prison population was said to have been addicted to the drug, yet no one from the Bureau of Prisons was asked to testify. Nor was anyone summoned from the Children's Bureau of the Office of Education to discuss the alleged prevalence of marijuana-smoking among the adolescent population. Had representatives from these agencies been given the opportunity to testify, they likely would have refuted the Treasury Department's claims that drug addiction among inmates or school children was a growing problem.[18]

Essentially the point Woodward was trying to make was that more legislation in this situation was not necessarily better. He argued that sufficient laws designed to control marijuana had already been passed. On the federal level was title 21, section 198 of the United States Code, the same statute that created the Bureau of Narcotics in 1930. Laws relating to marijuana already existed, and, as Woodward pointed out, if these statutes contained any weaknesses, the Secretary of the Treasury was to blame for not exercising stricter enforcement during the seven years they had been in effect. The so-called "twilight zone"—which Anslinger blamed for contributing to the narcotics problem—was a legal loop-hole between state and federal laws that allowed drug peddlers to evade prosecution and, according to Woodward, resulted from a lack of effort to coordinate the laws.

Dr. Woodward did not limit his criticisms to the state laws. Even the proposed federal marijuana taxing bill, he observed, contained several weaknesses. For the federal government to continually inspect the entire United States for the growth of marijuana would be physically impossible. Even if the government discovered a crop of the weed and obtained a search warrant, Woodward felt that prosecuting attorneys would encounter the same difficulties experienced under the Prohibition Act: inadequacy of the courts, inadequacy of the prosecuting attorneys, and inadequacy of the jails to hold all of the offenders.

In what was perhaps the most serious or amusing loophole, depending on the point of view, was the provision that defined "producers." As written in the bill, anyone who made use of marijuana was a producer. And a producer must be taxed, although he had the right to pay the tax and obtain the drug. An astute user of the drug could have deduced correctly that any addict who could pay the tax could register as a producer and purchase the drug for his own use. Woodward assumed that this oversight would be amended by the Treasury Department.

Dr. Woodward also thought it strange that Anslinger offered no information on why the states needed assistance. Even a major interstate trafficking problem did not necessitate a federal law. The doctor testified on several occasions that he advised the Commissioner of Narcotics to follow the practice of meeting annually with state officers to exchange information, as had been so successful in the Bureau of Public Health. Without the voluntary cooperation of the states, Woodward feared that the federal government would see little progress under the proposed legislation. He was convinced that through the conferences the states would be given incentive to enforce their own laws.[19]

As an attorney, Woodward was supicious and critical of the legal reasoning given for why marijuana was not simply added to the Harrison Act. In what resembled a modern Catch-22 situation, he argued that it did not make sense to him that there was so much concern about constitutionality. Since the constitutionality of the Harrison Act had been affirmed by the Supreme Court and since Treasury representatives testified that they were assured the bill was constitutional, there should be no reason why it could not be incorporated in the Harrison Act. If it was not constitutional, then obviously it should not be enacted.

Woodward was an unpopular witness at the hearings and he knew it. If there was any doubt in his mind, it was quickly erased in the interrogation that followed. The taxation of marijuana was relegated to a secondary role; Dr. Woodward became the focal point of the hearings. After the equivalent of eleven pages of testimony and questioning, Congressman Vinson expressed less interest in the regulation of marijuana than he did in Woodward's credentials.

As soon as Woodward presented his résumé, Vinson engaged the doctor in a petty squabble about an editorial published in a recent AMA *Journal* which, in the two-sentence excerpt the congressman read, appeared supportive of the bill. Vinson argued that the AMA was behind the bill. Woodward countered that in his brief quotation Vinson had distorted the tone and substance of the article. When the doctor could not divulge who wrote the editorial, Vinson suggested that Woodward was not an appropriate representative of the AMA.

Congressman McCormack continued the line of questioning on the editorial, followed by Congressman Chester Thompson of Illinois. When Vinson got his next opportunity, he asked Woodward to give the committee a statement on all the bills for which he testified as counsel for the AMA. When he replied that it was not possible to do that, Vinson narrowed the period to the past fifteen years.

In addition to the animosity Woodward aroused by his criticisms of the government's efforts to control marijuana, there was also a "partisan" hostility toward him. As an ardent New Dealer, Vinson vented his anger on Woodward for the AMA's opposition to the Title VI provision of Roosevelt's social security act which authorized $8 million for health benefits.[20]

Congressman Doughton was also not to be deprived of an opportunity to harass the doctor. Near the end of the hearings, the tone became even more bitter and condescending as the chairman pressed the doctor to justify his criticisms. Nearly every opinion expressed by Woodward was challenged by one or more members of the committee. The doctor never had a chance. He was even accused of being "peeved" because he was not consulted on the drafting of the bill. At the conclusion of Woodward's testimony—which was considerably longer than Anslinger's—Chairman Doughton dismissed him without even granting him the professional courtesy of a thank-you.[21] Dr. Woodward was accused of everything from misrepresentation and evasiveness, to giving inaccurate testimony and impeding important legislation.

When the hearings moved to the Senate two months later, Woodward wisely decided not to subject himself to further harassment. Instead of making a personal appearance, he submitted a one-page letter reiterating the reasons for the AMA's opposition to the bill.

"SOMETHING THAT IS CALLED MARIHUANA": DEBATE?

One week after the hearings, on 11 May, Chairman Doughton reported the marijuana tax bill, re-styled with amendments as H.R. 6906, to the full House. A month later it was presented for debate on the House floor. The same Congressmen who were determined not to allow Woodward's dissenting point of view to sway their judgment in committee hearings participated in the debate on the regulation of marijuana. Again they betrayed an appalling ignorance of the subject. They exhibited a cavalier attitude in debating the bill and approached it with an aloofness and indifference not commonly associated with the enactment of narcotics laws; it was almost as if they were annoyed with having to discuss it.

MR. DOUGHTON: I ask unanimous consent for the present consideration of the bill (H.R. 6906) . . .

MR. SNELL: Mr. Speaker, reserving the right to object, and notwithstanding the fact that my friend, REED, is in favor of it, is this a matter we should bring up at this late hour of the afternoon? I do not know anything about the bill. It may be all right and it may be that everyone is for it, but as a general principle, I am against bringing up any important legislation, and I suppose this is important, since it comes from the Ways and Means Committee, at this late hour of the day.

MR. DOUGHTON: I may say to the distinguished gentleman from New York that we have a unanimous report from the committee on this bill and there is no objection, and while we would like to get it passed, if there is any objection, I shall not insist, of course.

MR. SNELL: This is an illustration of the situation I was talking to the majority leader about a few moments ago. If we hold a session until late in the day and somebody brings up a piece of legislation, the average Member knows nothing about it, and while it is probably all right, it is hardly fair to take it up at that time.

MR. RAYBURN: Mr. Speaker, if the gentleman will yield, I may say that the gentleman from North Carolina has stated to me that this bill has a unanimous report from the committee and that there is no controversy about it.

MR. SNELL: What is the bill?

MR. RAYBURN: It has something to do with something that is called marihuana. I believe it is a narcotic of some kind.

MR. FRED M. VINSON: Marihuana is the same as hashish.

MR. SNELL: Mr. Speaker, I am not going to object but I think it is wrong to consider legislation of this character at this time of night.[22]

On 14 June Congressman Frank H. Buck of California presented the bill again, asking for unanimous consent. After less than thirty minutes of debate, which included no medical or scientific evidence, H.R. 6906 was read a third time and passed. From the House the bill went to the Senate for hearings conducted by a Senate Finance subcommittee chaired by Senator Pat Harris of Mississippi.

The Senate hearings were relatively brief, requiring just one session to examine only six witnesses including Anslinger. They were an abbreviated version of the House Ways and Means hearings. No new testimony or new evidence was presented; none of the witnesses—different people but representing the same birdseed and hemp interests—offered an original statement. Anslinger repeated his horror stories for the benefit of the committee and stated with absolute conviction that marijuana produced homicidal tendencies in the user's personality. In less than thirty pages of testimony the hearings were concluded. In the next few days the bill was reported favorably out of committee, passed with minor amendments, and sent back to the House where it was considered again. The Senate suggestions were quickly adopted. The major concern raised in the House was whether the bill was supported by the AMA. Congressman Vinson confirmed that the committee had heard testimony on the association's behalf and noted that Dr. Woodward testified at length.[23] On 2 August, President Roosevelt signed the bill into law; it was to take effect sixty days later on the first of October.

The law that banned a plant most people perceived as an evil weed and imposed an occupational tax on importers, sellers, dealers, and anyone handling cannabis. A transfer tax fixed at one dollar per ounce was charged for registered persons and $100.00 per ounce for those not registered with the government. Unlike alcohol during prohibition, possession was outlawed with penalties to fit an Assassin of Persia: violations were punishable by a $2,000 fine, five years' imprisonment, or both. Unlike prohibition and its advocates, this law marked only the beginning of the fight for Anslinger.

If the debate aroused in Congress seemed minimal, that aroused in the press was almost nonexistent. Ironically, the model for repressive narcotics legislation, which was to foster a heated debate over the next forty years, received little attention. In its 14 August issue, *Newsweek* devoted less than a column and a half to the new law commenting that "sensational press stories about its use in grade and high schools generally prove unfounded."[24] The *New York Times* reported its enactment on page four of its 3 August edition, stating only that "President Roosevelt signed today a bill to curb traffic in the narcotic marihuana, through heavy fines on transactions."

Aftermath

The Marijuana Tax Act was poorly conceived by Treasury Department officials and haphazardly debated by uninformed politicians who made little effort to understand the subject. Testimony at the hearings was given by experts like Clinton Hester who declared the drug deadly on the basis of a vague two-year study. Dr. James Munch, a government pharmacologist who subjected dogs to marijuana, concluded that it caused degeneration of the human brain. In addition to exaggerating stories of the drug's effects, Commissioner Anslinger felt confident enough to make medical pronouncements about marijuana. With the exception of Dr. Woodward, who opposed the bill, the only official testimony given at the hearings was from Treasury department personnel who initiated the legislation.

The provisions of the Marijuana Tax Act, of course, were not really designed to raise revenue or even regulate the use of marijuana. Their purpose was to provide the legal mechanisms to enforce the prohibition of all use of marijuana. Anslinger and others had capitalized on social and cultural conditions to gain passage of the law. They also benefited by presenting anti-marijuana legislation as moral reform necessary to protect innocent victims, especially children, from becoming addicted to an evil drug. The Tax Act was more a symbolic effort and bureaucratic victory than a solution to the threat of a marijuana epidemic. Nevertheless, Anslinger was convinced that marijuana was socially threatening and that strict control through law enforcement was essential. The bureau's educational campaign was stepped up, and within a few years every state had passed laws against marijuana that were often equated with laws concerning murder, rape, and other serious offenses. These laws also failed to distinguish one drug from another. Immediately following the Tax Act, most states specified that marijuana and heroin penalties be identical. Consequently, as heroin sentences were increased over the years, marijuana penalties were automatically re-adjusted upward.

THE CALDWELL CASE

The first case to be tried under the new law exemplified the excessively punitive attitude of many courts throughout the country. On Friday, 8 October, just one week after the act went into effect, United States District Judge J. Foster Symes of Denver imposed the first sentence. Samuel R. Caldwell, a 58-year-old peddler, was sentenced to a four-year term in Leavenworth Penitentiary and fined $1,000. Justice for Mr. Caldwell was unusually swift. Arrested by narcotics agents working out of the Denver bureau on Wednesday night, Caldwell was indicted by a grand jury on Thursday and sentenced on Friday. Remarkably, Caldwell, who had pleaded guilty, had been processed through the judicial system in a period of forty-eight hours.[25]

The punishment imposed by Judge Symes was in striking contrast to the manner in which cases involving marijuana had been handled in the past. Prior to the Caldwell case—and the Marihuana Tax Act—dope peddlers were usually treated much more leniently under city or state laws that under the new federal legislation that provided for sixty days minimum sentence and particularly under that handed out by Symes. In pronouncing sentence on Caldwell, the judge cited the viciousness of marijuana and emphatically warned other potential violators that they, too, would be dealt with severely in his court:

I consider marihuana the worst of all narcotics—far worse than the use of morphine or cocaine. Under its influence men become beasts, just as was the case with [Moses] Baca . . . who two weeks ago tried to murder his wife, the mother of three children. Marihuana destroys life itself. I have no sympathy with those who sell this weed. In the future I will impose the heaviest penalties. The government is going to enforce this new law to the letter.[26]

To Commissioner Anslinger, who once urged judges to "jail offenders, then throw away the key," Judge Symes's disposition of the Caldwell case was most satisfying.[27]

Anslinger continued to press for tough enforcement throughout the duration of his career. But soon after the act's passage, he began to tone down the hysterical reports of marijuana and even discouraged continued media attention. As a promoter of the Tax Act, he found it advantageous to publicize marijuana addiction among adolescents and its relation to violent crime. As an enforcer of the new law, however, Anslinger decided that it was much more pragmatic and expedient to minimize its effects. In a report written in 1938, he admitted that, although marijuana was a vital enforcement problem, "the abuse of Marihuana isn't as prevalent as some sensational accounts would indicate." When asked by Congressman Louis Ludlow during the appropriations committee hearings in December 1939 if there was an increase or decrease in the number of drug addicts, Anslinger replied that there was a "very definite decrease." He still regarded it as a potential danger to the younger element of the population but again conceded that some of the reported crimes and atrocities attributed to its use "have been authenticated and some have been disproved."[28]

MARIJUANA AND NARCOTICS

The Marijuana Tax Act, which is now a part of the Internal Revenue Code, has not produced any significant revenue, since few Marijuana Tax stamps have been issued to those wishing to officially register under the act. Still, as late as 1970, the Internal Revenue Service has tried to collect $100,000 per ounce of illegally possessed marijuana from those who have violated the act.[29] The obvious intent of the legislation was not to regulate or control the traffic in marijuana but to impose federal police powers in the area of enforcement.

By the time the Tax Act was passed in Congress in 1937, forty-one states had already outlawed marijuana throughout the adoption of the Uniform Narcotics Law, which made no distinction between marijuana, a nonaddictive hallucinogen, and opiates such as heroin and morphine. This blanket classification was indicative of the absence of scientific research, but at least the Bureau of Narcotics maintained a degree of consistency in disavowing any appreciable difference in drugs. In describing the effects of marijuana in the 1930s, Harry Anslinger and other FBN officials frequently claimed it was more dangerous than heroin or opium, although Anslinger backed away from some of the more outrageous claims after 1937. Thirty years later Donald E. Miller, Chief Counsel for the Bureau of Narcotics, was still reluctant to separate marijuana from more potent narcotics. He acknowledged that marijuana was not considered a narcotic drug under federal law; but because many states still considered it a narcotic, physical properties were of little significance. Since both laws, argued Miller, were designed to "control a substance which is socially unacceptable," it was "less important that the controls fit like some finely balanced formula under either the taxing clause or the commerce clause of the Constitution, or in a category according to its similarity with other dangerous drugs."[30] Charges made by critics of the FBN since its inception had at last been confirmed by one of the bureau's own: that, although the Narcotics Bureau did not create the marijuana scare in the 1930s, it was fully prepared to enforce prohibition of the drug.

LEGACY

In the nearly fifty years since the passage of the Marijuana Tax Act, a dramatic transformation has occurred with regard to the anti-marijuana legislation, the typical user, and perceptions of its effects. Decriminalization in the 1970s reversed the continual trend of escalating penalties, and no longer did a person who possessed or even pushed the drug risk life imprisonment. Many states, in fact, had reduced marijuana use to a misdemeanor punishable by no more than six months in jail; more likely sentences were six months probation. The 1990s may be a decade of increasing penalties, however. During the scare of the 1930s, smokers generally came from disadvantaged minority groups. Since then marijuana's popularity has ranged across the spectrum of socio-economic classes. Finally, marijuana no longer is portrayed as a contributing cause of violent crimes. There may be a correlation in some cases between marijuana and crime, but it is not considered as a causal factor in murder or rape as was reported in the mid-1930s.

The history of marijuana prohibition since the enactment of the Marijuana Act shares similarities with the prohibition of alcohol. Both proved to be extremely difficult to prohibit and both provoked enormous controversy resulting in either repeal or dramatic modification. The legislation was viewed by many as hastily adopted attempts to restrain individual behavior which the government, or agencies of the government, had determined was harmful and objectionable. In both cases, many have argued, the cure was more detrimental to the user's health than the ailment. The enforcement of alcohol and marijuana prohibition was in ways more threatening to society than the problems it created.

Combined state and federal enforcement was sufficiently effective by the end of the 1930s, according to the Bureau's annual report, to slow the volume of trafficking and diminish marijuana's popularity.[31] Anslinger and the Bureau of Narcotics appeared to have the drug problem under control. The commissioner proved his resourcefulness in protecting the bureau and displayed impressive bureaucratic talents. But Anslinger's outspoken manner and inflexible philosophical views made him a favorite target for those who saw him as tyrannical and narrow-minded. His passionate belief in hard law and order as a solution to problems ranging from drug addiction to juvenile delinquency to communist aggression insured that he would constantly be a subject of controversy. During his first decade as head of the Narcotics Bureau, Anslinger demonstrated his crusading spirit in securing the Marijuana Tax Act. He would need more than a piece of legislation, however, to survive the many internal threats and external challenges that followed him throughout his career.

4

Storm and Stress, 1930–1950

Harry Anslinger had no sooner assumed his responsibilities as the Commissioner of Narcotics when he was beset with a series of problems that potentially could have terminated his career. In one instance it was Anslinger's own carelessness and imprudence that provoked a Washington official to demand his resignation, but in the end the incident proved to be little more than a temporary embarrassment. Most of the difficulties confronting Anslinger, however, involved improper conduct and procedure on the part of bureau agents. Less than a year after his appointment, the commissioner was confronted with the first scandal within the bureau. Though it was an isolated incident, it was not the last time the reputation of the FBN would be tarnished by the ignominious behavior of corrupt agents.

Close Encounters

The first crisis in Anslinger's administration erupted in April 1931 when three federal agents of the local New York narcotics bureau were arrested as conspirators in an attempt to bribe a federal official.[1] Richard Nash and Charles Keane, both then with the bureau, and Philip DeStefano, who had recently resigned, were taken into custody and charged with attempting to bribe another agent, Arnold Lachenauer. At the arraignment it was reported that DeStefano had delivered $1,000 to Lachenauer to persuade him not to testify against a dealer in narcotics. The dealer, Peter Ellsinois, was indicted with thirty others in December 1930 as the result of a well-planned wholesale raid led by Lachenauer.

The alleged conspiracy began on 16 March 1931, when Keane, acting as go-between, offered the money to Lachenauer if he failed to identify Ellsinois. Lachenauer played along and agreed to accept the bribe, telling Keane to "bring the money in cash and I'll do the rest." Lachenauer then reported the incident to his immediate superior, Joseph A. Manning, who in turn contacted Anslinger in Washington. Anslinger instructed Manning to go along with Keane in order to lay a trap.

On 2 April De Stefano met with Lachenauer and delivered the $1,000 while they dined in a restaurant on Pearl Street. Approximately one hour later they left for a speak-easy on 52nd Street where they were joined by Nash and Keane. Shortly after they were seated, the three narcotics agents were apprehended by investigative agents from the Department of Justice who had been planted in the lounge. In addition to conspiracy, the agents were charged with subornation of perjury, attempted bribery, and obstruction of justice. During their trial in June, Keane was eventually acquitted; Nash and DeStefano were both found guilty and sentenced to five years in the Atlanta penitentiary and ordered to pay fines of $13,000 each.

Throughout Anslinger's career and after his retirement, scandals involving corrupt agents frequently rocked the bureau. The New York office in particular was constantly under investigation and became involved in what was probably the most damaging scandal (involving collusion between narcotics agents and heroin dealers) to the integrity of federal narcotics agents in 1968, as discussed in chapter 8.

Just eight months after the bribery incident, New York agents were again charged with illegal practices, this time by U.S. Congressman Loring M. Black, who accused them of protecting underworld figure Jack "Legs" Diamond.[2] Black asserted that narcotics agents interfered with the New York City police by preventing Diamond's release to the local authorities for interrogation and photographing. The congressman also accused the federal agents of spending $40,000 to equip an apartment in New York for the purpose of tapping the telephone of a wholesale drug distributor, which Black maintained was in violation of the law. Apparently he was unaware or indifferent to Secretary of the Treasury Morgenthau's tacit approval of wiretapping as a means of detecting violators of laws against narcotics, smuggling, and bootlegging.[3]

Congressman Black's charges may have been justified, but his demands for a formal congressional inquiry were likely politically motivated. The Democratic representative had been urging a congressional investigation of the narcotics situation for more than two years. In 1931 he and Representatives Fiorello H. LaGuardia and Hamilton Fish, Jr., both of New York, introduced measures calling for investigations, but none of them was passed. Only a month before the "Diamond protection," Black introduced House Resolution 98 "to investigate the Narcotics Bureau."[4]

Politically inspired or not, the charges against the Bureau of Narcotics for harboring a criminal and hampering local enforcement officials attracted only negative publicity which Anslinger could not afford if he wanted to retain his appointment. This was especially critical in a presidential election year, when it was obvious that the Hoover Administration, with which Anslinger was closely allied, was to be succeeded by the Democrat Franklin D. Roosevelt. The White House and the spoils of political patronage were about to be awarded to a new president and a different party. Harry Anslinger's situation in the early 1930s could best be described as precarious.

Ironically though, if anyone benefited from the strains of the Depression, it was Anslinger. Roosevelt was so immersed in organizing his National Industrial Recovery program through the first several months of his presidency that Anslinger and other second-level administrators who were left over from the outgoing administration enjoyed a reprieve. Even with the borrowed time, Anslinger almost managed inadvertently to arrange his own resignation. Two incidents within the next year not only embarrassed Anslinger, but aroused unnecessary and unwanted controversy for the commissioner.

William G. Walker, Chief of the Narcotics Division for the State of California and close friend of Anslinger, was charged by the *San Francisco News* with having permitted his records "to be recklessly distorted in the interest of a hysterical campaign," thereby "bringing the law and the state into contempt."[5] To justify his request for an additional appropriation, Walker admitted under pressure that he had fed stories to the *San Francisco News* and the *San Francisco Examiner* detailing the activities of a narcotics and white slave ring. Claiming that young women were picked up regularly at San Francisco employment bureaus, Walker described how the victims said they were turned into addicts within a week before being sold to a Sacramento ring where they were forced into prostitution so they could support their habit.

The Walker scam in itself would not have adversely reflected on Anslinger's reputation or lessened his chances for reappointment. But only four months earlier, in a letter to California state Senator Sanborn Young, Anslinger referred to the recent appointment of Walker as Chief of Narcotics and commented, "I knew Mr. Walker very favorably during the time he was an Administrator in the Prohibition Bureau, and I am sure narcotic enforcement in your State will go ahead under him."[6] Though Walker was not in the FBN, Californians and high-ranking politicians were aware that he had the commissioner's support. Obviously this kind of recommendation was a less-than-impressive display of Anslinger's judgment.

Though he was still in office at the end of 1933, Anslinger had not yet been asked to stay, and rumors were rampant that he was certain to be replaced. Even those who had no interest in politics—downtrodden drug addicts—were aware of Anslinger's fragile position in the new Roosevelt Administration. One of them, remaining appropriately and prudently anonymous, presented a pathetic but realistic picture of the plight of a drug addict in a sloppily handwritten letter to Postmaster General James A. Farley:

Mr. Farley—Anslinger, shaking and trembling, knowing you are going to can him, is making a big noise recently [about addicts and the drug problem] pinching a lot of poor <u>sick addicts</u>. And here is the <u>sad part</u>—a <u>genuine tragedy</u>—he conveys to society the impression that drug ad<u>dicts are</u> desperate criminals. Mr. Farley, drug addicts are the most <u>harmless</u> class of people in the country. A smart dick will tell you the same. <u>Not</u> a <u>Narcotic agent</u>.[7]

Drug addicts were not the only ones who would have preferred the removal of the commissioner. Still trying to secure his position in the last months of 1934, Anslinger triggered the second incident that nearly guaranteed his own demise. In a circular letter distributed to district supervisors in December, Anslinger alerted agents that an informer named Edward Jones was neither reliable nor satisfactory. Included in the memo was a physicial description listing his age, height, weight, and color, which Anslinger reported as "Medium and might be termed a 'ginger-colored nigger.' "[8] This time protest came not from below but from above.

Newly elected U.S. Senator Joseph F. Guffey of Pennsylvania, Anslinger's home state, was outraged and demanded that President Roosevelt ask for the commissioner's resignation. In a letter to Anslinger's immediate superior, Assistant Secretary of the Treasury Gibbons, Senator Guffey referred to the circular letter and expressed concern for the affront to the sensibilities of the black population:

> This circular letter has become public and the colored population of the State of Pennsylvania have been advised thereof. I am being deluged with complaints from our colored population because Mr. Anslinger has been so indiscreet as to refer to one of their race as a "ginger-colored nigger."
>
> It would seem to me that a man in such a responsible position as that held by Mr. Anslinger should have more discretion than to refer to one of such a large part of the population of this Country in the manner quoted above, and that I doubt very much that one so indiscreet should be allowed to remain in such a responsible position. Personally, I think he should be replaced, and I submit the matter to you for your consideration.[9]

Anslinger's gaffe did not pass without notice in the presidential circle either. Two weeks after the circular letter was publicized, Robert L. Vann of the Department of Justice forwarded a copy to Louis M. Howe, Secretary to President Roosevelt, suggesting that the president be informed about the incident and warned that "an avalanche of protest against Mr. Anslinger is headed toward the White House."[10] Vann, too, was furious with Anslinger's racial slur, stating that it was absolutely inexcusable for a communication of this nature to be distributed throughout the United States. More pragmatically, Vann was concerned that because it was so insulting, it would have a "tendency to lead colored people to believe that this is the type of treatment they may expect from the Roosevelt Administration." Though the letter came from outside the White House, Vann observed, likely without realizing the incredible faux pas he committed, that "In any event, the President gets the 'black eye.'"

From the press releases issued by the White House in March 1933, it appeared that, though Anslinger had not been reappointed, Roosevelt was expected to ask him to remain. When the commissioner was notified that he was chosen again to represent the United States in May when the League of Nations narcotics committee met in Geneva, many observers interpreted the move as assurance Anslinger would continue as head of the FBN.[11] But by summer another contender with impressive credentials and a more suitable political affiliation emerged.

Dr. L. S. Booker of Durham, North Carolina—who was enthusiastically endorsed by Senator Robert R. Reynolds and Congressman William B. Umstead, both members of the North Carolina Congressional delegation—was regarded as a serious candidate for the $9,000-a-year position. After recommendations were presented to Postmaster Farley, a major North Carolina newspaper reported that Anslinger would probably be removed, with Dr. Booker to be named as his successor.[12]

Over the next several months additional names surfaced as possible replacements for Commissioner of Narcotics. In a memorandum to President Roosevelt on 28 November 1933, four individuals were discussed along with their "qualifications" for the office. Charles Hand was suggested for the appointment because of his involvement in Al Smith's presidential campaign and the popularity he enjoyed in Texas as an aide to Congressman John Nance Garner, who had since become Vice President of the United States. Perhaps most important, it was thought that Hand would "meet with Hearst's approval."[13] Since the publishing magnate had proved himself an ardent and faithful supporter of strict narcotics enforcement and exerted national influence, this was a prime consideration. Bill Lawby was also mentioned bcause of his long years with the Hearst company, and New York Deputy Police Commissioner Phil Hoyt was suggested although it was feared his Tammany connection might be a handicap.

It is not unusual for politicians and affected business interests to lobby for patronage appointments; quite the contrary, it has become an accepted and expected practice. What was surprising about the endorsements above was that they came not just from Democratic congressmen seeking favors, but from Louis Ruppel, Anslinger's assistant and second in command of the Narcotics Bureau. Needless to say, "Louis Rubbish," as Anslinger loyalists within the bureau commonly called the deputy commissioner, enjoyed a far shorter tenure than his boss.

Competition for Anslinger's job also came from aspirants who lacked the benefit of political influence and attempted to promote their own candidacy. In a four-page letter to Louis Howe, Dr. Walter F. Enfield presented a detailed outline of his assets and emphasized that he, more than Anslinger, was capable of controlling the country's drug problem. Writing from Bedford, Pennsylvania, approximately thirty miles from Anslinger's hometown of Altoona, Enfield discussed his loyal support for the President and stressed Anslinger's political connections with Pennsylvania Republicans and critics of the New Deal.[14]

Despite political patronage, more qualified competition, embarrassments, scandals within his agency, and the fact that he was a conservative Republican in a liberal Democratic administration, Anslinger managed to hang on and win reappointment. Had he introduced an innovative program for rehabilitating drug addicts, adopted an effective benevolent approach to enforcement, or established a reputation for nailing big names in the criminal underworld as J. Edgar Hoover was doing at the FBI; it would have been logical for Roosevelt to keep Anslinger. But the commissioner could claim no accomplishments of that magnitude. What he did have, though, was a loyal, influential following, a knack for making himself seem indispensable, and a preservationist instinct.

While Roosevelt was inundated with partisan endorsements for a new narcotics commissioner, he was also entreated by staunchly conservative newspaper editors, influential Washington politicians, and a powerful pharmaceutical lobby to keep Anslinger. Among the drug companies that supported Anslinger—and nearly all of them did—three were especially valuable to the Commissioner and the Narcotics Bureau. Merck & Company in Rahway, New Jersey; Mallinckrodt Chemical Works in St. Louis; and New York Quinine & Chemical Works in Brooklyn were the largest manufacturers of pharmaceuticals in the United States and formed the nucleus of "Anslinger's Army."

As Commissioner of Narcotics, one of Anslinger's most important duties, in addition to the enforcement of drug laws, was to monitor the internal control of manufactured drugs. The simplest way to exercise control was to authorize only a limited number of pharmaceutical firms to import raw opium which was used for the production of various medicinal drugs. Obviously the companies that were permitted to manufacture the drugs, especially since there were so few, stood to gain tremendous profits. The arrangement was mutually convenient for both Anslinger and the manufacturers. The drug companies made money, and Anslinger was given control of a powerful lobby. Eventually a fourth company, Hoffman-LaRoche in Nutley, New Jersey, was granted authorization to import opium, and by 1936 Parke-Davis & Company in Detroit, Eli Lilly in Indianapolis, Sharpe & Dohme, in Philadelphia, and E. R. Squibb & Sons in Brooklyn were added to Anslinger's exclusive list.[15] The intense competition within the drug industry for a lucrative import license contributed greatly to Anslinger's influence.

While President Roosevelt remained indecisive about reappointing the narcotics commissioner, Anslinger kept his name in the newspaper by declaring a war against race track owners who were lax in preventing the doping of horses with cocaine, heroin, caffeine, and even strychnine. The problem was confined to a relatively small number of tracks, but Anslinger maximized the emotional effects of cruelty to animals. Even Drew Pearson commented in a 1933 column that Anslinger was getting much publicity by exposing the doping of horses.[16]

Publicity was exactly what Anslinger wanted; and, by threatening involvement of the Bureau of Narcotics to expose this nefarious practice, he generated more notoriety. Anslinger assigned several agents to work undercover at various tracks, and through the use of recently developed saliva tests for horses, several individuals were arrested. Anslinger could not be criticized for going after such unscrupulous people who would risk the lives of thoroughbreds so they could guarantee winning horses. But he was extremely reluctant to interfere with the track owners. In a letter to William Randolph Hearst, Anslinger expressed his appreciation to the Hearst newspapers for their support of his effort to suppress horse-doping and stated that, though he would not waver in his purpose, he would not involve the federal government in the regulation of horse racing.[17]

By publicizing federal agents' raids on several race tracks but actually taking minimal preventive measures, Anslinger drew attention to the Narcotics Bureau. The numerous arrests of trainers—who received 10 percent of the purse if the horses won—put Anslinger in the role of a protector for which the owners—usually very wealthy—were most appreciative. They were also pleased that Anslinger had not held them legally responsible or charged them with abuse or negligence. The owners expressed their gratitude in their support of him as narcotics commissioner. Thus, Anslinger adroitly exploited the situation to both his and the track owners' advantage. The latter group was satisfied that the problem was being solved, causing them minimal inconvenience; the commissioner managed to prove his *raison d'être* and gain favorable publicity.

The horse-doping scandal first aroused Anslinger "sometime about 1932."[18] Through 1936, frequent references to it appeared in many newspapers, including the *New York Times* as well as several articles in racing periodicals like *Post Time* and *Polo,* and in magazines with general circulations such as *Esquire* and *Liberty.*[19] By 1937, however, the controversy had suddenly subsided. During the next twenty years, the problem appeared infrequently in the media. But since more correspondence appears in Anslinger's archives relevant to race tracks in the period 1932 to

1934 than the following two decades, it appears that the commissioner capitalized on horse-doping as a political issue to insure his job security much in the same way he exploited the marijuana menace to facilitate the adoption of a federal law.

Anslinger's supporters, who enabled him to survive the Roosevelt landslide and the Democratic takeover of the White House in 1933, included a strange alliance of conservative law and order politicians (who equated any drug usage with anti-Americanism), pharmaceutical executives who wanted to protect their monopoly in the importation of opium, and racetrack owners embarrassed by horse-doping scandals.[20] Having quickly established influential allies, Anslinger effectively neutralized an early threat to his status as narcotics commissioner. But other setbacks would occur, not quite as threatening as the possibility of presidential removal perhaps, but serious enough to cause some anxious moments for Anslinger when he contemplated his future as Commissioner of Narcotics.

Consolidation and Investigation

One of the most formidable threats to Anslinger's position was not an overt move by political opponents to oust the commissioner, but the economic exigencies brought on by the Depression which necessitated severe cuts in funding for government agencies. To lessen federal expenditures in 1933, Director of the Budget Douglas introduced a plan for reorganizing several bureaus under one head. Included in Douglas's proposal was the transfer of the Bureau of Narcotics from the Treasury Department to the Attorney General's office in the Department of Justice where it would merge with the Prohibition Bureau. The budget director convinced the Commissioner of Prohibition, A. V. Dalrymple, that the consolidation of the two bureaus for the purpose of economic gains would encourage the interaction between narcotic and prohibition agents, resulting in more effective law enforcement and greater operational efficiency.[21] Attorney General Homer S. Cummings was also favorably impressed with the proposal because "it would save a great deal of money," although he could not estimate how much.[22]

Several objections raised to the Douglas plan, however, exposed serious weaknesses in a merger. First, as Stuart J. Fuller, a State Department representative with expertise in narcotics, pointed out, reorganization of this nature would be in violation of Article XV of the 1931 Geneva Convention (in which Anslinger participated as an American delegate) requiring that each signatory maintain a separate, central narcotics office. Furthermore, Fuller cautioned, the proposal was in effect a bureaucratic step backward since it was likely that the enforcement of narcotics laws would be no different than it was before the Bureau of Narcotics was created in 1930.

Obviously, Anslinger did not support a merger that would diminish his power and authority and possibly cost him his job altogether. The inclusion of Article XV binding the United States to an international agreement was largely the work of Anslinger, who capitalized on the opportunity to guarantee his autonomy as narcotics commissioner. If the federal government reneged on the separate bureau clause, other countries would interpret it as a lack of commitment on the part of the United States to fight the illicit traffic in narcotics. Anslinger also took great pride in the bureau as a model law enforcement agency that was admired at Geneva for its efficiency and administration. To dismantle it would be a grave injustice to the people who contributed so much time and energy to its operation.[23]

Writing to Frank W. Russe of the Mallinckrodt Chemical Works on 5 April 1933, Anslinger was dubious about his status as the American delegate to Geneva for the annual convention because he had not yet received instructions to attend the conference. He was anticipating that, though he was uncertain about the present situation, "there will be some reorganization involving the Bureau."[24] Less than two weeks later, President Roosevelt ended any speculation when he told Undersecretary of State William Phillips that in deference to the Geneva treaty obligations there would be no merger.[25] The defeat of the proposed merger plan once again underscored the bureaucratic skills of Anslinger in the management of federal narcotics policies. By 1935 he had survived the election of Roosevelt and an attempt to swallow his bureau through restructuring within the Treasury Department.

Anslinger barely had time to regroup from the Douglas merger plan in 1933 when Secretary of the Treasury Morgenthau proposed the unification of all the Treasury enforcement agencies (Narcotics, Customs, Intelligence, Secret Service, and Alcohol and Tobacco Tax) to create a super agency that would rival the Federal Bureau of Investigation in the Justice Department. Since the early 1930s, J. Edgar Hoover had been given increasing recognition as the director of a prestigious law enforcement agency, which had not gone unnoticed at the Treasury. What worked for the Justice Department, Morgenthau reasoned, could also benefit the Treasury Department.[26]

At the request of Secretary Morgenthau and with the approval of President Roosevelt, Congressman Robert L. Doughton introduced H.R. 11452 on 24 January 1936 to "provide for the more adequate protection of the revenue, a more effective enforcement of the revenue and other laws administered by the Treasury Department, and for other purposes."[27] When no action was taken on the bill, Congressman Doughton resubmitted it unchanged as H.R. 10586 on 25 February. At a glance the bill appeared to be nothing more than an effort to improve the investigatory and enforcement activities of agencies within the Treasury Department. What was especially alarming to Anslinger and his supporters, however, was the provision in the bill to create a Secret Service Division in the Treasury under a chief appointed by the Secretary of the Treasury who also was to appoint an assistant chief and five deputies. Hence, the legislation became known as the Secret Service Reorganization Act. The new chief was to be given the powers formerly held by the Enforcement Division of the Alcohol Tax Unit, the Intelligence Unit of the Internal Revenue, the Customs Agency Service, and the Bureau of Narcotics. Morgenthau had designed it as an effort to unite into one bureau the various enforcement activities of the Treasury.

Anslinger was no less opposed to reorganization in 1936 than he was to the merger plan three years earlier and vigorously protested the proposed legislation. The work of the Bureau of Narcotics, he maintained in a four-page memorandum, was largely of an administrative and regulatory nature and was not meant to be included in the same division with enforcement agencies. Moreover, Anslinger again cited the Geneva Convention of 1931 which he stated necessitated that the narcotics regulation in any single country should be concentrated in a single office.[28]

Hearings on the bill were held on 28 February, just three days after it was presented as H.R. 11452. Of the nine witnesses who testified, only Clinton Hester, legal counsel for the Treasury Department, was supportive of the bill. The remaining eight witnesses represented the American Drug Manufacturers, the Federal Wholesale Druggists, the World Narcotic Defense Association, and the National Hotel Druggists Association, all of whom obviously had a vested interest in the ramifications of any reorganization affecting the Bureau of Narcotics. Representatives were also present from the General Federation of Women's Clubs and the National Woman's Christian Temperance Union, organizations that were concerned that the act might hinder the Bureau's enforcement of narcotics laws.

Once again "Anslinger's Army" was mobilized to prevent the Narcotics Bureau from being absorbed by other agencies. Testimony by Hester during the hearings that reorganization would in no way alter or affect the regulatory activities of the FBN did little to allay the fears of pharmacists and wholesale druggists. Even when assured that the bill was supported by the AMA, members of the drug industry were not placated. Their concern over the Doughton bill was twofold. First, they were not comfortable with the idea of being supervised by Secret Service personnel who were not specially trained and qualified in the area of narcotics. Pharmacists and drug manufacturers particularly, did not want the regulation and enforcement of narcotics to be given over to a police agency. The second reason for their opposition also had to do with enforcement practices. Not only were they apprehensive about agents ill-trained in the dispensing of narcotics, but druggists were fearful that Secret Service personnel would be unreasonable in exercising enforcement, with no recognition of the difference between a technical and a criminal violator. Because they felt they were harassed in the past by inspectors from the Alcohol Tax Unit, some of whom were taken from the Works Progress Administration relief rolls, they had become fiercely opposed to any supervision of their trade outside of the FBN.[29] The manufacturers and dispensers of controlled drugs understandably preferred the flexibility and tolerance the narcotics agents allowed them.

Anslinger's files contain dozens of letters between his office and numerous organizations and individuals who opposed the legislation, usually on the ground that it represented a potential danger to pharmacists and that instead of promoting efficiency it would severely weaken enforcement. Letters from the National Association of Retail Druggists, the WCTU, Women's Clubs, and the National Congress of Parents and Teachers flooded the White House in protest of any reorganizational scheme that included dismantling the Bureau of Narcotics.

In late March President Roosevelt announced that he had abandoned plans to consolidate Treasury law enforcement agencies. Foremost of the reasons he gave for his decision was his fear that such a merger "might be the first step in the development of a centralized secret police state such as the German Gestapo or the Russian Ogpu."[30] The *New York Times* reported that Secretary Morgenthau, who had long cherished consolidation within his department, was personally responsible for the President's decision to drop the plans, apparently realizing that a merger would not have been significantly more cost-effective. The most reshuffling Morgenthau could manage was the appointment of Elmer Irey, the former Internal Revenue agent who was responsible for nabbing Al Capone, as the coordinator of all Treasury enforcement.[31] Curiously, White House officials made no public mention of the opposition from the drug industry's letter-writing campaign.

The relationship between Morgenthau and Anslinger fell short of mutual admiration. Unable to push his reorganization plan and the merger of the Narcotics Bureau through Congress, Morgenthau tried to limit Anslinger's authority more indirectly but just as effectively. In a conference on his farm in August 1936, the secretary informed Anslinger that in the future, all investigative work abroad having to deal with illicit traffic in narcotics was being transferred from the FBN to Customs. Narcotics agents working in Europe would be required to report their activities to Customs officials.[32] Such a change would dramatically limit the bureau's jurisdictional authority. It would also severely affect its contacts in foreign countries or the source of the drug production where Anslinger felt it was necessary to stop the illegal trafficking.

Morgenthau also told Anslinger that he was not satisfied with the work being done by the Bureau of Narcotics either here or abroad and that he still intended to reorganize the bureau by dividing its activities between enforcement and permissive work. He assigned Deputy Commissioner Will S. Wood exclusively to permissive functions, and Special Agent A. C. Palmer of the Intelligence Unit, under Anslinger's supervision, to all criminal investigations and enforcement work. When Anslinger defended the record of the bureau for imprisoning more criminals per agent than any other federal enforcement organization, Morgenthau cynically commented that "the bulk of the Bureau's defendants were petty violators, chiefly peddlers and addicts."[33]

Once more Anslinger's allies had preserved his autonomy and saved the bureau from subordination, if not extinction. Not until the 1960s, after Anslinger had retired, would another concerted attempt to merge the Bureau of Narcotics with another agency surface. That did not mean, however, that the commissioner was no longer subjected to criticism from disparagers or exempt from an intense evaluation by those who questioned his abilities and narcotics policies.

One such individual was Representative John M. Coffee, a first-term Democrat from Washington, who introduced in April 1938 House Joint Resolution 642 "to provide for a survey of the narcotic-drug conditions in the United States by the United States Public Health Service."[34] Before he was elected to Congress, Coffee was a practicing attorney whose views on the enforcement of narcotics laws were in accordance with those expressed by the *St. Louis Post-Dispatch,* which criticized the Harrison law as costly and totally ineffective. Rather than tougher penalties, the newspaper recommended that the act should be repealed and replaced with a license system that would eliminate the drug traffic completely. Among other improvements, this new approach would "substitute sanity and realism for a law that has its roots in ignorance and hypocrisy."[35] Because he believed the Harrison Act had been misinterpreted, Congressman Coffee felt that the responsibility for narcotics enforcement had been inappropriately entrusted to the wrong agency. On 14 June he urged that Congress approve legislation that would transfer the enforcement responsibilities from the Federal Bureau of Narcotics to the U.S. Public Health Service where it belonged.

In requesting an appropriation for his resolution in Congress, Coffee first addressed the economic aspects of the narcotics situation. Quoting estimates calculated by the American Association on Drug Addictions, the congressman stated that the annual cost to American taxpayers for the federal government's war on narcotic addiction was $2.735 billion or the equivalent of $80.00 per family. This was an unjustified and needless financial burden, he argued, that was imposed on the American public not because the problem of addiction was so catastrophic, but because of the "mistaken interpretation of law made by the Federal Narcotics Bureau."

If this claim is justified, the Narcotics Bureau stands as the costliest bureau or government department in the world, and the Commissioner of Narcotics ranks as far and away the costliest man in the world.[36]

Continuing his attack on Anslinger's Narcotics Bureau, Coffee then discussed the harmful effects of the Harrrison Act and questioned the wisdom of denying medical treatment for addicts and imprisoning them:

In examining the Harrison Special Tax Act we are confronted with the anomaly that a law designed (as its name implies) to place a tax on certain drugs, and raise revenue thereby, resulting in reducing enormously the legitimate importation of the drugs in question, while developing a smuggling industry not before in existence. That, however, is only the beginning. Through operation of the law, as interpreted, there was developed also, as counterpart to the smuggling racket, the racket of dope peddling; in a word, the whole gigantic structure of the illicit-drug racket, with direct annual turn-over of upward of a billion dollars.[37]

To substantiate his claim that the Harrison Act had been misinterpreted since its inception, Congressman Coffee argued that the law contained no reference to the uses of narcotics nor any mention of drug addicts or drug addiction. He then cited Supreme Court decisions in the *Linder* case (1925) and the *Nigro* case (1928) which held that the Harrison Act exercised no control over the practice of a profession, specifically physicians who were often harassed by narcotics agents.

Regarding the treatment of addicts, the congressman accused the Bureau of Narcotics of ignoring those court decisions and charged that it had cavalierly assumed the authority to prevent doctors from even attempting to cure drug addicts unless under confinement. That the Supreme Court declared that addicts were victims of a disease and should be treated as patients while the Narcotics Bureau treated them as criminals was especially ironic. After reminding Congress that less than a decade earlier the federal government passed legislation for the construction of two narcotics farms designed specifically to treat addicts, Coffee noted the development of a paradoxical situation: on one hand both the Supreme Court and Congress had interpreted and passed laws favorable to the rehabilitation of narcotics addicts, but on the other hand Anslinger and the Bureau of Narcotics independently decided to prosecute them as criminals.[38]

To more fully understand why there was a resistance to permitting the law to operate, Congressman Coffee proposed that a formal investigation be initiated:

> The opposition [to the Harrison law] comes from a small coterie of persons in authority, who are in a position to benefit by the status quo. These persons will be brought into the open by such a congressional investigation as this bill proposes. There will then be opportunity to subject to official scrutiny the records of these opponents of law reform.
>
> Specifically, there will be opportunity to question the Commissioner of Narcotics—and to observe how he may endeavor to justify the activities that cost the American people not far from $3,000,000,000 a year, and give the Commissioner himself status as the costliest man in the world.[39]

After he enumerated several factors contributing to the narcotics problem, the congressman referred to the problem of corruption in the Narcotics Bureau which he thought had become pervasive in the agency. Only a few days earlier Chris Hanson, the chief narcotics agent for the state of Nevada, was arrested and convicted for selling narcotics to a gang of Chinese racketeers. Because the Commissioner of Narcotics took no active role in the initial investigation, Coffee felt that Anslinger's "dubious partisanship amounted to effective championship of the dope peddler—and seems inexplicable on any other basis."[40]

Finally, Coffee questioned the hypocrisy in the Narcotics Bureau's philosophy on treating addiction. If, for example, alcohol addicts or nicotine addicts were permitted to receive treatment without the risk of involuntary confinement, why were morphine or heroin addicts not allowed the same privilege? The congressman concluded that the obvious answer had to be that the "pushers" would be put out of business, as would the entire drug racket. But that only prompted another question: Why would persons in authority want to keep the drug pusher in business and encourage the billion-dollar narcotics traffic? For Congressman Coffee that answer was obvious, and he challenged Congress to assume greater responsibility:

> I submit that an official answer to that question would be not merely of interest, but of truly vital importance to every American citizen. If we, the representatives of the people, are to continue to let our narcotics authorities conduct themselves in a manner tantamount to upholding and in effect supporting the billion-dollar drug racket, we should at least be able to explain to our constituents why we do so.[41]

John Coffee was seemingly conscientious and sincere in his concern for the plight of the drug addict and the effectiveness of the federal narcotics policies in general. In his remarks on the floor of Congress, he articulately and coherently justified the purpose of House Joint Resolution 642 to investigate the activities of the FBN. Unfortunately the resolution never made it out of committee. Despite the fact that he was a Democrat whose party was in control of both houses, Coffee never even attracted a co-sponsor of his bill in the Senate. Hearings, which could have revealed much about the operations of the Bureau of Narcotics and might well have prompted dramatic changes in policies and personnel, never occurred. Congressman Coffee introduced legislation to investigate Anslinger's bureau the following year in 1939 and again in 1940, but each time it remained bottled up in committee. Since by the end of his first decade in office Anslinger had cultivated strong congressional ties, he did not publicly respond to House Joint Resolution 642 except in Geneva through the League of Nations. Anslinger's papers contain only one brief reference to the congressman, a letter from state Senator Sanborn Young who cautioned the commissioner that "the President is chummy with 'John' (Coffee) and you may hear from him."[42] The congressman's ten-year campaign against the Federal Bureau of Narcotics ended in 1946 when he was defeated for re-election. It would be another decade before anyone else would mount a serious campaign to oust Anslinger.

The War Years and After

During the 1930s, in large part because of the pressures of the world-wide depression, the semblance of world order that had been established after World War I unraveled at a frightening pace. In 1931 the Japanese invaded the Chinese industrial province of Manchuria. Six years later, in 1937, they initiated a war against China proper, slaughtering thousands of civilians. Between the anti-Western Japanese militarists who badly wanted to extend their sphere of influence in the Pacific and Hitler's Nazis who were storming through Europe, war seemed inevitable. Though popular sentiment supported non-intervention, President Roosevelt recognized that because the international situation was so volatile, it was paramount that the United States stand as the "arsenal of democracy."

Several years before the Japanese attacked the American naval base at Pearl Harbor, Commissioner Anslinger also anticipated the adverse effect that global war would have on the flow and distribution of narcotics used for medicinal purposes, and he adopted plans to insure that the Bureau of Narcotics would be able to do its part in the war effort. In 1935 Anslinger reported to Secretary Morgenthau that the current supply of narcotics, which was entirely in the hands of retailers, would last only until January 1937. The federal government had no supply at all. If war would involve the United States, a shortage was surely imminent. To prevent that from happening, Anslinger recommended that the federal government order 169,000 pounds of opium for 1936, of which 30,000 pounds would be held on reserve in London or Amsterdam. Morgenthau was in agreement with Anslinger's reserve plan, but he was puzzled by Anslinger's desire to deposit the drug abroad where it was not easily accessible. Perhaps the Commissioner judged his agents and other Treasury personnel to be less trustworthy than Morgenthau did. When Anslinger replied that he was concerned about theft, the Secretary assured him that his fear was "perfectly ridiculous" and suggested that "we bring the narcotic to this country and keep it in vaults here in the Treasury."[43] Morgenthau then approved an order for 130,000 pounds of opium to be distributed among retailers and an additional 50,000 pounds to be kept in the Treasury's vaults in Washington.

In the next few years Anslinger made purchases of the precious painkiller drug from sellers in Turkey, Yugoslavia, Bulgaria, and Afghanistan. By 1940 the Narcotics Bureau had stockpiled 300 tons of opium in the Treasury vaults in Washington, which had become vacant when the gold reserves were transferred to Ft. Knox. Normally seventy-seven tons of crude opium were legally imported annually; Anslinger had hoarded enough to last nearly four years. In December 1941 he testified before the House Appropriations Committee that in addition to making the various opium derivatives available for American civilians and armed forces personnel, the FBN was also supplying the medical needs of allied nations such as the Netherlands, Indies, the Soviet Union and some South American countries.[44] But even the casualties suffered by these armies did not exhuast the Bureau's 300-ton opium stockpile, much of which was still held in peacetime. Some of the drug was allocated for use at veteran's hospitals; the unused portion remained locked in the Treasury vaults.[45] The effect of Anslinger having virtually cornered the opium market during the war years was staggering—the price soared an incredible 300 percent.

The disruption in communications and commerce as a result of the war temporarily alleviated the narcotics problem in the United States. International trafficking was drastically curtailed. Despite the diminution of drug usage due to unfavorable conditions and the belief that illegal drug production was looked upon as unpatriotic, Anslinger urged harsher enforcement. In a report he helped to compose for the League of Nations in 1942, he exhorted the American public that more than in peace time it was important to guard against the development of drug addiction, resulting either from extensive reliance on painkillers or through the theft of narcotics supplies.[46]

Since the war had seriously interfered with the normal patterns of international drug distribution and made for a starving time for addicts, Anslinger was left with comparatively little to do during the war years but to focus on the use of narcotics in the military. He also anticipated an addiction epidemic that he was certain would emerge in the post-war period just as it had in the years following World War I. The drug of particular concern to Anslinger was not any of the opium compounds but the old menace, marijuana. The controversy over its effects in the previous decade extended into the 1940s.

In 1943 an editorial in *Military Medicine* addressed the use of marijuana among American soldiers and concluded that the drug was found to be especially appealing to "recruits of low mentality."[47] A year and a half later two doctors in the Army Medical Corps reported the results of a study they conducted with thirty-five marijuana addicts. Among their findings they disclosed that marijuana users revealed "pronounced disturbances" in the Rorschach tests, exhibited homosexual traits, conveyed a "deprecatory attitude" toward women, frequently engaged in self-mutilation and were "overtly hostile, provocative, and intransigent." It should be noted that of the thirty-five subjects who participated in the study, only one was white and "nearly all were of low or very low social and economic background."[48] The myths of race associated with marijuana were still supported by research.

Anslinger reported to Appropriations Committees during the war years the rate of marijuana addiction declined. The obvious reason for the drop in popularity of the drug, which he had to realize but never bothered to mention, was that only marijuana could be home grown in the United States and that it was not susceptible to chaotic international conditions. The commissioner and his agents worked diligently, not only to keep the addiction problem under control, but also to prevent soldiers from seeking a discharge as marijuana addicts. Anslinger was of the belief that any soldier who was found guilty of such behavior should not be discharged but dealt with severely in a court-martial. In February 1944 he launched his campaign against drug addiction in the army by involving his agents in 3,000 investigations of marijuana cases in or around military camps.[49]

Documented cases of marijuana smoking among military personnel, as well as incidents of addiction to morphine, did exist. But they were comparatively isolated and never reached the number reported during World War I, nor did they approach the epidemic proportions Anslinger predicted they would. On the contrary, the feared epidemic of drug use among GIs did not materialize. The country was more concerned with the task of demobilization and re-establishing patterns of normality than with narcotics addiction. Anslinger had been victimized by his own propaganda, and he was unable to obtain increased appropriations for the bureau for a problem that did not exist. "Our funds are so low," he wrote to an old friend in 1947, "that we couldn't even send an agent across the border from El Paso unless he walks and doesn't spend any money for gasoline."[50]

Still, that did not deter Anslinger from sounding an alarm that the

United States was as much in danger from an invasion of narcotics as it was from enemy troops. Whatever political and social changes were to occur after the war, Anslinger was convinced that it was critical that the United States take an active role in maintaining the international control and regulation of narcotics, which he helped to accomplish in London as a delegate to the new United Nations organization. Convinced in 1942 that Japan had started its war on Western civilization ten years earlier by using narcotics as weapons, Anslinger claimed that the Japanese had committed many "Pearl Harbors" prior to the actual outbreak of war in 1941.[51] When interviewed on a radio broadcast, Anslinger stated that Japan was working on the theory that a "drug-sullen nation is an easy conquest and cannot offer adequate resistance to attack."[52] In the 1940s Anslinger asserted that Japan, with its strategy of spreading opium addiction, would destroy the Western world. During the next twenty years, however, Anslinger would accuse other aggressor nations of trying to subdue the United States by drug addiction—claiming each was a greater threat than the one before.

Though Anslinger was not a politician in the purest sense, his influence in formulating and enforcing narcotics laws often brought him into contact with members of official Washington. By the late 1940s Anslinger's notion that narcotics addiction and communism were synonymous inseparable evils made it difficult to keep the Narcotics Bureau separate from politics. Consequently, as he divulged in his book *The Murderers,* he found himself caught in the middle of a tense situation.

In this particular incident, one of the most influential members of Congress, whom Anslinger did not insist should be sent to the federal hospital in Lexington, became a narcotics addict. Anslinger described him anonymously as the head of one of the most powerful Congressional committees whose "decisions and statements helped to shape and direct the destiny of the United States and the free world." On discovering that this legislative leader was a confirmed morphine addict who vehemently resisted help to control his addiction, Anslinger was fearful that, because of the congressman's role in sensitive issues, there was an "imminent danger that the fact would become known," which would do irreversible damage to the integrity of the American government.

The commissioner instructed agents to contact the congressman to persuade him to accept medical treatment. When he flatly refused any suggestions to seek help, Anslinger confronted the addict himself. The congressman was intractable; he defied Anslinger to cut off his source of supply and threatened to go directly to the pushers if the Narcotics Bureau interfered with his habit. Realizing the power wielded by the congressman and the potential for public scandal that Anslinger feared would embarrass the country, the commissioner agreed not to force him into hospitalization or to expose him. Instead, Anslinger secured a pledge from him not to go to the pushers; in return, the addict would be supplied with all the drugs he needed. Anslinger was uncomfortable with the arrangement but rationalized his action on the premise that he was acting out of loyalty to his country. He also justified maintaining the addict's habit because he could control the supply, since the prescriptions would be filled by Anslinger's personal pharmacist. When Anslinger's trusted druggist leaked the story to a syndicated columnist, the commissioner warned the reporter of the Harrison Act's two-year jail provision for anyone revealing the narcotics records of a drug store.[53]

Evidence suggests the mystery politician was Senator Joseph R. McCarthy. As a senior agent and one of a handful who were in frequent contact with Commissioner Anslinger, John T. Cusack thought McCarthy was probably the congressman, though he could not officially confirm the link: "I think the facts were that McCarthy was being prescribed morphine by his doctor for some, whatever the reason was." He also commented that "some doctors, I think, did use morphine to bring people off alcohol." McCarthy's excessive drinking had potential detrimental effects on his performance; therefore, his use of morphine, a contemporary treatment to combat alcoholism, would not be surprising. The agent also remarked that if a physician was filling a prescription for McCarthy, "Anslinger would want discretion there."[54] According to the commissioner, "No one beyond this addicted lawmaker and myself—and an obscure druggist on the outskirts of Washington—knew what was happening." The official cause of McCarthy's death was listed as "hepatitis, acute, cause unknown."[55] On the day the anonymous politician died, Anslinger wrote, "I thanked God for relieving me of·my burden."[56]

Harry Goes to Hollywood

Much discussion and little research about marijuana smoking in the 1930s provided little knowledge and only muddied the controversy to the point that, among the relatively limited number of Americans who were aware of a problem, few possessed any clear understanding of what marijuana was. Jazz musicians did more to promote marijuana's popularity than any other single group. They generated publicity not so much by smoking the weed (though many did), but by using its terminology in their music. Provocative song titles such as "Sweet Marijuana Brown," "If You're a Viper," "Reefer Song," "Sendin' the Viper," and "That Funny Reefer Man" glamorized marijuana smoking.[57] Of course these songs did not escape Anslinger's attention nor did many of the musicians who performed them, including Count Basie, Cab Calloway, Duke Ellington, and Louis Armstrong.[58]

One of the most popular performers of jazz in the 1930s, Milton "Mezz" Mezzrow, a clarinetist, provided a glimpse into the deviant practice of marijuana smoking within the subculture of musicians in his autobiography *Really the Blues*. Published in 1946, Mezzrow's book described the effects of marijuana and contradicted nearly every argument the Bureau of Narcotics made against its use. Mezzrow wrote that none of his fellow musicians who smoked the weed ever thought it was addictive and felt that it had been erroneously classified as a narcotic. He and his fellow musicians were also convinced that a marijuana cigarette was no more "dangerous or habit-forming than these other great American vices, the five-cent Coke and ice-cream cone, only it gave you more kick for the money."[59]

Actually Anslinger was almost as fascinated with the popularity of drugs among entertainment personalities as he was with international criminals who manufactured and distributed them around the world. The bureau suspected many musicians as users of narcotics and arrested several of those lesser known during the late 1930s and early 1940s. The biggest catch made by the Narcotics Bureau, however, was that of swing-band leader and drummer Gene Krupa in January 1943. Arrested by narcotics agents in San Francisco, Krupa was charged with contributing to the delinquency of a minor because he sent a seventeen-year-old boy to his hotel room for marijuana cigarettes. The popular musician was also found with marijuana in his possession. On 18 May Krupa pleaded guilty to a misdemeanor charge and was sentenced to ninety days in the county jail and fined $500.

For the felony charge of corrupting a minor, he was sentenced to one to six years in San Quentin to run concurrently with his misdemeanor sentence.[60] The arrest and conviction of Krupa as reported in *Time* magazine was little deterrent to more than a few musicians who were willing to take the risk. Under the influence of marijuana, it was said, the user's musical abilities were heightened beyond imagination. In July 1943 *Time* magazine also noted that the drug was much less mysterious than had been publicized:

> If it [marijuana] could be universally detected, it would land a great many jazz musicians behind prison bars. It is no secret that some of the finest flights of American syncopation, like some of the finest products of the symbolist poets, owe much of their expressiveness to the use of a drug. But the nature and effects of marijuana, specifically, are a good deal more of a secret than they need be.[61]

Five years later, in 1948, Anslinger's Narcotics Bureau moved from the jazz subculture into the movie industry when Los Angeles agents arrested a thirty-one-year-old rising screen star, Robert Mitchum. Discovered in a secluded three-room cottage on the outskirts of Hollywood, the $3,000-a-week idol of "bobby-soxers" and three others were charged with possession. At the Los Angeles County jail Mitchum rambled endlessly about the escapade and was certain the arrest would be the end of his marriage and his career. He confessed to having been a marijuana smoker since he was a teenager and said he realized that he would likely one day be caught.

At the time of Mitchum's arrest, Hollywood was trying to shake a hedonistic reputation by projecting an image as a typical American community of hard-working people. It was imperative that the Mitchum affair be resolved as quickly and quietly as possible. Since Mitchum was under contract with RKO at the time, the studio quickly persuaded the star to retract his confession and claim he had been framed. To insure Mitchum's chances for acquittal, famed Hollywood criminal lawyer Jerry Geisler (who had successfully defended Errol Flynn on a charge of statutory rape and Charles Chaplin on a Mann Act charge) was retained. This time Geisler was less successful.

On 10 January 1949, Mitchum was found guilty of conspiracy, and on 9 February he entered a plea for probation. Despite the efforts of Attorney Geisler and the defendant's earnest appeal, Mitchum was sentenced to one year in jail, which was later suspended, and two years' probation. In September, however, the district attorney moved to reopen the case, and on 31 January 1951, Mitchum pleaded not guilty. The case was quietly dismissed. Neither Mitchum nor Anslinger generated any publicity over the incident.[62]

Through Kenneth Clark, a long-time personal friend of Anslinger, the bureau was able to monitor the activities of Mitchum and other celebrities like blues singer Billie Holiday and singer and actress Judy Garland, both of whom died from narcotics overdoses. Oddly enough, in the case of the latter, Anslinger informed Louis B. Mayer of MGM Studios in 1948 that "our investigation shows that Miss Garland is not now and has never been addicted to the use of narcotic drugs."[63]

The commissioner also met with Mayer in 1948 to discuss a growing problem among several actors who relied on drugs to alleviate depression and insomnia. On his prepared agenda Anslinger noted "The case of Peter Lorre" and "Case of Errol Flynn," followed by a cryptic hand-written notation "Ms. to sober up—pre-addiction." The FBN must have spent considerable time and energy investigating Hollywood behind-the-scenes for Anslinger to suggest that Mayer have the studio head "call in Bogart, Flynn, and Wells, and lay down the law." In regard to Judy Garland, Anslinger wanted to reinforce the opinion of the public in Washington, Philadelphia, and Pittsburgh who have "noticed the deterioration in her physical condition."[64]

But Anslinger was not satisfied with simply making arrests of entertainment figures. In 1949 he became involved in a fight against what he considered to be objectionable material in films. Though the FBN had no power to censor movies, Anslinger issued an unofficial ban against *Drug*

Addicts, a first-prize winner in the Canadian Film Awards. To Anslinger, who oppposed "propaganda on the danger of drug addiction because it 'advertised' the use of drugs and stimulated curiosity about their effects," the graphic scenes of the habits of addicts and illicit distribution were totally unacceptable. It was a measure of Anslinger's influence that on his insistence the United States government made a "friendly request" of the Canadian government that the film not be shown in this country.[65]

A few years later Anslinger again was outraged by a film which he felt exercised no discretion in the treatment of a sensitive subject matter. Through Joseph Bransky, the FBN's Philadelphia District Supervisor, Anslinger characterized *She Shoulda Said No* as "insidious propaganda that would teach juveniles the method of using narcotics," and asked the Pennsylvania Board of Censors to sustain a ban on the film. Since methods of smoking marijuana "not generally known to the public" were graphically demonstrated, he was fearful young people would be influenced by the movie.

Anslinger aroused the most publicity in his censorship campaign when he attacked the Otto Preminger film *The Man With the Golden Arm,* featuring a new actor, Frank Sinatra, in the leading role. Although Anslinger admitted he had not viewed the film, he vociferously objected to the depiction of an addict driven to suicide even though the user conquered the habit and the story had a happy ending. In an interview with *Variety,* a theatrical trade paper, Anslinger stated that in some instances where he had prior knowledge of "dangerous" themes scheduled for radio or television, he made his views known to the station and the program was not aired.[66]

Anslinger may have objected to questionable presentations of drug-related plots in television or theatre films, but he heartily supported those he personally judged to hold some redeeming value. He obviously approved of the 1948 movie *To the Ends of the Earth* starring Dick Powell; in it Commissioner Anslinger played a bit part as himself. In 1958 he approached a representative from Screen Gems studio about transforming the film into a television series, but nothing ever came of it.[67]

The increasing number of lurid reports of Harlem tea pads, or apartments where jazz devotees congregated to listen to music and share a marijuana cigarette, impelled New York City Mayor Fiorello LaGuardia to uncover the facts and fallacies about the "weed of madness." Personally skeptical that marijuana was capable of causing the bizarre behavior that had been attributed to smoking the drug, Mayor LaGuardia was determined to organize an impartial, scientific, city-wide investigation. To conduct the study, the popular LaGuardia appealed to the prestigious New York Academy of Medicine. In October 1938 the Mayor's request was referred to the Academy's Committee on Public Health relations which authorized a special subcommittee. Serving on the committee were two internists, three psychiatrists, two pharmacologists, one public health expert, and the commissioners of Health, Hospitals, and Corrections, and the director of the Division of Psychiatry.[68]

In addition to this special scientific core, commonly referred to as the "Mayor's Committee," a number of physicians, chemists, and sociologists also served. Their primary responsibility was to organize and conduct a two-part study. The first phase involved a sociological examination of the extent of marijuana smoking and the methods by which it was obtained. Included were what areas of the city were affected, among what races it was most prevalent, what social conditions figured in its use, and what relationship, if any, there was between its use and criminal acts and antisocial behavior. The second phase of the study focused on the clinical aspects of marijuana. Researchers conducted controlled experiments to observe the physiological and psychological effects on different personality types to determine whether it caused physical or mental deterioration.[69]

No aspect associated with marijuana smoking was ignored. To facilitate the extensive investigation, the committee also received the full cooperation of the New York Police Department. Six police officers were trained as special investigators to assist the committee on a full-time basis. The entire medical staff of Riker's Island, New York's prison hospital, was actively involved, and the Goldwater Memorial Hospital provided the committee with two wards of office space and a staffed laboratory. Obviously this was more than a half-hearted attempt to score political points in an election year. Never before or since has such a thorough and extensive study been conducted on marijuana.

The Mayor's Committee either challenged or refuted virtually every notion about marijuana advanced by Anslinger and the Bureau of Narcotics over the past decade. One of the committee members visited a Harlem tea pad where he observed that the individuals were relaxed and "free from the anxieties and cares of the realities of life."[70] Contrary to the belief that marijuana smokers were aggressive and belligerent, the investigator found that "a boisterous, rowdy atmosphere did not prevail." Nor was it evident that marijuana stimulated erotic behavior. As to its relationship to crime and juvenile delinquency, marijuana was not identified as a significant contributing factor. Interviews of police officers furnished no proof that major crimes were associated with smoking marijuana. They did state that petty crimes were committed but that the criminal career usually existed prior to the time the individual smoked his first marijuana cigarette.

Among the committee's conclusions made in the sociological study was the belief that marijuana smoking did not lead to addiction in the medical sense of the word.[71] It did not lead, as Anslinger by then believed, to morphine, heroin, or cocaine addiction; it was not widespread in school yards and among school-aged children; nor was addiction directly associated with the practice of smoking marijuana. In perhaps what represented the most serious challenge to Anslinger was the committee's finding that "the publicity concerning the catastrophic effects of marihuana in New York City is unfounded." Mayor LaGuardia was relieved to know that the marijuana menace in his city was more exaggerated than real, but as he stated in the introduction to his committee's report: "I shall continue to enforce the laws prohibiting marijuana until and if complete findings may justify an amendment."

The report submitted on the clinical effects of marijuana was equally contradictory to Anslinger's claims about the drug. To study the physiological and psychological effects, seventy-seven volunteer prisoners in a hospital ward were observed over a period of several weeks while numerous experiments were administered. The clinical studies showed no alterations in personality traits or behavior patterns that would sustain popular beliefs that marijuana was the cause of insanity or violence. As to its addictiveness, marijuana was found to be less habit-forming than alcohol or tobacco. In fact, it was reported that marijuana likely continued therapeutic properties that merited further study for easing the agony of withdrawal from heroin.

Because the Mayor's Report flatly contradicted most of the myths advanced by the Bureau of Narcotics, it was subjected to bitter attack. Even before the report was released, rumors circulated that it would be suppressed. Anslinger vigorously discredited the report, labeling critics of the bureau as "dangerous" and "strange" people. When two members of the Mayor's Committee, Doctors Samuel Allentuck and Karl R. Bowman, published a preliminary article entitled "The Psychiatric Aspects of Marijuana Intoxication" in the *American Journal of Psychiatry* in 1942 suggesting there might be more reason for concern about tobacco or alcohol than cannabis, Anslinger openly attacked the authors and the report.[72]

A month after a December 1942 editorial in the *Journal of the American Medical Association (JAMA)* referred to the Mayor's Report as a "careful study" and mentioned the therapeutic possibilities, Anslinger responded in a letter to the editor that on the behalf of law enforcement officials, he felt that Allentuck and Bowman should not have stated as fact that marijuana did not lead to physical, moral, or mental degeneration. Anslinger was especially concerned with how readers unfamiliar with the drug (though unlikely since this was a professional journal geared specifically to physicians) might interpret the Allentuck and Bowman article as the "final word."[73]

Throughout 1943 and 1944 an exchange of views on the marijuana controversy continued in the *JAMA* between Anslinger, Jules Bouquet of the Narcotics Commission of the League of Nations, and Allentuck and Bowman. By 1945, when the Mayor's Report was finally released, *JAMA* had published numerous articles from experts eager to register their support or criticism of the report.[74] Anslinger's arguments had not succeeded in reversing anyone's position in the marijuana controversy; that was not his primary objective. Divide and conquer seems to have been his strategy, since he was successful in isolating the AMA from other members of the scientific community. He also accomplished his goal of minimizing the findings of the Mayor's Report so effectively that its impact was negligible in the media.

By 1950 Anslinger and the Bureau of Narcotics had endured a series of close encounters both internal (scandals and reorganization) and external (investigation and the Mayor's Report). Each time Anslinger survived the threat; each time he emerged more powerful and more influential. By 1950, the Commissioner of Narcotics had again demonstrated his resiliency, bureaucratic resourcefulness, and political acumen.

It was clear that twenty years in Washington had made Anslinger wise about the ins and outs of federal bureaucracy. His frequent close involvement with the State Department established a satisfactory working relationship with the Department of Justice (Hoover's FBI); he also developed important congressional contacts. Especially mindful of who was in a position to help the bureau financially, he was not reluctant to outwardly demonstrate his appreciation for their support. On one occasion he assigned an agent to Paterson, New Jersey, hometown of Congressman Gordon Canfield, who chaired the House Appropriations Committee, even though there were district offices nearby in Newark and New York City.[75]

Anslinger's involvement in politics was more than that of a lobbyist for budget considerations. In 1952 a group of independent Democrats, who were trying to balance the elitism of Adlai Stevenson, decided they wanted "a combination of Pennsylvania Republican (industrial northeast), a crime buster (conservative and pragmatic) and a man experienced in international affairs (in the midst of McCarthyism) to run for Vice President." Commissioner Harry Anslinger was their choice.[76] An old acquaintance of his, Judge William T. McCarthy of Boston, even wrote a letter of support to Speaker of the House John McCormack.[77] Though Anslinger fit their qualifications perfectly, he declined the offer, no doubt realizing that his chances of gaining the nomination were hardly realistic.

Perhaps it was coincidental, but also in 1952 Anslinger experienced a scare that rivaled that of 1933, when only days after the election, the *Washington Star* reported that under the incoming president, Dwight D. Eisenhower, "Harry Anslinger is due to get the axe."[78] As it turned out, however, the commissioner's appointment was only temporarily held up.

By December his "Army" was reactivated and a torrent of letters from the old stand-bys—the WCTU, pharmaceutical firms, and church organizations—flooded the White House.

Anslinger's most ardent supporter was his close friend and editor of the *Bangor Daily News,* Reginald Kaufman, who attracted attention in an editorial when he praised the commissioner and chided the incoming administration for playing politics with the Narcotics Bureau. The publicity generated by the Kaufman camp included U.S. Senator Margaret Chase Smith, who enclosed a copy of the editorial in a letter to General Eisenhower. Though she did not know Anslinger personally, Senator Smith found it difficult to believe that because he was a Republican, he would be replaced "under a spoils system any more than you would replace J. Edgar Hoover by some action."[79] Anslinger's reappointment was all but assured.

With the Bureau of Narcotics firmly secured as a durable agency, Anslinger no longer needed to maintain a defensive posture. He welcomed the 1950s as a new era in which he could move the bureau forward with a stronger reputation and new approaches to the narcotics problem.

5

Retreat into the Future, 1945–1961

The only constant during the first twenty years of Anslinger's official life as commissioner was scarcity. In the early years, Anslinger found it irritating that his agents were not provided with adequate firearms or enough automobiles. Worse, it was always difficult to find capable men who were willing to stay with the bureau for any length of time, and it was virtually impossible for him to obtain a sufficient appropriation to increase the number of field agents.

From Famine to Feast

From 1930 through 1949 the budget of the Narcotics Bureau never exceeded $1.5 million. During that period Anslinger was fortunate if he could maintain his budget from one year to the next. Beginning in 1950, however, due largely to Anslinger's growing influence and increased media attention resulting from the postwar addiction epidemic and a threat of communism that generated additional congressional support, the FBN budget steadily increased.

The appropriation for 1950 was increased by $160,000 from 1949 to $1.6 million, and the trend continued through the rest of the decade and into the 1960s.[1] Anslinger's testimony before the House Appropriations Committee seems to have had a direct relationship to the amount of the appropriation. The two largest single increases in the 1950s coincided with the introduction of major pieces of antinarcotics legislation. In 1951 Anslinger's budget was allotted a hefty increase of $650,000 (or half of his total budget for 1947) to $2.5 million. Then again in 1956, when the second anti-narcotics law was passed, the bureau's appropriation was increased by $530,000 to $3.7 million.

Anslinger's success in convincing Appropriations Committees to allocate his bureau additional money was due to more than the added burden of enforcing recently enacted anti-narcotics legislation. It was also attributable to a core of mostly conservative congressmen who were responsive to Anslinger's alarmist preachments on the evils of narcotics and who were supportive of his punitive approach to the narcotics problem.

A close examination of the *Congressional Record* for the period 1951–1956 shows a dramatic increase in the number of Washington legislators who proposed federal statutes for greater control of narcotics. In 1951 twenty-six bills (twenty-two in the House, four in the Senate) related to drug enforcement (increased penalties, deportation, and hospitalization of addicts) were introduced. The number decreased over the next three years. But in 1955, when Anslinger again began to campaign for tougher penalties, congressmen obliged him by introducing numerous bills. Anti-narcotic legislation peaked in 1955 when fourteen bills and twelve resolutions were introduced and in 1956 when sixteen more were proposed (thirteen bills, three Senate Resolutions), most of them to accommodate the commissioner's plea for lengthier sentences for repeat offenders.

A combination of the Narcotics Bureau's scare tactics, a prevailing fear of communism in the McCarthy era, and congressional response to the public's anxiety about drug addiction enabled Anslinger to attract and sustain a loyal following on Capitol Hill. These factors also fostered complacency and prevented any significant advances in either the treatment of drug addicts or in slowing illegal narcotics trafficking. The common and popular solution in the 1950s had been to regard the addict as a fugitive and adopt tougher sentencing laws to deter drug smugglers. Neither approach was effective in alleviating the problem of drug abuse.[2] Philosophically Anslinger had ceased to progress, having taken the Bureau of Narcotics and federal drug policies a giant step backward.

Two factors leading to the enactment of the Boggs Act, sponsored by Hale Boggs of Louisiana, produced a flurry of anti-narcotics bills introduced in 1951 and influenced Anslinger's testimony during the 1950 Kefauver Committee hearings on Interstate Commerce in Organized Crime, which linked organized crime syndicates to drug trafficking. Reflecting Anslinger's "get tough" attitude and growing congressional support for a more punitive approach, the Boggs Act increased the already severe penalties against narcotics violators. Not only did the act make it easier for prosecuting attorneys to secure convictions, it also stipulated that first offenders would be subject to a sentence of not less than two years or more than five with the possibility of probation. Second offenders received a mandatory five to ten years with no probation or suspension of sentence permitted. Three-time losers faced a mandatory twenty years with no probation or suspension of sentence. All offenses also carried fines up to $2,000; prior to the Boggs Act the penalty was a ten-year maximum sentence.[3]

Those who criticized the Boggs legislation did so on several counts. First, they argued that the penalties were inordinately oppressive and were a reflection of attitudes more prevalent in ancient times than the mid-twentieth century. They also challenged the language and effectiveness of the act. Because its penalties fell primarily on the victims of the drug trafficking—the addicts—and not on the dealers and distributors, the law was suspect. One of the bill's critics in the House of Representatives, Congressman Victor L. Anfuso of New York, agreed that the Boggs penalties were misdirected and argued that imposing severe jail sentences would not prevent the traffic because the profits were too lucrative not to take the risk.[4]

Moreover, no distinction was made between the violator who was profiting from an illegal practice and the addict-violator who was in a sense a victim of the drug itself. Both the trafficker and the addict were subject to the same penalties. Unfortunately, because the addict was usually destitute and resorted to committing "street crimes" (robberies and burglaries, for example) he was easily apprehended. The pusher was more difficult to arrest, primarily because he enjoyed greater financial and legal resources. This enabled him to evade the authorities or leave the country, making prosecution nearly impossible.

On introducing H.R. 3490 on 3 April 1951, "to amend the penalty provisions applicable to persons convicted of violating certain narcotics laws," Congressman Boggs justified the necessity for such legislation as a deterrent to the dramatic increase in narcotics use, particularly among juveniles in the period 1948–1951.[5] The Congressman was an Anslinger "loyalist," and his bill would not have been considered inconsistent with his conservative political views. However, other circumstances motivated him to introduce such drastic proposals.

As Boggs was gaining national recognition for his bill, a political faction in his home state was in a position to overthrow Earl Long, brother of Louisiana's best known politician, Huey Long. Earl Long had been governor since 1948, but he had come under attack in 1951 for corruption and mismanagement of state affairs. The recent inquiry by the Kefauver Committee of criminal racketeering in New Orleans and throughout the state exposed widespread corruption and further weakened Long's position by making him more vulnerable in his campaign for reelection in 1952. If Boggs could project himself as a strong proponent of law and order, he would have more appeal with the Louisiana voters.

Confident he could unseat the incumbent, Congressman Boggs finally made it official that he would be a candidate for the Louisiana state house. But charges of mismanagement in the Long administration notwithstanding, unseating the popular governor would be difficult. Polls conducted by Boggs' workers, though, indicated that support for Long in the middle-class New Orleans district he represented was weak. What Boggs needed was to identify himself with a "safe non-political" issue as well as with working-class voters who were most likely to vote for Long. Once the Congressman discovered the narcotics problem in New Orleans, which was the racket involving the smallest number of people, he had established the foundation for his gubernatorial campaign.[6]

The hearings on H.R. 3490 opened on 7 April 1951, and lasted three days. The first witness to testify was Congresswoman Edith N. Rogers of Massachusetts who wanted the regulation of over-the-counter sales of barbiturates assigned to the Bureau of Narcotics.[7] Anslinger was not opposed to such regulation, but he had been reluctant to assume the enforcement responsibilities over barbiturates prior to Congresswoman Rogers' bill and continued to oppose similar proposals throughout his career. He knew his already overburdened agents could not possibly enforce the laws pertaining to barbiturates with any degree of efficiency or effectiveness. Anslinger maintained that these enforcement activities would be more appropriately assigned to the Food and Drug Administration.

The testimony given by other witnesses was notable for several reasons. When discussing the validity of the "stepping-stone" theory with Congressman Boggs, Anslinger contradicted his own statement given in the Marijuana Tax Hearings in 1937 about marijuana leading to harder drugs. In the 1951 hearings, when asked if he found marijuana users graduating to barbiturates, he responded: "No we do not find that." In 1937 he argued convincingly that the use of marijuana would unquestionably lead to experimentation with even more dangerous drugs. Anslinger also seemed to have softened in his view of the effects of marijuana when he commented that "only a small percentage of these marijuana cases was anything more than a temporary degree of exhilaration."[8]

When asked who he thought he was most responsible for the traffic in narcotics, Anslinger stated unhesitantly that it was "all underworld." The commissioner then lamented that the "big fellows" were not given long enough prison sentences and chastised the judicial system for not keeping them in confinement. The judges, Anslinger argued, were too easy on peddlers who served light sentences and went right back into dealing. "We are on a merry-go-round," he remarked, and implored Congress to pass legislation with longer minimum sentences.[9]

By the time the bill was debated on the House floor, opposition to some of its provisions had become substantial. The most vocal opponents, Congressmen Emanual Celler of New York and Richard M. Simpson of Pennsylvania, agreed that the penalties should be increased but expressed misgivings about the mandatory minimum sentences. Congressman Celler's greatest concern, echoed by Congressman Simpson, was that the bill would make it impossible for a judge to impose any sentence less than two years, thereby denying him all discretionary power. In addition, juries would be reluctant to convict a small-time peddler who faced such a harsh mandatory minimum sentence. In defending his bill, Congressman Boggs assured his colleagues that there was no intended encroachment on judicial authority, but Celler remained unconvinced and refused to support the bill.[10] By the conclusion of the debate, opposition to H.R. 3490 cut across party lines, with both Democrats and Republicans arguing that, though the penalties were not too severe for the professional trafficker in narcotics, they might be an injustice to helpless addicts who fell victim to the drugs. Nevertheless, the bill was approved by a voice vote and sent to the Senate. On 2 November 1951, it was signed into law by President Truman.

Almost immediately Anslinger reported a "startling decline" in the illicit use of narcotics by juveniles. Commenting on the television show "Battle Report," he attributed the drop-off in the number of juveniles requesting treatment to the heavier penalties imposed in the new Boggs Act. Because the new law provided heavier penalties, the commissioner said, law enforcement agencies could reduce the sale and use of narcotics so that one day they will "no longer be a danger or threat to our society."[11]

The extraordinarily harsh and inflexible penalties of the Boggs Act were scarcely entered in the federal criminal code as statutes when Anslinger began to agitate for even tougher laws. During the 1951 hearings he referred to Communist China as a point of origin for heroin and twice made formal charges before the United Nations Commission on Narcotic Drugs against the Chinese Communist regime for selling heroin and opium as a means of subverting free countries. By 1955 the fear of being over-run by communists wielding hypodermic needles rather than rifles had become a major concern to Washington politicians. In 1954 seven members of Congress spoke on the floor about the evils of communism and either cited Anslinger directly or included articles written by him in the *Congressional Record*. One of them, Congressman Fred E. Busbey of Illinois, felt that even the long sentences provided for in the Boggs Act were insufficient for communist-supplied dope peddlers who were poisoning America's juvenile population. To get "at the very heart of the whole treacherous narcotics problem" Congressman Busbey introduced H.R. 8700, which would make the death penalty or life imprisonment mandatory for anyone convicted of selling narcotics to persons under twenty-one years old.[12] The "life and death" bill did not reach a vote in 1954, but it was indicative of the public's frustration with what it perceived as an addiction problem of epidemic proportions which threatened American young people.

While Congress continued debating on the most effective methods of dealing with drug offenders, the American Bar Association (ABA) was evaluating federal narcotics policies, particularly in regard to enforcement. In 1954 the legal society created a special committee on narcotics and the following year joined with the AMA in recommending that the Harrison Act and the Narcotics Bureau be objectively and scrupulously studied by a congressional investigation.[13] Too many Congressmen, however, were unsympathetic to the ABA-AMA's plea for more statutes, and on 14 January 1955, forty-two senators co-sponsored a bill which provided for even stiffer sentences, including the death penalty for second offenders who supplied drugs to teenagers. [14] But two months later, on 8 March 1955, the Senate did adopt Senate Resolution 67, which authorized the first nationwide investigation of the illicit narcotics traffic, drug addiction, and the treatment of drug addicts, with the objective of improving the Federal Criminal Code and enforcement procedures dealing with marijuana and other drugs. [15]

The sponsor of the resolution and the head of the special subcommittee was Senator Price Daniel, a conservative Democrat from Texas. Described as "colorless but effective," Senator Daniel, much like Congressman Boggs in 1951, needed name recognition to establish himself as a front-runner in the 1956 Texas gubernatorial campaign. Chairing the subcommittee for eight months in cities throughout the country—while managing to conclude the hearings within the allotted time and $15,000 under budget—was in itself a remarkable achievement sure to fuel the "Eisencrat's" campaign for governor. [16]

From the testimony at the hearings, which began on 27 May 1955, it was apparent that the congressional review of the narcotics traffic in the postwar era was almost a replay of past investigations. The FBN enthusiastically favored the resolution and was represented by Anslinger and Malachi ("Mal") Harney, officially a Technical Assistant to the Secretary of the Treasury but actually the brain trust behind the bureau's enforcement policies. Just as with the Tax Act Hearings of 1937, outside expert witnesses corroborated Anslinger's assertions about how dangerous narcotics addiction was to the future of the United States. A number of public officials, including Dr. Frank B. Berry, Assistant Secretary of Defense for Health and Medicine; Dr. Kenneth Chapman, Director of the Federal Narcotics Hospital in Lexington, Kentucky; and Dr. George Hunt in the Bureau of Medical Services, offered variations on the exaggerated effects of marijuana. [17]

Anslinger was the first witness, and he testified only minutes before the discussion of drug addiction turned to marijuana as a first step to the use of other narcotics. Nearly twenty years had elapsed since the passage of the Marijuana Tax Act in 1937; yet, despite the heated controversy and the scientific research that indicated otherwise, Anslinger's regard for marijuana as the "killer weed" was just as obvious as it had been when he testified in 1951:

SENATOR DANIEL: Now, do I understand it from you that, while we are discussing marihuana, the real danger is that the use of marihuana leads many people eventually to the use of heroin, and the drugs that do cause them complete addiction; is that true?

MR. ANSLINGER: That is the great problem and our great concern about the use of marihuana, that eventually if used over a long period, it does lead to heroin addiction. . . .

SENATOR DANIEL: As I understand it from having read your book [*Traffic in Narcotics*], an habitual user of marihuana or even a user to a small extent presents a problem to the community, and is a bad thing. Marihuana can cause a person to commit crimes and do many heinous things; is that not correct?

MR. ANSLINGER: That is correct. It is a dangerous drug, and is so regarded all over the world.[18]

As if needing further assurance that marijuana really was that vicious, Senator Herman Welker of Idaho pressed Anslinger to specify. The commissioner, who had never passed up an opportunity to discuss the evils of marijuana, agreed with Senator Welker that it was indeed a horrible drug, but Anslinger was reluctant to implicate marijuana in all violent crimes:

SENATOR WELKER: Mr. Commissioner, my concluding question with respect to marihuana: Is it or is it not a fact that a marihuana user had been responsible for many of our most sadistic, terrible crimes in this Nation, such as sex slayings, sadistic slayings, and matters of that kind?

MR. ANSLINGER: There have been instances of that, Senator. We have had some rather tragic occurrences by users of marihuana. It does not follow that all crimes can be traced to marihuana. There have been many brutal crimes traced to marihuana, but I would not say that it is the controlling factor in the commission of crimes.

SENATOR WELKER: I will grant you that it is not the controlling factor, but is it a fact that your investigation shows that many of the most sadistic, terrible crimes, solved or unsolved, we can trace directly to the marihuana user?

MR. ANSLINGER: You are correct in many cases, Senator Welker.

SENATOR WELKER: In other words, it builds up a false sort of feeling on the part of the user that he has no inhibitions against doing anything; am I correct?

MR. ANSLINGER: He is completely irresponsible.[19]

Later in Anslinger's testimony, when the questioning focused on the treatment of addicts, Senator Welker was interested to know the commissioner's reaction to members of the legal and medical professions who felt that narcotics should be legalized and addicts given free treatment to help them conquer their addiction. In voicing his opposition to what he considered a preposterous idea, Anslinger referred to the failure of the drug clinic system in the United States in the early 1920s and how many individual states, pressured by the Narcotics Division, forced the clinics to shut down. When Senator Daniel asked Anslinger if he was aware of recently published articles in national magazines advancing the legalization of drugs for confirmed addicts, the commissioner claimed that they were "full of misinformation" and written by two doctors who he doubted had ever seen a drug addict.[20]

Anslinger's testimony was not totally comprised of opinionated generalizations devoid of factual information. On the issue of addiction rates, he estimated that at the time there were about 60,000 addicts in the United States who spent an average of ten dollars a day to support their habits. "Dr." Anslinger, as he had often been addressed (his L.L.B. degree was seldom recognized as the equivalent of the more contemporary J.D. degree), told the subcommittee that his figures were taken from a five-year survey conducted by the Bureau of Narcotics since 1953. Based on this study, Anslinger provided an exceptionally precise state-by-state breakdown of the number of addicts. Of the 60,000 addicts nationwide, which contrasted sharply with the one in 10,000 rejected for military service in World War II, New York state was the highest with 9,458. Second was Illinois with 7,172, followed by California with 2,350.[21] Many of Anslinger's critics found it remarkable how the bureau could produce such exact numbers of addicts, since it was hardly likely that a person would admit to having an addiction problem. Impartial authorities around the country also were astounded by Anslinger's compilations and his figure of 60,000 addicts nationwide, since it had been estimated that there were 20,000 in New York City alone.

Anslinger felt that the narcotics problem was so pervasive and so established that it would not matter "if you had the Army, the Navy, the Coast Guard, the FBI, the Customs Service and our [narcotic] service, you would not stop heroin from coming through the Port of New York." To that Senator Daniel asked if an increase in funding and additional agents would enable the bureau to conduct more investigations. Anslinger's obvious answer was that an increase in appropriations would be extremely beneficial.[22] With the exception of a handful of attorneys and doctors who were opposed to severe penalties and the treatment of the addict as a criminal, testimony during the hearings was a resounding affirmation of Anslinger's policies and capabilities as chief narcotics administrator.

By October 1955, after listening to former prizefighter Barney Ross's dramatic account of his addiction to morphine, Senator Daniel announced that he would urge the investigating subcommittee to include in its recommendations to the Committee on the Judiciary the death sentence for narcotics smugglers.[23] Two months later, in a parallel inquiry headed by Congressman Boggs of a House Ways and Means subcommittee, Representative Anfuso also called for the death penalty for the selling of narcotics to deter what he referred to as "a crime worse than murder."[24] There was little doubt that the already severe penalties created by the Boggs hearings in 1951 would be made even more harsh; only the degree of severity was in question.

On 9 January 1956, after hearing 346 witnesses who provided more than 8,600 pages of testimony taken in thirteen cities, Chairman Daniel submitted his committee's report to Congress. The proposed legislation, entitled the Narcotic Control Act of 1956 (NCA) provided for an entirely new chapter in Title 18 of the Federal Criminal Code. In addition to the provision which completely outlawed heroin in the United States, the act included dramatically escalated penalties for smuggling and selling narcotics.

The penalty for selling heroin to juveniles stipulated a $10,000 fine and a minimum sentence of ten years' imprisonment. It also carried as a maximum sentence of death upon recommendation of the jury for any person who sold or gave heroin to a person under eighteen. Penalties for offenses related to marijuana were also increased, depending upon the nature of the illegal activity. Maximum fines and sentences under the NCA, which were more severe for selling than they were for possession, essentially doubled those provided for by the Boggs Act. For the first possession offense, the penalty was two to ten years' imprisonment with probation or parole. For the second possession or first selling offense, there was a mandatory five to twenty years with no probation or parole; and, for the third possession or second selling and subsequent offense, the violator was sentenced to a mandatory term of ten to forty years with no probation or parole.[25] The provision for mandatory sentences, which was an infringement on the judges' discretionary power, was to insure that drug dealers would not be let off with lenient sentences, though there was no real evidence that the courts pampered the convicted pushers.[26]

In addition to these excessive sentences, the NCA contained provisions that greatly expanded enforcement activities for the Narcotics Bureau. Both the FBN and the Customs Bureau were given the authority to carry firearms, serve search warrants, and make arrests without warrants for "violations committed in their presence." In an effort to better prepare its agents, the bureau was authorized to organize a training school. Special permission was also granted for intercepting telephone calls between suspected narcotics traffickers, providing consent was obtained from federal court.[27]

When Senators Price Daniel and Frederick G. Payne, co-sponsors of Senate bill 3760, opened the floor debates in late May, they asked for favorable action by noting that the NCA was the first real concerted effort in solving the narcotics problem undertaken by the federal government in many years. Senator Payne also emphasized that its greatest benefit was that it "will give Harry Anslinger . . . a chance to put the fear of God into the hearts of those who deal in this type of traffic."[28]

As convincing as the senators' arguments may have been, the bill met with opposition from several sources. Senator Herbert L. Lehman of New York felt that the punitive approach, which had already been tried unsuccessfully, was not likely to be effective. Senator Lehman was also concerned, after reading a report by the New York Academy of Medicine, that the bill made no mention of a treatment facility for drug addicts. Instead of seeking ways to devise longer prison sentences, he felt the government should be giving more consideration to possible methods of rehabilitation.[29]

Senator Joseph C. O'Mahoney of Wyoming and Senator Wayne B. Morse of Oregon also had reservations about the bill. Primarily they opposed what they perceived as "precedent for the expansion of wiretapping by Government agents . . . to invade a citizen's home."[30] Senator Daniel defended the wiretapping provision by reminding his colleagues that the Attorney General had been tapping certain telephones in subversion cases for the last twenty years with the approval of Presidents Roosevelt, Truman, and Eisenhower. Without further opposition, Senate bill 3760 passed the Senate on 31 May.

On 21 June the House of Representatives unanimously passed the bill but refused to accept the Senate death penalty clause. However, the next week a joint Senate-House conference approved a compromise measure which included the death sentence from the Senate version and the stiff penalty schedule from the House version. Less than three weeks later, both houses had passed the bill and sent it to the White House, and on 18 July 1956 President Eisenhower signed the Narcotic Control Act into law.

The sweeping regressive reforms contained in the NCA represented the most punitive and repressive anti-narcotics legislation ever adopted by Congress. All discretion to suspend sentences or permit probation was eliminated. Parole was allowed only for first offenders convicted of possession, and the death penalty could be invoked for anyone who sold heroin to a minor. The only progressive measure, providing for hospitals and treatment facilities for addicts, introduced by Senator Lehman, received no consideration.

Armed with its most powerful weapon yet, the Federal Bureau of Narcotics began an immediate nationwide battle against drug trafficking. With the addition of forty new agents and $300,000, it also stepped up its foreign operations. The most effective provision of the Narcotic Control Act, according to Commissioner Anslinger, was the mandatory five-year prison sentence for first offenders convicted of selling any narcotics. With the new legislation, Anslinger declared an all-out war against heroin, which he said was now coming primarily from Lebanon, Syria, Turkey, Mexico, and Communist China.[31] The enactment of the NCA with its oppressive, inflexible penalties was a total victory for Anslinger and the Bureau of Narcotics. Appropriations were increased, tough laws guaranteed more convictions, and few critics publicly opposed the commissioner. With the NCA Anslinger had moved the Bureau forward by reverting to simplistic and faulty notions of a past era to solve contemporary social ills.

Because of its unprecedented penalties, the Boggs Act first aroused the attention of the ABA and AMA in the early 1950s. During the course of the Daniel hearings when it was apparent that those laws would be made even tougher, the special joint committee created by these associations initiated an examination of the narcotic drug traffic and related problems. In 1955, with the appointment of delegates from the ABA and AMA, the investigation was officially under way.[32]

Under the direction of Judge Morris Ploscowe of New York, the committee was composed of accomplished men from both professions. Among those participating in the study were attorney Rufus King, Chairman; Judge Edward S. Dimock and Abe Fortas of the ABA; Dr. Robert H. Felix, Director of the National Institute of Mental Health; and Dr. Issac Starr, professor of medicine at the University of Pennsylvania, both of the AMA. In its early months, the committee was beset with problems stemming primarily from a lack of consensus on methodology and funding. Eventually agreement was reached on the specific issues to be investigated; and, in October 1956, twenty months after the initial ABA resolution, the Russell Sage Foundation awarded a financial grant to the Joint Committee.[33]

Within the next year, the committee conducted a preliminary evaluation of numerous aspects of the narcotics problems and, in November 1957, announced that it would focus on five related objectives: (1) to assess the possibilities of establishing an out-patient experimental clinic for the treatment of drug addicts; (2) to engage in on-going research to learn more about the causes of addiction, (3) to evaluate the educational campaigns on narcotics, (4) to examine the relationship between state and federal drug laws, and 5) to study the administration and effectiveness of existing policies. Along with these recommendations, Judge Ploscowe wrote a summary and commentary entitled "Some Basic Problems in Drug Addiction and Suggestions for Research," outlining the history of federal narcotics policies beginning with the Harrison Act of 1914.[34]

Like its predecessor the LaGuardia Report a decade earlier, the ABA-AMA Joint Committee was intended to be administered as an independent scientific study of the narcotics situation that would ultimately produce viable solutions to combatting drug addiction and trafficking. Unlike the panel that compiled the Mayor's Report, however, the joint committee was in frequent communication with Commissioner Anslinger and extended several invitations to him to attend various conferences, all of which he declined. Immediately following the publication of the committee's findings in its *Interim Report,* Judge Ploscowe wrote to Anslinger suggesting, "It would be very helpful to sit down with you at your convenience in order to discuss the enclosed materials."[35] Ploscowe and the joint committee were anxious for a meeting with representatives from the Bureau of Narcotics to provide for a free exchange of reactions and criticisms, but Anslinger opposed the idea. In writing a response to Judge Ploscowe in March 1958, the commissioner explained the reasons why he could not participate in the committee's study. After stating that he was grateful to have a copy of the report, Anslinger found it "incredible that so many glaring inaccuracies, manifest inconsistencies, apparent ambiguities, important omissions and even false statements could be found in one report."[36] Anslinger also stated in the letter that he did not wish to censor the report; but, when it was scheduled for publication by the Indiana University Press, a federal narcotics agent began making inquiries about the document. The agent was interested in the reasons for publishing the book, the number of copies to be printed, and particularly how it was financed. When asked by a *Washington Post* reporter why the agent had been sent to the university, Anslinger stated that he was only instructed to purchase a copy of the book. Records of the *Post,* however, showed that the Deputy Commissioner of Narcotics ordered the book for the Bureau on 30 March 1961; the agent did not appear in Bloomington until 4 April.[37]

More than twenty-five years later, the bureau's confrontation with the ABA-AMA remains a sensitive issue with Henry L. Giordano, the deputy commissioner at the time. When the matter was raised during an interview with the man who later succeeded Anslinger as commissioner, Giordano bristled at the mention of Dr. Alfred Lindesmith, a sociologist and long-time critic of FBN policies at Indiana University who was actively involved in the publication of the Joint Committee Report.[38]

Under Anslinger's directive, the Bureau quickly published its own study, *Comments on Narcotic Drugs,* which was a compilation of refutations gathered from more than two dozen "experts," such as Congressman Hale Boggs, Dr. Edward Bloomquist, Senator Price Daniel, Judge William T. McCarthy (a personal friend of Anslinger), Alfred L. Tennyson (chief counsel, Bureau of Narcotics), and Malachi Harney. In refuting the findings of the joint committee, many of those contributing to the bureau's defense resorted to highly emotional and sometimes irrational arguments. The most vilifying attack in the bureau's comments, which at

185 pages is twice as long as the Joint Committee Report, came from Harney, who doubted that it was even worth his time to react to what he regarded as far less than a legitimate investigation.

The bureau's former legal adviser and later superintendent of the Division of Narcotic Control for the State of Illinois did not limit himself to general commentary on the committee's recommendations but delivered scathing personal attacks against each individual member.[39] Harney labeled the committee members "special pleaders presumably making some sort of an objective study of the drug addiction problem" who were nonetheless "entitled to express whatever opinions they have, however bizarre." As a panelist in a symposium on narcotic drug addiction in March 1958, while the Joint Committee was preparing its conclusions for publication, Harney accused those who advocated the treatment of addicts as out-patients of being propagandists who relied on "a technique reminiscent of the Hitler 'Big Lie.'"[40] He also reproved a lax and inadequate judicial system for making it difficult for police and narcotics agents to secure convictions. Harney believed that the Narcotics Bureau and similar agencies were targets of a conspiracy. In the *Comments* report he bitterly complained, "We are presently the victims of a Supreme Court majority which to me seems almost hysterical in its desire to suppress any freedom of action of law enforcement officers."[41] Those kinds of scurrilous remarks were too much even for Anslinger, who announced on 18 March 1960 that he had ordered the Narcotics Bureau to remove an "objectionable" reference to the Supreme Court. After Justice William O. Douglas requested President Kennedy to ask for Anslinger's resignation, the publication was withdrawn from public sale.[42] Anslinger never issued a formal apology or any kind of explanation, commenting only that the statement "escaped all of us."[43] Anslinger may have been conciliatory in public, but privately he shared Harney's notion that the judiciary was at least partly responsible for allowing too many narcotics violators to go unpunished. A year after he expressed his regret for Harney's attack on the Supreme Court, the commissioner wrote his old friend, Judge McCarthy: "It is incredible what the courts are doing these days. If we go down the drain it will be because of courts, criminals, and communists."[44]

Anslinger's decision to halt further publication of the document came too late. The bureau's commentary was no longer in print, but anyone who was interested in the report could obtain it. The bureau did not even bother to delete the insulting references to the Supreme Court, merely penciling them out. Anslinger himself continued to assail the ABA-AMA Joint Committee as a body of "bleeding hearts" who only sought to complicate the bureau's enforcement of narcotics laws.

As one contemporary journalist observed, "The whole tenor of the document indicates that Anslinger does not want to win the discussion as much as he wants to eliminate it."[45] Rather than continue to expend the time, energy, and financial resources to persuade the commissioner to adopt their recommendations, the ABA-AMA Joint Committee decided to be patient and wait for Anslinger to reach the mandatory age for retirement in 1962.

Once again, as with the testimony of Dr. Woodward in 1937 and the LaGuardia Report in 1945, the bureau continued to cast a suspicious eye toward those who had opposing points of view. Anslinger scoffed at the "out-patient proposal" and was not likely to concede that there might be alternatives to his punitive approach. The publication of *Comments on Narcotic Drugs* was yet another example of the Narcotics Bureau's inflexibility and unwillingness to experiment. As it became more difficult for Anslinger to challenge the credibility of independent scientific investigations that recommended advancements in the treatment of drug addiction, Anslinger and the bureau continued an ideological retreat into the future.

By the end of the 1950s, mostly in response to the Narcotic Control Act and the *Comments* report, bureau critics had become more numerous and more vocal. Most were the more liberal-minded members of academia like Lindesmith at Indiana University, but they also included physicians and attorneys who wanted to treat the drug addict with compassion, as a sick person, much like a recovering alcoholic would be treated for his "disease," rather than as a criminal. But because of the stringent laws and Anslinger's disdain for rehabilitative clinics, many physicians preferred not to handle patients with drug-related problems. Dr. Herbert Berger, a consultant to narcotics for the United States Public Health Service, claimed that his profession had been scared out of treating addicts by the FBN and charged that the Bureau was run by "Harry J. Anslinger, a despot interested only in maintaining the status quo."[46]

Dissent

A handful of judges also deplored the Bureau's heavy-handed philosophy toward drug addicts. In his book *Who Live in Shadow,* published in 1959, New York City Chief Magistrate John M. Murtagh acknowledged that Anslinger was an honest, conscientious cop, but felt that the enforcement of narcotics laws was misplaced.[47] To achieve greater efficiency, Judge Murtagh suggested that enforcement be transferred from the Treasury Department to the FBI in the Department of Justice.[48] Murtagh saved his sharpest criticism, however, for a press conference on the publication of his book in May 1959. He stated that the Narcotics Bureau was doing little more than arresting addicts while ignoring the more powerful distributors and called for Anslinger's resignation to make way for sweeping reforms. He vehemently condemned the bureau's policy of fining and jailing narcotics addicts and accused Anslinger and his agents of carrying out a "reign of terror" against physicians.[49]

Not the bureau's attitude but its policing methods were what offended Judge David Bazelon of the United States District Court of Appeals for the District of Columbia. He lashed out at Anslinger's policies in his decision in a 1959 case involving informers. Judge Bazelon found it particularly hypocritical that the bureau should cooperate with and pay a person for information while that person himself was constantly engaged in illicit activities.[50]

Perhaps the most direct challenge to Anslinger's authority came from a young circuit attorney in St. Louis, Missouri, who sponsored a new state law that allowed first offenders against narcotics laws to be paroled or placed on probation. Under the old Missouri law and the recently enacted Narcotic Control Act, first offenders had to be sentenced to at least two years in the penitentiary. Circuit Attorney Thomas E. Eagleton lobbied for the statutory change in lieu of imprisonment to permit probation and to allow judicial latitude. Eagleton was not sympathetic toward drug violators, but like Congressmen Celler and Simpson, who opposed the Boggs Act, he realized that a first offender charged with possession was not likely to plead guilty regardless of the evidence against him if the judge had no discretion but to hand out a minimum two years.[51] The accused person might as well plead not guilty and let the jury determine his fate. By amending the law to allow the judge the option of probation for first-time offenders or to permit a jury to impose a lesser sentence than the mandatory minimum of two years, Eagleton was striving for procedural efficiency and judicial flexibility in the disposition of narcotics cases.

Attorney Eagleton also had been influenced by a technique developed in Oakland, California, in the late 1950s, which required periodic testing of the offender during his probationary period. Usually reporting once a week, the defendants were administered nalline, a drug that caused the pupils in the eye to dilate, enabling an examiner to detect the use of narcotics. The only drawback was that nalline also reacted to caffeine as well as it did to heroin; thus it was never adopted for widespread use.[52]

Anslinger was furious. Never before had a public official had the audacity to defy the commissioner so brazenly. He had no authority to interfere with state laws, but he did have control over federal enforcement in Missouri, and in September 1959 he announced that as of 31 October, most agents in the state would be withdrawn. The St. Louis branch would be reduced from four to one, and the Kansas City office was scheduled to be cut from three to two.[53] Anslinger never offered a reason for withdrawing the agents, but it was obvious to any observer that he was expressing his dissatisfaction with Missouri's new law.

The Missouri press was outraged that the federal Commissioner of Narcotics, charged with impartial enforcement of the laws, would exploit his powers to punish its citizens for changing their own law. After a series of editorials in the city newspaper, Anslinger did relent somewhat and announced he would retain two agents in St. Louis rather than one; the Kansas City staff remained unchanged. Missouri kept its new law, but the message from Commissioner Anslinger clearly indicated that he would not tolerate dissent and that he would move quickly to smother any challenge to bureau policies.

On the inside, too, it seemed the Narcotics Bureau could not escape the problems that plagued it since its inception in 1930, when the initial choice for commissioner, Levi Nutt, was excluded from consideration because of his involvement in questionable record-keeping practices. Anslinger was confronted with numerous scandals within the bureau throughout his career. Although he was spared any scandals of major proportion while he was commissioner, several lesser incidents occurred, one of which was embarrassing if not ignominious.

In 1952 Assistant United States Attorney Thomas A. Wadden was put in charge of a special unit organized specifically to break the syndicates which controlled gambling and narcotics in Washington, D.C. Almost immediately in his investigation of the narcotics laws, Wadden realized that the local statutes had been so loosely enforced that it was relatively safe for dope peddlers to sell heroin, cocaine, and marijuana openly on some street corners.[54] On loan to aid in the special investigation were two detectives from the Metropolitan Police Force and several agents from the Federal Narcotics Bureau. The Wadden unit's probe into the city's narcotics trafficking was extremely successful, as it was responsible for jailing 300 violators in a one-year period.

Perhaps the strangest case, however, unfolded during the interrogation of a small-time peddler named Jim "Yellow" Roberts, who told of at least one major wholesaler in the district who had a direct connection to the Treasury Department vault. A few days later on 15 April, Wadden heard the story repeated by another narcotics user, Leroy Troy, who identified the connection as "Walter." Not wanting to interfere with the Narcotics Bureau's internal affairs, Wadden informed an agent working with the special investigation and suggested that he report to Commissioner Anslinger.

On 16 April Walter Morant, a janitor at the Treasury Department, admitted that since 1949 he had received approximately thirty deliveries of cocaine from another Treasury janitor, Eddie Gregg. One of the largest distributors of cocaine in Washington was employed by the Treasury Department and literally was stealing from under the nose of officials in the Federal Narcotics Bureau. The janitors should have been easy to apprehend. Obviously the best way to establish a strong case for conviction was to nab him with the stolen narcotics. However, for some unknown reason, when bureau agents met with Gregg to set up a buy, they took him into custody not only without an arrest warrant but before they could catch him in the act of stealing the cocaine. Surprisingly the Bureau gave little time and attention to a dealer who later confessed to having stolen up to 150 ounces of cocaine and between fifty and seventy-five pounds of marijuana. The street value of these drugs was estimated at approximately $250,000.[55]

When Eddie Gregg appeared before a grand jury, skeptical Bureau representatives asked how the janitor got into the Treasury Annex room where the drugs were stored. FBN officials found it difficult to envision someone getting through a heavy iron-barred door without a key, but when the Treasury employee demonstrated how, with a piece of cord used for wrapping packages, he was able to turn the knob from the inside, they were astounded.

Gregg's testimony incriminated several major narcotics dealers who had eluded the Narcotics Bureau for years, yet because it had been so humiliated and was fearful of the publicity, the bureau discouraged Attorney Wadden from bringing the case to trial. Commissioner Anslinger actually impeded the investigation, asserted Wadden, by making "public statements which tended to disparage our claims."[56] Eventually Anslinger admitted that there might have been some pilferage, but he "could see no reason for all the fuss." When Wadden was preparing to round up five major dealers identified by Gregg, the bureau requested that he postpone his raid for four hours. Wadden refused and picked up his suspects, but he was prevented from going from after more when the commissioner organized his own raids. With sixty agents, marshals, and police, accompanied by newspaper reporters and photographers, Anslinger personally led the city-wide seizures. The commissioner was taking no chances with the next morning's headlines.

The public was not aware of the Wadden investigation until the District Attorney published his story in 1953. The grand jury, however, issued a report which accused the Bureau of negligence and berated it for "inadequate and unorthodox methods which greatly hampered the grand jury in procuring the proper evidence upon which to return indictments."[57] As potentially damaging as these charges may have been, they did little to discredit the reputation Anslinger had developed as a crime fighter.

Despite criticisms aired by opponents of the Bureau's philosophy, Anslinger was generally able to cultivate and sustain an image as a proficient bureaucrat and a capable administrator. Critics could charge that his punitive methods were outdated and ineffective or that he was inflexible, but they never doubted his tenacity.

The testimony of George H. White, senior narcotics agent and supervisor and one of the bureau's most capable investigators over the preceding twenty years, was totally unforeseen when, during Senate hearings on juvenile delinquency in 1959 and 1960, he revealed that the Narcotics Bureau and the Bureau of Customs tacitly agreed to establish a "sphere of influence" for enforcement purposes. When asked by Chairman Thomas C. Hennings of Missouri to describe the narcotics situation in Mexico, Agent White stated that very little had been accomplished there by the FBN. According to the agreement, the Bureau of Customs was responsible for enforcement in the Orient and Latin America; the Bureau of Narcotics had Europe. This "dog-in-the manager" policy, as White referred to it, precluded one agency from investigating a case in the other's "sphere of influence."[58] Because of this policy, Agent White believed that it was impossible to enforce federal narcotics laws in either Mexico or Hong Kong.

With each additional bit of information White offered, the committee members became more astonished that such an agreement existed and more intrigued with how it originated. Chairman Hennings wanted to know whether it was a written or verbal agreement and who was responsible for it, to which White replied that it was "decided upon by the Secretary of the Treasury after consultation with the Bureau of Customs and the Bureau of Narcotics."[59] When Senator Roman L. Hruska of Nebraska asked White if he had knowledge of any discussions of the agreement at the Cabinet level, the agent replied cryptically: "I am not prepared to answer that. I imagine that there have been some recently."[60] Either Agent White was a very careful witness, or he presumed that some discussions had taken place. In either instance he was never pressed to clarify his statement.

The agent testified further that he believed that the narcotics laws were about the only popular laws that Customs enforced and that under the agreement narcotics agents would not interfere with their border jurisdiction. White expressed his frustration when he related how he had made repeated attempts to conduct an investigation in Hong Kong where he had trailed major smugglers, only to be told by Customs agents that they did not want him there. In another unrelated case, while hunting down traffickers who crossed the United States border, White told of how he followed them into Mexico in "violation" of the agreement. The narcotics agent emphasized how a "dog-in-the-manger" policy resulted in an intra-departmental conflict which made effective enforcement impossible. At this point Chairman Hennings promised that when the hearings returned to Washington "we are going to dig into this thing and find out about these conflicts of authority and jurisdiction."[61]

On 22 January 1960, the special Senate subcommittee returned to the capital and resumed its hearings. True to his word, Chairman Hennings continued his inquiry first with A. Gilmore Flues, Assistant Secretary of the Treasury, who acknowledged that there was competition from time to time between the two bureaus. When the Assistant Secretary later asserted that a "little rivalry" is a healthy thing, Chairman Hennings suggested that for expeditious law enforcement "healthy cooperation" might be a more appropriate characterization.[62]

When Flues was asked to account for Agent White's testimony that the Narcotics and Customs Bureaus divided their jurisdictions and responsibilities, the Assistant Secretary preferred not to respond and called upon Commissioner Anslinger. Apparently trying to minimize the impact of White's testimony, Anslinger described the veteran agent as a capable man but one who had "a strong personality and frequently clashes with many law enforcement agencies."[63] By depicting White as a "maverick" who often acted independently, Anslinger made it sound as though the problem was more a personality conflict among individuals than an intradepartmental clash.

Anslinger recalled that White had never submitted any kind of formal complaint to Washington but that he had occasionally "grumbled" about it. In recalling White's testimony two months earlier, Senator Hennings informed the commissioner that Agent White was not "grumbling" when he last appeared before the subcommittee, but that he stood up and testified with enough force to be heard not only by those in the courtroom where the hearings were held but by passersby in the corridors.[64] At this point Chairman Hennings and other members of the committee became annoyed by the direct conflict between the disclosures in the testimony of George White, who was at that time District Supervisor for the FBN in San Francisco, and the testimony given by Assistant Secretary Flues and corroborated by Commissioner Anslinger. The committee was also puzzled as to why Anslinger informed Chairman Hennings in a letter dated 20 October 1959 that he would be unable to appear and suggested that Agent White be called to testify because "no one is better qualified to discuss the California situation with your subcommittee." Yet Anslinger stated on 22 January 1960, after White had told about the agreement, that "Mr. White was not always aware of what was going on."[65]

The reasons for White's whistle-blowing were never brought out during the hearings, and one can only speculate what might have provoked the agent to choose that occasion to so vigorously vent his dissatisfaction with the longstanding "sphere of influence" agreement. What was more curious, as observed by Chairman Hennings, was that White's testimony was purely voluntary, initiated by him, and did not evolve from a cross-examination intended to uncover any specific problem. It might have been a lack of communication between White and Anslinger which resulted in conflicting testimony, but that scenario is plausible but not likely. Anslinger was too experienced to commit that kind of oversight and he had come to regard White as his "best enforcement man."[66] Nor was Secretary Flues in a position to settle the dispute, since the agreement was made long before he joined the Treasury and his only meeting with White was a brief exchange of pleasantries in Washington. Most likely was that White, who was extremely volatile, had grown weary of coming out second best in the rivalry with Customs and decided to even the score against the agency that consistently made bigger seizures and more arrests than the Bureau of Narcotics.

Whatever the cause of the White-Anslinger breach, it was evident that by 1960 the bureau had become involved in activities without the knowledge or approval of even top-level Treasury officials. It was also clear that the Federal Bureau of Narcotics had not functioned in isolation but had begun to branch out into peripheral enforcement activities that Congressman Porter never would have imagined when he introduced his bill to create the bureau in 1930. One of those activities was the commissioner's relentless pursuit of his most hated, almost natural enemy that he first encountered as a twenty-three-year-old laborer for the Pennsylvania Railroad—the Mafia.

6

Anslinger Goes After the Mob, 1930–1962

At least since the frenzied days of Prohibition in the 1920s, the American public has viewed the personalities and activities associated with organized crime almost in reverential fear. Mob-related exploits as they are divulged in front-page headlines across the country have continuously reinforced this long-held fascination with the existence of an underworld during the past half century. More recently the production of numerous books and films has reawakened the popular view of organized crime as a cavalier and romantic—although deadly—adaptation of an urbanized western. Often perceived as a fusion of fantasy and reality, organized crime still has a mystique that is irresistible to a vast segment of the American population.

That this notion still exists was evident in the wake of the typical gangland-style slaying on 16 December 1985 of Paul Castellano, reputed head of the Carlo Gambino crime family in New York City. The hit, which was perfectly suited for the tabloids and six o'clock news, fired the public's curiosity and for days drew hundreds of inquisitive on-lookers to the scene of the crime in front of Spark's Steak House in midtown Manhattan.[1]

Genesis

Organized crime's structure, activities, and the nature of its existence, are responsible for a plethora of descriptions from scholars, journalists, government officials, and even former members who cannot agree on even the most fundamental questions ranging from what defines it to how it originated. Perhaps the greatest lack of consensus of opinion is about the most controversial form of organized crime, the Mafia.

The many students of this complex criminal organization have described it as a secret society of Sicilian origin (Andrew Varna, Edward J. Allen, and Ed Reid), as an informal family affair (Frederic Sondern), as an Italian sub-group of the syndicate (Hank Messick), and as an "invisible

127

government" (Fred J. Cook). Others have even argued that the Mafia does not exist (Daniel Bell) and that the so-called Mafia myth has been perpetuated as a result of media distortions and erroneous interpretations of evidence presented in congressional investigations.[2]

Correspondence and official documents contained in his papers, show that Harry Anslinger never doubted the existence of a Mafia. He could not forget his alleged fateful encounter with the "Black Hand" when he was a young man working for the "Pennsy" in Altoona, and he was convinced that the modern-day Mafia was transported to the United States by Sicilian immigrants in the late 1800s.[3] At first, according to Anslinger's interpretation, the organization's criminal activity was limited to extorting money from Italians outside the Mafia, but Prohibition provided new opportunities to reap extraordinary profits through the production and distribution of bootleg liquor. When the "Noble Experiment" was repealed in 1933, mob criminals looked to other illicit enterprises such as gambling, prostitution, and eventually narcotics as sources of revenue.[4]

As late as 1962, contrary to Anslinger's theory, some law enforcement officials had accepted the notion that there may have been a loose association of criminals operating in various cities throughout the United States but that there was no evidence of a tightly-knit nation-wide syndicate controlling or coordinating illegal operations. Indeed one of the most respected adherents to this theory was J. Edgar Hoover, Director of the FBI, who wrote in the January 1962 issue of *Law Enforcement Bulletin* that "no single individual or coalition of racketeers dominates organized crime . . . , but there were loose connections among controlling groups."[5] For forty-eight years, the head of the nation's premier law enforcement agency refused to believe that there was such a thing as a Mafia and kept his agents' attention on bank robberies, political dissidents, and stolen cars.[6] The FBI began to focus seriously on the corporate structure and economic power of the mob only after Hoover's death.

Several hypotheses have been advanced about why Hoover was so reluctant to acknowledge the existence of the Mafia when his counterpart in the Narcotics Bureau was so insistent that there was such an organization. In a study of the FBI, Fred J. Cook suggested several possibilities. One commonly cited reason was that Hoover feared that by taking on adversaries more cunning and resourceful than the common street criminal, he risked tarnishing the FBI's near perfect record of convictions. Another less plausible theory was that since Hoover enjoyed cordial relations with Congress and realized that many politicians were "bought" for protection, he felt that by going after the Mafia he would jeopardize his political support.[7] Cook's first theory is acceptable only to a limited degree; his second is illogical. By the early 1960s Hoover was well established as the most powerful bureaucrat in Washington, virtually immune to presidential politics and hardly in need of congressional favors. If Hoover eschewed any manifestation of organized criminal activity, it was not because he feared antagonizing a handful of corrupt politicians.

One hypothesis among the several formulated by Donald R. Cressey in his examination of organized crime as a corporate venture suggested that a jealous rivalry between Hoover and Anslinger prevented any interdepartmental cooperation.[8] Since Anslinger believed the Mafia existed, the theory goes, Hoover denied it. Cressey himself questioned this hypothesis, and not without justification. Whatever Hoover's reasons were for steering the FBI away from the Mafia—and they are not within the purview of this study—no evidence indicates that a rivalry was the cause. None of the correspondence in Anslinger's papers—beginning in 1933 and continuing, albeit sporadically, through 1970—hints of friction between the two crime-fighters that would negate an alliance of the two agencies for the purpose of fighting the Mafia.[9]

In direct contrast to Hoover's avoidance of the mob, Anslinger insisted that organized crime, whether it was called the Black Hand, the Mafia, or Unione Sicilione, was a real and dangerous threat to American society. Thus Anslinger has been credited as the first official on the federal level to have discovered the Mafia.[10] Anslinger claimed to launch his anti-Mafia campaign as early as 1931 when the bureau suspected Lonnie Affronti of operating a drug ring in Kansas City. Affronti, however, was not well-connected and, as Anslinger observed in a Bureau Report, was forced to "take flight . . . to evade prosecution for violation of the narcotics laws."[11] Though the Bureau was well aware of the Kansas City organization throughout the 1930s, it was unable to identify the real power behind the illicit traffic because Anslinger noted it "was on the hands of dangerous criminals and so highly organized as to make approaches to the 'higher-ups' by outsiders a very difficult and tedious procedure."[12]

In the early years of the 1940s, however, agents were able to make narcotics transactions that furnished them with enough evidence and information to arrest Carl Carramusa and three of his associates. In 1942 Carramusa submitted a statement in which he described the nature of narcotics distribution in Kansas City and implicated all the members of the Kansas City syndicate. Carramusa also told of how his organization maintained a distribution point in St. Louis that functioned as the major source of heroin and opium.[13]

Through his investigation of Affronti and the subsequent arrest and testimony of Carramusa, Anslinger quickly learned that these people were part of an established network and that they did not operate independently but as part of a criminal system. In his detailed report of the Affronti case, Anslinger referred to the mobster's organization as "the local chapter of the Italian Mafia Secret Society (Unione Sicilione or the Black Hand)."[14]

He also learned about the structure of the organization and described it as one would characterize a legitimate business corporation:

> They hired a legal advisor, a supervisory board, a general manager, a traveling representative, a bookkeeper and an extensive sales force. Through its business-like tactics this organization developed contacts with the major sources of illicit narcotics, and was able to supply not only the Kansas City area, but carried on an extensive trade in the States of Missouri, Kansas, Arkansas, Oklahoma, Colorado, Nebraska, Iowa, and Illinois.[15]

Oddly, though, in detailing the functions of the "Kansas City Syndicate," Anslinger referred to the Affronti gang as "this subsidiary of the Italian Mafia Secret Society." By using the word "Italian" as modifier of Mafia and then penciling it out, Anslinger apparently decided that the organization was not limited to that ethnic group, and he was exercising caution to avoid another racial slur.[16] The commissioner had learned much from the Affronti/Carramusa incidents; and in the area of combatting organized crime, the Bureau of Narcotics was well ahead of its rival enforcement agencies.

Despite the fact that most of Anslinger's proselytisms about a crime organization drew little attention, the commissioner remained unshaken in his determination to expose such nefarious activities. The FBI might not have recognized the existence of criminal associations, but that would not deter him from alerting his fellow law-enforcement officers. In a speech before the International Association of Chiefs of Police in October 1931, he warned that the murder of children in New York City due to the use of illicit narcotics could be directly traced to "organized gangsters in that city."[17]

In his crusade against mob crime, Anslinger did not limit bureau investigations solely to the distribution of narcotics. In 1937 Agent H. T. Nugent described how one group, operating the Nation-Wide News Service, also published the *Daily Racing Form* for the purpose of transmitting information on horse races to practically every principal city in the country.[18] Normally such a publication would not have warranted an investigation by a federal agency. However, this wire service included the list of all horses entered in the races at a particular track and the approximate odds on each horse based on the calculations of the handicapper. This information was then transmitted to major cities and relayed to smaller towns within the region. Essentially this network service provided the "morning line" used by all bookmakers in quoting odds to bettors prior to the actual running of the races.

The changing odds on each horse, received by telegraph in key cities, were relayed by telephone to hundreds of cigar stores, pool rooms, newstands, and other establishments where individual bookmakers covered the bets. Subscribers to the wire service usually paid Moses L. "Moe" Annenberg, a former Hearst circulation manager, $100 a week. The Internal Revenue Service's investigation of the Annenberg syndicate revealed that his wire service was one of the largest rackets in the United States. In 1940 Annenberg was charged with operating a monopoly of the telegraph service and income tax evasion, which resulted in his conviction and a three-year prison sentence.

After years of untangling Annenberg's corporate affairs, Elmer Irey (who coordinated Treasury Department law enforcement activities) was able to produce sufficient evidence that the man who ran real estate, insurance, liquor, and laundry companies was convicted for evading taxes totaling $3,258,809. Annenberg died in 1942 shortly after he served two years in prison, but his wire service was taken over by a Cleveland syndicate and continued to flourish. Much of the Annenberg empire was dismantled through court settlements in the early 1950s, but Annenberg's son Walter, who had been indicted with his father in the 1940 tax evasion case—charges were later dropped—was appointed as ambassador to England in 1969, likely because he made substantial contributions to Richard M. Nixon's presidential campaign.[19]

The bureau's involvement in the wire service syndicate was an exception, since most of its investigations naturally focused on narcotics-related activities. Over a twenty-year period, from 1930 to 1950, when no one seriously considered the concept of organized crime, Anslinger's agents continually arrested people connected with syndicate or criminal organizations. In 1938, again under the direction of Irey, the Narcotics Bureau broke up the Ice House gang of heroin peddlers. FBN agents arrested four leaders of the gang who were headquartered near an ice house in New Orleans, and who were eventually convicted and sentenced from one to three years in prison.[20]

Bureau of Narcotics agents also developed a case against Nicolo Impostato in the early 1940s that resulted in his conviction and two-year sentence in a federal penitentiary. The professional killer and member of the Kansas City narcotics syndicate was identified as "an alleged member of the infamous Italian Mafia" who was a "lieutenant of Joseph De-Luca."[21]

In 1947 Garland H. Williams, District Supervisor for New York, persistently monitored the activities of Joseph "Pip the Blind" Gagliano when the bureau had long suspected him of heading one of the largest narcotics rings in the country out of uptown East Side Harlem. Upon Gagliano's arrest, Supervisor Williams filed a report in which he linked the Sicilian to the "mysterious 'Mafia' organization."[22] If the Mafia was still something of a mystery to the public and a nonentity to other enforcement agencies by 1950, it was well known to Anslinger and his narcotics agents.

Anslinger was also aware that narcotics trafficking by organized crime was not exclusively the domain of a Sicilian Mafia or that these gangs operated without the benefit of international ties. During the 1930s, bureau officials believed that one of the "most powerful operations in narcotics traffic was that of the Newman brothers."[23] Though not commonly mentioned in historical studies of organized crime, George, Charles, and Harry Newman (an alias for Neiditch) reportedly distributed narcotics worth $25 million on the street from 1934 to 1938. With their principal offices in downtown Manhattan, they were believed to be the source for drugs distributed by "Big" Bill Hildebrandt in Minneapolis, the Kayne-Gordon gang in Chicago, Louis Ginsburg in Dallas, and Arthur Flegenheimer (Dutch Schultz) in New York. The brothers also had an international reputation and were well connected with the Lyon-Bacula organization in France. To evade suspicion, the Newmans operated hotels as fronts of their illegitimate activities, including gambling, bookmaking, confidence games, stock frauds, liquor smuggling, and, of course, narcotics. Fortunately, though, for the Narcotics Bureau, the trio was careless with their record-keeping, and they, like Capone and Moe Annenberg, were indicted and convicted on charges of income tax evasion.[24] Securing the convictions of the Newmans was not an easy task, but they comprised another fraternal organization operating internationally that Anslinger later considered the most "ambitious task I ever hoped to accomplish during my entire career."[25]

The Eliopoulos brothers, George and Elie, enjoyed a lifestyle that most accurately fits the stereotype often depicted in the Hollywood productions of the suave and cultured racketeer. Posing as bankers and industrialists, the two Greek nationals established themselves on a high social plane, frequenting fashionable resorts, living in luxurious hotels, and hobnobbing with leaders of finance and industry while occasionally accepting the hospitality of diplomats. They also boasted the friendship of kings and princes and had close political associations throughout Europe until World War II made it hazardous to travel in belligerent nations. More than altering the Eliopoulos brothers' social lives, however, the Nazi invasion resulted in the collapse of their drug empire. Believed to be the largest illicit dealers in drugs "ever to come to the attention of the narcotics police of the world," the brothers sold drugs in $50,000 and $100,000 lots, which brought them $10,000 to $20,000 a week in the Depression years. They were the suppliers for what constituted a substantial directory of American criminals, including the Newman brothers, Louis "Lepke" Buchalter, Samuel Bernstein, August ("Little Augie") Del Gracio, "Legs" Diamond, and Dutch Schultz.

In 1941 Elie and George fled to Greece where Elie collaborated with Nazis. They were soon forced out of that country when Greek freedom fighters wanted them caught and tried as traitors. Ultimately they escaped to South America and eventually to New York City. When it became public that Elie and George were on the run, Anslinger and the Bureau of Customs began a surveillance of their movements. For the next two years, the two agencies, in a cooperative effort, gradually amassed enough evidence to make a case against them. In 1943, after a lengthy investigation, the Eliopoulos brothers were convicted by a jury in Brooklyn for their involvement in a shipment of 17,500 cans of narcotics on the steamship *Alesia.*[26]

The Newmans and the Eliopoulos brothers may have qualified as two of the most powerful and extensive organizations in the sale and distribution of narcotics, but among the enemies of the FBN they were not the most dangerous. That heinous category Anslinger reserved for two of the most publicized and notorious mobsters in the twentieth century, Louis (Lepke) Buchalter and Salvatore Lucania, more popularly known as Charles "Lucky" Luciano.

By the later 1930s, Louis Lepke, the son of Russian immigrants, had become an old nemesis for the Narcotics Bureau. Garland Williams first tangled with the Jewish gangster in the 1920s when Lepke was earning his reputation for brutality.[27] Over the next several years Lepke's involvement as a racketeer in the fur, garment, and baking industries in New York City was well publicized, as were his numerous arrests. Lepke's reign of terror as an extortionist was superseded only by his connection with "Murder, Inc.," a Brooklyn "Murder-for-profit-syndicate which he ran in association with Emanuel 'Mendy' Weiss." Because of Lepke's power and connections, Anslinger thought he was virtually untouchable.[28]

Lepke's involvement in extortion or murder did not ultimately result in his conviction. "Public Enemy No. 1," as he was labeled by Hoover, was also involved in an intricate narcotics smuggling ring which imported drugs from Tientsin, China. Between 1935 and 1937 the FBN estimated that the ring imported more than $10 million worth of heroin and other narcotics through the New York Port of Customs.[29] Lepke apparently had too many rackets in operation at the same time to insure that each was adequately protected. Because narcotics trafficking had become increasingly risky, even the more cunning and powerful Meyer Lansky withdrew. Lepke, however, continued his drug-smuggling.[30]

Since March 1932, when the Bureau of Narcotics listed Lepke as "#3 in the Confidential List of suspected major violators," Anslinger tried unsuccessfully to build a case against the gangster. But five years later, when the commissioner learned of a large smuggling syndicate operating in New York, he initiated an extensive investigation. In November 1937 the bureau decided to secure indictments in the case. On the basis of primarily circumstantial and documentary evidence, a preliminary secret indictment was obtained, which named thirty persons, including Lepke, for violating narcotics laws. The bureau had the indictment, but it did not have Lepke.

Twenty-one of those indicted were arrested almost simultaneously, and their testimony made conviction a certainty. Lepke, however, went into hiding and could not be found. The Bureau of Narcotics and other law enforcement agencies began advertising for him. District Attorney Thomas E. Dewey, who also began to move against Lepke, devoted total concentration and energy to the manhunt. The FBI, which called Lepke "The most dangerous criminal in America," offered a $5,000 reward, which District Attorney Dewey increased to $30,000, dead or alive.[31] When the reward still produced no Lepke, Anslinger, Hoover, Dewey, and New York Police Commissioner Lewis J. Valentine agreed to coordinate their efforts and share information.

Had it not been for the influence of Meyer Lansky, who saw an opportunity to eliminate the competition and pressured Lepke to surrender, the fugitive might have remained at-large indefinitely. Since Lepke was no ordinary criminal, a dramatic plan was devised to bring the gangster in. Convinced that cooperation with the authorities would earn him a lighter sentence, Lepke agreed to surrender to Hoover, thinking that the FBI's charges against him for crossing state lines would be dropped. Lepke never left New York City.[32] The intermediary chosen to meet with the fugitive was Walter Winchell, the flamboyant radio and newspaper commentator.

Under instructions from Hoover, Winchell announced on the air and in the *New York Mirror* that Lepke would be guaranteed safe delivery to FBI agents. After three and a half weeks of rendezvousing with representatives of "Murder, Inc.," Lepke finally met Winchell alone late Sunday night on 25 August 1939 near Madison Square Park. Several minutes later Hoover joined them, and the most publicized manhunt since that of Bruno Hauptmann in the Lindbergh kidnapping came to an end.[33]

After a fifteen-day trial in which Lepke was charged with ten offenses, he was convicted on 20 December 1939 on a charge of conspiracy to violate laws relating to narcotics drugs. On 2 January 1940, he entered guilty pleas to nine other charges relating to unlawfully importing heroin, failing to pay duties on specified storage trunks upon entry to the United States, and bribing a federal government employee. The sentences imposed upon Lepke totaled fourteen years' imprisonment. He was also fined $2,500 and placed on ten years' probation.[34]

While Lepke was serving the first year of his sentence in 1940, the Narcotics Bureau was also collecting evidence against Mendy Weiss, Lepke's principal associate in "Murder, Inc." In March narcotics agents discovered that Weiss and four other syndicate members were operating a chemical plant for the purpose of manufacturing morphine. Weiss's partners were apprehended easily, but a nation-wide search was required to bring in Weiss himself, who was captured by narcotics agents in Kansas City, Missouri, in December. While Weiss awaited trial in New York, the government deferred pressing charges until a stronger case could be built against him on a murder charge.

In November 1941 Weiss and Lepke were prosecuted for the 1936 slaying of a Brooklyn candy store owner, and Lepke alone was charged with ordering the death of a truck driver who was prepared to testify on racketeering in the garment and fur industries. With thirty-three witnesses and fifty-four exhibits, the prosecution produced evidence that, as the head of "Murder, Inc.," Lepke had ordered the deaths of sixty to eighty people and simultaneously manipulated over two hundred illegitimate businesses.[35]

When the jury in King's County Court found Lepke guilty of murder in the first degree and Judge Franklin Taylor sentenced him to death, the mobster stood pale and trembling, gasping for breath. Lepke's lawyers immediately appealed the case, but the New York State Supreme Court unanimously upheld the lower court's decision, and on 4 March 1944 Lepke was executed at Sing Sing Prison on Ossining, New York.[36]

Despite Anslinger and the Bureau of Narcotics initiating the investigation and producing the evidence that enabled the government to secure a conviction, the FBI benefited most from the publicity in the Lepke case. Dewey later was elected governor of New York, and in 1944 he launched a presidential campaign based predominantly on his reputation as a crime-fighter. Anslinger, the person who was denied credit for his role in the case and the only one who insisted that there was a Mafia that functioned as a subsidiary of organized crime, had to be satisfied with knowing another notorious criminal was rendered inactive. Anslinger was far ahead of Hoover in realizing that certain criminal activities were highly organized and especially in recognizing that "what others call the 'organization' . . . is not only the Mafia itself but other related groups."[37]

Lepke Buchalter might have been "stolen" from the Bureau of Narcotics, but that was not the case with Charles "Lucky" Luciano, one of the most notorious American criminals in the twentieth century. Anslinger had been after Luciano from the time Lucky became "the Boss" in 1931 until his death in a Naples airport in 1962. The commissioner even wrote a fictionalized biography of Luciano but carefully deleted obvious references to the Mafiosi by name, referring to him only as "the Boss."[38]

Like Lepke's, Luciano's involvement in criminal activities began as a youth in New York City.[39] An associate of Arnold Rothstein and an alumnus of the infamous "Five Points Gang" that spawned Al Capone,

Luciano had enjoyed virtual immunity from the law after he arranged the murders of Joe Masseria and Salvatore Maranzano in 1931 and set himself up as the new "Boss."[40] Through his connections at Tammany Hall, City Hall, the state government at Albany, and even Washington, Luciano was able to control New York's Italian underworld so tightly that no racket operated without his approval. Anslinger was convinced that one of Luciano's rackets was distributing narcotics, though he lacked sufficient evidence for prosecution. Since he was involved in so many high risk rackets, it was especially surprising to Anslinger and other enforcement officials that Special Prosecutor Dewey charged Luciano in 1936 with ninety counts of "compulsory prostitution." The Narcotics Bureau had by this time gathered enough evidence for Dewey to prosecute for narcotics distribution and extortion, but the commissioner and the prosecutor agreed to press only for the numerous white slavery counts. By the time Luciano was brought to trial, evidence showed that he employed over 1,200 women in parlors throughout the United States, producing an annual revenue of $10 million.[41] The original ninety counts had been reduced to sixty-two, but that made little difference in the outcome of his trial. Though some of the witnesses were of questionable character and Lucky protested that he had been framed, the verdict was obvious. On 17 June 1936, the jury convicted Luciano on all counts. The Judge gave him an extraordinary sentence of thirty to fifty years at Dannemora Prison in upstate New York.

At Dannemora, Luciano was the model prisoner. He freely lent money (which is as important inside prison as outside) to inmates, and on one occasion even donated funds to a local church that desperately needed repairs. Luciano was popular with the prison inmates, but he was unable to convince state officials of his rehabilitation. When his appeal was heard by the New York State Court of Appeals in 1938, he was turned down; the United States Supreme Court refused to even review the case. Five years later, in 1945, Luciano again petitioned the state Supreme Court, this time for a reduction in the sentence, arguing that his cooperation with American naval intelligence during the war merited reconsideration of his case. He also appealed to the parole board, which accepted his request for executive clemency and unanimously recommended to the governor that he be released and exiled forever from the United States. The exact nature of Luciano's wartime services, which were the basis for his appeal, has never been determined conclusively. Accounts of Luciano's contributions to the war effort in "Operation Underworld" vary widely. Most likely he did order Joe Adonis, who controlled the waterfront area of New York, to cooperate with the Navy in preventing sabotage and espionage. He also allegedly provided Naval Intelligence personnel with information that facilitated the landing of American troops on Sicily and Italy. But when

Lieutenant Commander Charles R. Haffenden, who was instrumental in organizing "Operation Underworld," was asked about Luciano's role, he commented only that Lucky had been of "value."[42]

On another occasion, Haffenden stated that he was unable to gauge the value of information supplied to the armed forces by Luciano. The retired Naval officer did admit that Luciano had been transferred from the remote Dannemora in northeastern New York to the Great Meadow Prison north of Albany, where he could more easily pass information to Joseph "Socks" Lanza who in turn relayed it to Naval Intelligence. Haffenden made it clear, however, that what came from Luciano was nothing extraordinary and that he could not cite any particular advantage gained from the mobster's information or recommendations.[43] When it was suggested that Luciano provided the names of Sicilians in New York who were familiar with the coastal areas of their native land, Haffenden contended that Luciano was like all other informers and that he did no more than any good American citizen. The head of the wartime secret service, William J. Donovan, however, denied emphatically that Luciano deserved any special recognition or generosity for his aid during the war.[44]

Shortly before his death in 1962, Luciano himself disavowed his role in helping the Navy. "I was getting tired of sitting up there in prison," Luciano claimed, "and I had my lawyers dig up everything they could on a very prominent official. When they finished they gave me a book." By his own account Luciano threatened to have the "book" published if he was not released. "That got me out," he boasted.[45]

In 1951 FBN Agent Joseph Amato filed a confidential memorandum from Italy in which he reported that, during the questioning of a reliable source, he learned that the sum of $150,000 had been paid as the initial installment to the "right people" for Luciano's parole. The total cost to the mob for the "Boss's" release was said to be $500,000. It also was believed that Luciano worked assiduously from Italy to elect Dewey to the presidency in 1948, thinking that he would issue a presidential pardon and allow Lucky to re-enter the United States.[46] According to Agent Amato's source, the Mafia thought it had a "sure thing" and was at a loss to figure out what went wrong when Harry Truman won the election.

No specific details were provided in the Amato report, but in 1952 Michael Stern published a story in *True Magazine* which corroborated the narcotics agent's memorandum.[47] On the basis of an interview with Luciano, who swore the journalist to secrecy, Stern related Luciano's story that the Mafia did pay $500,000 to Moses Polakoff, Lucky's lawyer, to secure his release. This information was supplied to Anslinger by Agent Charles Siragusa in Rome, who was asked by Stern to furnish personal anecdotal information on Luciano for his article. Polakoff, in turn, passed the money to Charles Breitel, the former law partner of Governor Dewey.

Luciano would not confirm who received shares of the payoff, but he did imply that Breitel was paid the "lion's share," that ex-Navy Commander Haffenden received a sizable portion, and that "maybe Governor Dewey himself also received a cut."[48] Siragusa also noted that Breitel was under consideration for appointment by Dewey to the New York Supreme Court at the time.

The Stern account is an engaging explanation of why Luciano was released, and it provided tremendous publicity for the writer. But because Stern offers no supporting evidence except his private interview with Luciano, his story must be viewed with suspicion for several reasons. First, Luciano was not the kind of person to violate *omerta* (believed to be the Mafia's code of silence) by revealing incriminating evidence to an unknown reporter. Second, Stern may have been sworn to secrecy, but Luciano was not so naive as not to know that once Stern left Italy the story would become instant headline material. Moreover, Luciano desperately wanted to return to the United States; and, though it was not likely that would happen, it would have been incredibly foolish of him to reveal the details of a pay-off involving the governor of New York. A third possibility was that Luciano simply wanted to embarrass Dewey for prosecuting him on what Lucky felt were unsubstantiated charges. Finally, Governor Dewey did not initiate the commutation (it was not a pardon, as erroneously reported in many press releases) of Luciano's sentence. He merely followed up on the parole board's recommendation that Lucky be released and deported to Italy, never to re-enter the United States.

Just how much value Luciano was to the Navy has been shrouded in mystery and controversy. It also has caused considerable embarrassment to Governor Dewey, who acted favorably on the parole board's recommendation and commuted Luciano's sentence. Rumors that a deal was made between Dewey and Luciano haunted the governor and two-time presidential candidate for years. In 1954 when Dewey was trying to decide among running for a fourth term as governor, accepting a cabinet post in the Eisenhower administration, or retiring from politics, stories began to circulate that he pressured a publishing company to delay the release of a book about racketeers, in particular Lucky Luciano. Whether it was the Luciano issue or other factors, Dewey apparently decided that his political appeal was waning and withdrew from politics.[49]

Lucky Luciano was a personality whom the media loved to write about, and the Bureau of Narcotics enjoyed touting him as the major organizer of the international distribution of narcotics. The bureau knew that not even prison walls prevented Luciano from giving orders to his underworld cronies. Anslinger also suspected that he continued the importation of narcotics into the United States while living in exile on the exotic Isle of Capri.

Because of Luciano's extensive network and far-reaching power, Anslinger became extremely apprehensive when he learned in February 1947 that Luciano had been living in Cuba for four months.[50] When he was asked why he moved to the small island country less than a hundred miles from the United States, he replied that he wanted to be closer to his relatives and that he found the climate more suitable. It was more convenient for his sister to visit him, but he also received many friends like Joe Adonis, Frank Costello, the Fischetti brothers, and Willie Moretti, all allegedly involved in criminal activities as members of the Mafia.

Anslinger was furious that Luciano had been able to secure an Italian visa and Cuban passport while he had been so closely watched. He also suspected that Luciano's real motive for taking a Havana address was to facilitate his narcotics distribution and eventually control the island's gambling business. What he most feared, though, was that Luciano's move to Cuba was an organized effort to pave the way for his re-entry into the United States, which the Commissioner considered a "terrible thing."[51]

To exert pressure on an uncooperative Cuban police force that refused to arrest Luciano, Anslinger announced that the United States would halt the shipment of legitimate drugs to Cuba for as long as the "czar of organized crime" remained there. The next day Luciano was taken into custody by the Cuban secret service and was held for forty-eight hours; he was then sent back to Italy. By exerting power that normally fell within the State Department, Anslinger demonstrated that his influence extended beyond the American borders.

Because he was so well known as a Mafia boss, Luciano often was implicated in crimes on the basis of flimsy, circumstantial evidence. Usually the evidence emanated from the Federal Bureau of Narcotics, which claimed he was running a worldwide narcotics ring while in exile. The Italian police, continually watching Luciano, protested that if that were true, "Lucky must be a magician."[52] No doubt Lucky was a clever operator, but it was the tendency of the FBN to exaggerate his versatility and diverse activities. During a congressional hearing on the control of narcotics in 1951, Congressman James G. Donovan of New York even testified that when Luciano was first convicted, he was not only a drug peddler but an informer for the Bureau of Narcotics.[53]

Throughout his life Luciano maintained that he had been repeatedly accused of crimes he did not commit and that the Narcotics Bureau was constantly and unjustifiably badgering him. Not surprisingly Lucky tremendously resented the relentless persecution heaped upon him by the Narcotics Bureau and its agents. Since his imprisonment at Dannemora, when he refused to cooperate in an interview with Agent George White, an almost natural enmity evolved between FBN agents and the crime boss which lasted until Luciano's death. In particular, Lucky detested the

Commissioner of Narcotics, whom he often referred to as "Esslinger," a deliberate disparagement. Luciano also was critical of Anslinger's grand-standing investigative methods. "Hitler was an angel in comparison to what 'Esslinger' is," Luciano observed. But Lucky apparently felt no such antagonism for J. Edgar Hoover who "makes no announcement about what he is going to do, . . . he don't shoot his mouth off. He's got efficiency."[54]

The one-time Mafia "Boss" spent his last years haunted by the image of the Narcotics Commissioner, and not without cause: Anslinger prevented him from living in Cuba and forced his deportation back to Italy. Anslinger also persuaded the Italian authorities to revoke Luciano's passport and influenced the *carabinieri* to ban him from Rome. From Luciano's perspective Anslinger seemed to be everywhere. "When the Russians land on the moon," the mobster bemoaned, "the first man they meet will be Anslinger, searching for narcotics."[55]

Discovery

Officials of the Bureau of Narcotics had consistently believed in the existence of the Mafia since at least the early 1940s. They were also aware of other criminal organizations that were not Sicilian in origin. Encounters with Lepke Buchalter and Lucky Luciano, who was described by Agent Siragusa as "one of the royal family of syndicated gangs," were sufficient evidence that organized crime was a reality. But the Mafia was not given official recognition as a nationwide crime enterprise by the federal government until the opening of the special Senate committee hearings in 1951. Chaired by Senator Estes Kefauver of Tennessee, the seventeen-month-long investigation of organized crime televised the testimony of eight hundred witnesses from fourteen cities around the country.[56]

For the American public that was able to view hours of testimony in the comfort of their living rooms, the Kefauver hearings had a profound impact. With the benefit of a Presidential Executive Order, the committee gained access to income tax returns and was able to pose penetrating questions from which it arrived at four general conclusions: (1) there was a nationwide crime syndicate known as the Mafia, (2) Mafia leaders usually controlled the most lucrative rackets, (3) leadership appeared to be a centralized group rather than a single individual, and (4) the Mafia was the bridge that linked the Costello-Adonis-Lansky syndicate of New York with the Accardo-Guzik-Fischetti syndicate of Chicago and other criminal groups around the country who kept in touch with Luciano in Italy.[57]

Unfortunately, the hearings turned out to be more an exercise in style than substance. They provided hours of entertainment and transformed Kefauver from an obscure politician to a household word, but they accomplished very little. Since many of the witnesses invoked the Fifth Amendment, almost no new information surfaced. Even those who did testify either denied that they had even heard of a Mafia, or they denied membership in the Mafia. By not inviting outside specialists, such as sociologists, criminologists, and journalists who might have had knowledge about such an organization, the committee deprived itself of potentially valuable insight and expertise. Rather than elicit the opinions of independent experts or other governmental agencies, it relied entirely on the reports of the Bureau of Narcotics as presented by Anslinger, and by Agents Charles Siragisa and George White, the committee's investigators, who testified that organized crime pervaded American society at all levels. Because groups like "Murder Inc." smuggled into this country and distributed enough narcotics to supply one-fifth of the entire addict population," the commissioner also recommended that the committee include in its recommendation that the 1951 Boggs bill, containing stringent penalties, be enacted by the Eighty-second Congress.[58]

When questioned about how he thought organized crime was structured, Anslinger asserted that he did not think "the activities in one part of the country occur as a result of instructions given in other parts of the country."[59] He felt that crime was "pretty well co-ordinated through a decentralized form of organization, not under the control of a single individual but by a national panel of 'leading mobsters' throughout the country" who constantly conferred with one another. His encounters with Lepke Buchalter, Lucky Luciano, and others who were deeply involved in the distribution of narcotics influenced Anslinger to modify his earlier assessment of mob crime—that there was no nation-wide syndicate controlling criminal operations. Augmenting his theory on the structure of organized crime, Anslinger submitted a bureau list of eight hundred suspected criminals directed by a syndicate with centers in New York, Florida, and California.

Despite the extensive testimony and its national television exposure of many alleged underworld figures, the Kefauver Committee could not prove the existence of a Mafia. The investigation was even negligible as a deterrent to syndicate crime. In most cities where the hearings were held, syndicate activities temporarily halted but resumed in full swing when the publicity faded, usually with the same people in control. Probably the greatest service performed by the Kefauver Committee was actually a by-product of the investigation.[60] The Boggs Act may have been enacted eventually, but when Senator Kefauver introduced it in Congress with the endorsement of Commissioner Anslinger as a weapon against organized crime, it attracted more support. With a punitive precedent established, it was easier to establish even lengthier prison sentences as part of the Narcotic Control Act, which resulted in significant action against organized crime drug activity.

Harry Anslinger did not need the Kefauver Committee's official recognition of the Mafia or any other form of organized crime to know that it existed. He was aware not only that the Mafia was running various rackets but that it had also penetrated legitimate businesses, including the entertainment industry. As a result of an investigation by Agent Howard W. Chappell, working out of the bureau's office in Los Angeles, the Bureau of Narcotics became embroiled in an investigation that involved agents from California to Rome. Chappell had received information that reputed Mafia boss Thomas Lucchese (alias "Three Fingers Brown") of New York had attempted to take over an interest in the internationally known singer and actor Mario Lanza.[61]

To confirm his information, Agent Chappell made arrangements to meet with Al Teitelbaum, a close friend and manager of the singer who also owned 10-percent interest in Lanza Enterprises. After Chappell related what he knew about the alleged takeover, Teitelbaum exposed Lucchese, Irving Berman, and an unidentified Jewish racketeer from New York as the people who tried to muscle in on the earnings of Lanza. Along with the performer's business, they also attempted to obtain interests in various movie productions in Hollywood.

A few days after talking with Teitelbaum, Agent Chappell interviewed Lanza, who impressed the investigator as being very cooperative. Lanza recalled that in the spring of 1955 he was in a serious financial bind, a fact generally known throughout the entertainment business. In May, Rocky Marciano, the former heavyweight prizefighter, introduced Lanza to Berman, who was also involved in professional boxing. The three men engaged briefly in a casual conversation, and Berman left.

About a week later Berman returned with Lucchese and a third person Lanza identified as a "tough-looking Jew from New York" who wanted to discuss the singer's finances. They advised Lanza that if he would be willing to work for Lucchese, his financial problems would be resolved. To convince Lanza that he was true to his word, Lucchese pointed out that a few years earlier Frank Sinatra had been in a similar financial bind and commented, "Look what we have done for him." When Lanza advised his three visitors that he was not interested in listening to their proposition, the unidentified man became irritated and in a threatening tone told the singer that they could do a great deal for him with their movie company, the Eagle Lion Corporation. They also suggested that "under the table" contracts could be made for the purpose of tax evasion. Lanza stated that he still refused to consider the offer.

At the conclusion of the interview with Lanza, Agent Chappell reported that Marciano then told how he had been required to turn over 50 percent of all his earnings to the syndicate in order to divorce himself from contact with the racketeers. The boxer did not indicate, however, whether he was being "bought" by the same group that was interested in Lanza. Nonetheless it was obvious that the mob was attracted to Hollywood personalities.[62]

Not only the American Mafia had a penchant for Mario Lanza and the movies. When Lanza was in Italy in 1957 to film *The Seven Hills of Rome,* he was greeted warmly by the popular post-war mayor of Naples, Achille Lauro, who was financially supported by Luigi Campolongo, the "unofficial mayor" of Naples as reported by Agent Charles Siragusa. While Lanza was filming the movie, the seventy-year-old Campolongo, known throughout southern Italy as "Mr. Mafia," informed him that he had taken it upon himself to arrange an open air concert in a local square that would benefit the mayor in the forthcoming municipal election. Lanza told Siragusa that he had to refuse Campolongo because his contract precluded an interruption of the shooting schedule and that his producer would not permit him to leave the set. According to Lanza, Campolongo met with the producer and cautioned him that he might be risking a tremendous loss at the box office of his fifteen Neapolitan-owned theaters. The following Sunday Lanza entertained over 100,000 people in a public square.

Lanza maintained that he had no connection with any gangsters and that he refused offers from night club owners Frank Costello, Willie Fischetti, and Tony Accardo to sing for high weekly under-the-table payments.[63] Though he was never seen associating with any undesirables and Siragusa believed that Lanza might have been sincere in his statements, the agent remained suspicious. The bureau, however, was never able to establish any criminal connection between the celebrity and the Mafia.

Through the 1950s, the Narcotics Bureau continued to investigate the Lanza affair and dozens of other cases involving organized crime in the United States and Europe. But with the conclusion of the Kefauver hearings in 1951, questions pertaining to the existence of a Mafia generated little controversy. The Mafia remained a nonissue until the occurrence of two unrelated events in 1957.

The first development was the formation of the Senate Select Committee on Improper Activities in the Labor and Management Field. Known more popularly by the name of its chairman, Senator John L. McClellan of Arkansas, the committee was organized in February 1957 as an outgrowth of studies conducted by the Senate Committee on Government Operations concerning certain procurement activities of the federal government. In addition to Chairman McClellan, the committee was composed of several prominent and ambitious men: John F. Kennedy of Massachusetts (whose brother Robert F. Kennedy was chief counsel for the Committee), Joseph R. McCarthy of Wisconsin, and Barry Goldwater of Arizona. The McClellan Commitee was a permanent committee formed as a follow-up to the Kefauver investigation, which uncovered evidence of mob involvement in labor unions.

Since the Kefauver Committee revealed organized gambling and corruption, the McClellan Committee expected to find racketeering but did not expect to find a "gathering of racketeers."[64] Nor did it expect to find the Mafia as a major force in organized crime; that evidence was introduced and advanced by Commissioner Anslinger and Agents Joseph Amato, John Cusack, and Martin Pera, who testified at length about their experiences with the mob and who also made observations on the origin, structure, and activities of the secret organization.

While the McClellan Committee was sifting through papers documenting embezzled union funds, extortion against management, and mob infiltration of the garbage collection industry, three seemingly unrelated incidents passed almost without notice. In May 1957 Frank Costello, Mafia boss and associate of Lucky Luciano, was the target of an unsuccessful assassination attempt. The following July, Frank Scalise, an underboss of a New York Mafia family, was murdered in the Bronx. Just three months later in October, Albert Anastasia, who was Lepke Buchalter's successor in "Murder Inc.," was killed in the barbershop of the Waldorf Astoria in midtown Manhattan. Unknown at the time, these slayings were not random murders but planned hits that were the result of one faction attempting to wrest power from another within the Mafia. This internecine mob warfare, which has occurred several times since, was not unlike that of a political coup in a Latin American country.

The New York murders were generally regarded as unrelated killings of no particular significance until the second major event of 1957 unfolded. On 14 November, Sergeant Edgar D. Crosswell at the Bureau of Criminal Investigations of the New York State Police discovered a convocation of the nation's criminal cartel leaders at Joseph Barbara's home in the bucolic hamlet of Apalachin (pronounced Ap-a-LA-kin), twelve miles from Binghamton, New York.[65] Since 1944 Crosswell had suspected that Barbara was affiliated with the underworld, but he had no proof. During the next thirteen years, Crosswell watched closely for any legal infraction that would provide him with confirmation that Barbara was, in fact, a member of the Mafia. But even tapping Barbara's telephone and auditing his bank account produced no incriminating evidence.

Crosswell's persistence paid off, though, when on the night of 13 November he discovered that the ailing Barbara had reserved three rooms for out-of-the-state guests at the local hotel. Upon further investigation he also learned that several automobiles were parked at Barbara's $150,000 eighteen-room English-style manor estate. The sergeant had seen a number of cars at Barbara's home before, but this time he called for assistance and, with additional police, set up a road block. When

Crosswell drove up to Barbara's residence, men dressed in silk suits ran from the backyard barbeque pits for their cars or into the woods. Most, however, were apprehended when they came out onto the road leading to the estate. Wearing pointed shoes and white-on-white shirts, they were hardly attired for a cross-country get-away or equipped to endure a pouring rain. One by one they were rounded up, bedraggled, soaking wet, and tired. Others chose to hide out for days in the Barbara cellar until they could slip away unnoticed.

Though no one has ever confirmed exactly how many men were gathered at Apalachin, Crosswell testified that sixty-two suspects, including "two characters of Barbara's," were arrested.[66] Regardless of the exact number of participants—the number ranges from fifty-eight to seventy-five—the exposure of the Apalachin meeting had a devastating effect on the American public. The media immediately, and without proof, called Apalachin a "convention of crime" and clamored for an investigation of the men in attendance and their reasons for meeting at the Barbara home.

The Federal Bureau of Narcotics, as represented by Agent Siragusa, believed that Apalachin was a meeting of the Mafia "Grand Council," which consisted of delegates from all principal cities in the United States. According to Agent Pera, who also testified, bureau studies conducted over a period of many years indicated that members of the Mafia are structured along family lines and that they "grow into" the organization rather than being recruited from outside the group. It was a loose organization, Pera observed, with no autonomy, but was composed of a group of individuals who discussed with each other what was mutually beneficial. The agent spoke with authority on the nature of the Grand Council, but when Senator Karl Mundt of South Dakota pinned him down on how many men the council included, Pera could not say.[67]

The Narcotics Bureau also believed that one purpose of the Apalachin gathering was to discuss the problem arising from a generation gap in the Mafia.[68] The elder statesmen gave orders for the organization to get out of narcotics. According to Charles Siragusa—the first government official to reveal that a contact had been made between undercover agents and persons connected to the underworld—the struggle for power would continue to spawn a series of reprisals for disobedience within the gangland organization. Speaking at a symposium on narcotics at Manhattan College in 1960, the agent also stated that some of the older members were morally opposed to drug dealing.

But the "Young Turks" refused to go along with the older leadership, which resulted in episodes of violence like the two murders and one attempted assassination that preceded the Apalachin meeting.[69] Commissioner Anslinger also believed that the possible purpose of Apalachin was to finance the acquisition of political control of the state of Nevada. The

FBN reasoned that if the Mafia controlled key political figures, it would also provide police protection for the control of gambling, drinking, and prostitution in that desert state, which would compensate for the huge loss of revenue from narcotics.[70]

Anslinger's Narcotics Bureau conducted all of the original investigative work (the FBI still held on to the position that large criminal syndicates did not exist or if they did they were state and local law-enforcement problems) and coordinated the nationwide arrests of Apalachin defendants. The FBN was also aware that Apalachin was the most recent in a series of meetings held by different groups of the criminal syndicate. The first had been held in Atlantic City, New Jersey, in late 1956 and consisted primarily of delegates from Philadelphia. The second meeting took place in Miami in early 1957 and was attended by members of the Chicago and Pittsburgh syndicates. A third, held during the summer in Los Angeles, was called by southern California and Chicago representatives.[71]

Apalachin, the McClellan hearings, and the revelations they produced created an ideal situation for Anslinger, the most vocal proponent of the existence of the Mafia. The discovery of a Mafia "summit" in upstate New York and testimony heard in the Congressional investigations supported Anslinger's hypotheses. With these developments, the commissioner unabashedly presented the FBN as the "only law enforcement agency which has revealed the existence of the Mafia." Narcotics was, of course, the primary responsibility of the bureau, but by the late 1950s, when he realized that he stood alone in chasing underworld criminals, Anslinger began to see the Mafia as an opportunity to one-up his competition. He correctly reasoned that the notoriety of the mobster was directly proportional to an increase in two areas that always concerned him—publicity and appropriations. However, Anslinger did not exploit the Mafia issue in the same way he used the marijuana myth in the 1930s. With marijuana Anslinger needed only to fuel the media with horror stories and testify before uniformed congressional committees about the drug's terrible effects. He could not create a Mafia myth so easily without actually proving that such an organization existed.

From breaking up the Affronti drug syndicate in Kansas City in 1931 to the conviction of Vito Genovese in 1960, Anslinger demonstrated repeatedly that the Bureau of Narcotics was not reluctant to penetrate the invisible empire of the Mafia. Nor did Anslinger concentrate solely on mob activities within the United States. When Agent Siragusa traced the distribution routes of illegal heroin coming into the United States, Anslinger knew that stopping the traffic would necessitate infiltrating internationally organized drug rings. In 1953 Siragusa identified Beirut, Lebanon, and Turkey as the points of origin for most of the opium shipped into Europe by Sicilian Mafia.[72] From the points in Italy it was transported to

French-Corsican associates in Marseilles who converted the poppy extract into heroin and morphine. From that French port city the drugs were smuggled to Montreal, Canada, and distributed from there to New York and other major cities in the eastern United States.

By 1960 the Bureau had arrested Angelo Tuminaro of New York and French trafficker Etienne Tarditi who were involved in the actual distribution. But the arrest of Harry Stromberg (alias Nig Rosen) of Philadephia and New York effectively disrupted what has since been popularized as the "French Connection." Stromberg was not only the brains of the Marseilles to Montreal connection; he paid for the heroin through financial machinations involving anonymously numbered Swiss bank accounts. Once Stromberg's heroin reached the United States, such Mafiosi as Vito Genovese and Frank Scalise bought it and distributed it as far south as Miami. With the arrest of Stromberg, the financier of an international drug ring and former close associate of Lepke Buchalter in 1958, the bureau had disrupted at least temporarily a major supply of heroin. On 23 April 1958 Stromberg was sentenced to five years in prison and fined $10,000, a ridiculous sum for a man who was running a $20 million-year business.[73]

On one occasion Anslinger was himself a defendant in a lawsuit filed by a reputed Mafia boss. In an article published by Jack Anderson in the 21 January 1962 issue of *Parade* magazine, the commissioner claimed that Santo Sorge was the "No. 5 backstage boss who ruled the underworld."[74] During the McClellan hearings in 1958, Agent Pera testified that Sorge was a close associate of Lucky Luciano, but few observers of Mafia activities regarded the alleged boss as a high-ranking Mafia chieftain.

In filing the libel suit against Anslinger in 1965, Altoona attorney James M. Dente charged that the commissioner by then retired, had intended to "injure the plaintiff in his good name, fame, credit, and reputation." Also included in the complaint entered by Dente in the Common Pleas Court of Blair County, Pennsylvania, were Anslinger's accusations that Sorge was a "participant in . . . acts of organized crime, illegal gambling, drug peddling, white slavery, . . . lawless Mafia activities, murder missions and bribery and corruption." As part of a total $1.6 million suit, Sorge sought $750,000 as compensation for the ridicule and contempt he suffered among his acquaintances and $50,000 for loss of his job as an international coordinator for an Italian corporation.[75]

On 18 February the United States District Court granted a removal petition from the federal government to have the trial moved to Pittsburgh. But before the case reached the next stage, the Italian government reported that it had issued a warrant for Sorge's arrest as a participant in Mafia-related crimes in that country. Realizing his client's case was seriously weakened by this disclosure, Attorney Dente requested that the libel suit be dismissed.

The Sorge incident neither seriously embarrassed Anslinger personally nor damaged his career. He had been retired three years by then and was secure in knowing the case would never come to much. If anything, the publicity enhanced his reputation as a tough, outspoken, no-nonsense cop who has not intimidated by the mob. Always image-conscious, Harry Anslinger enthusiastically welcomed the recognition he and his agents received for the courage they exhibited in their indiscriminate enforcement of the narcotics laws. But the FBN, the government's primary force in the fight against drug trafficking, was also involved in activities which would have proved extremely embarrassing to Anslinger and damaging to the reputation of the Narcotics Bureau had they been known at the time.

7

Tentacles, 1943–1965

With the end of World War II, the United States and the world entered a new era. The atomic bomb forced an immediate surrender of the Japanese, and the nation celebrated victory with visions of a brighter, safer future. Unfortunately, however, the agreements drafted during the war to achieve stability and security after the surrender quickly became strained, creating tensions in Europe and the United States. Naturally political leaders and top-level military advisers in Washington were deeply concerned with the constantly deteriorating status of international diplomatic relations. The Commissioner of Narcotics—who since before the war had been fearful of the United States being invaded by an enemy country whose primary offensive armament was not atomic weaponry but narcotics—was no less troubled.

Though Anslinger insisted that the United States was the target of a communist narcotics offensive, how he determined that to be accurate or why he perpetuated it throughout the remainder of his career is unclear. Anslinger's advocacy of the "Communist menace" was particularly controversial during the Cold War period, but other debates about bureau activities occurred that appear to be disconnected and for which there are no definite answers. Nevertheless, it is important to introduce them and examine their significance as they related to federal narcotics agents.

In the midst of postwar tensions and a growing anxiety over volatile international conditions, most Americans were concerned about their nation's role as an undisputed world power. In that respect, Harry Anslinger shared their apprehension, but his perception of the world situation and what he viewed as the country's most formidable challenge differed considerably from those of most contemporary observers. More than marijuana, the spread of heroin horrified Anslinger when he considered its deadly effects and potential for the mass ruination of innocent people. Anslinger could not be faulted for anticipating an increase in the illicit traffic of narcotics after the war. He assumed that a surge in addiction rates would occur when American G.I.'s returned home from Europe and the Pacific, similar to that in the post–World War I era. The channels of distribution that had been obstructed or shut off entirely in the 1940s had been reopened and were more profitable than ever. But Anslinger's fear of invasion and his identification of dangerous aggressor nations followed a curious pattern that suggests the Bureau of Narcotics was involved in more than the enforcement of narcotics laws during the war years.

Prior to World War II Anslinger contended that Japan, which had repeatedly committed belligerent acts throughout the 1930s, had adopted a three-fold plan for acquiring desired possessions. The commissioner warned that beyond gaining additional revenue and corrupting Western nations, the Japanese were intending to "demoralize and enslave the peoples of lands already invaded or marked for eventual invasion."[1] By the late 1940s, the McCarthy scare reinforced Anslinger's theories, convincing him that the increase in narcotics traffic and addiction was not limited to the Japanese but was part of a sinister communist plot. Anslinger's intense fear and hatred of a perceived communist takeover approached a level of paranoia shared by his counterpart, J. Edgar Hoover. The commissioner was convinced it was only a matter of time until the United States succumbed to an Oriental "Fifth Column" of heroin addiction.[2]

When, as a delegate to the United Nations Commission on Narcotic Drugs in 1952, Anslinger charged that the communists in the Far East had organized a narcotics traffic ring, he drew a heated response from the Russians. Soviet delegate V. V. Zakosov, resentful of the affront, in turn accused the United States of subjecting the Japanese and Koreans to the addiction to heroin and other atrocities such as brandings, use of poison gas, and bacteriological warfare.[3] The narcotics epidemic in Communist China is beyond dispute. Who was responsible for the mass addiction, however, is subject to different interpretations.

In 1953 Anslinger continued to blast Communist China when he testified before a Senate subcommittee on Juvenile Delinquency that the heroin coming from that country was responsible for the increase in addiction rates in areas west of the Rocky Mountains. When asked by Senator Estes Kefauver of Tennessee for an appraisal of the situation, Anslinger stated that the West Coast was being besieged with heroin that was 90 percent pure as compared to the heroin from Europe that was only 5 percent pure.[4] In claiming that "California heroin" was more potent than what Easterners were using, the commissioner apparently wanted to impress his audience with the potential threat of an Asian-inspired invasion. Anslinger also dazed the senators when he used the phrase "Communist narcotics infiltration" but strengthened his position with key congressional leaders who treated him as a recognized authority on Asian foreign policy. Only a few months earlier he reported to the United Nations Commission on Narcotic Drugs that "Red China's nefarious purposes are financing heavy outlays of the Korean War" and that the "Communist dope kings have been given special instructions to concentrate on soldiers of the United Nations' army."[5] Few politicians, who did not want to risk being labeled as communist sympathizers, challenged Anslinger's claims. In 1953 and 1954, at the height of McCarthyism, eight senators and congressmen either specifically mentioned Anslinger by name or alluded to articles he had written in their remarks on the floor of Congress.[6]

Anslinger antagonized the communist members of the United Nations a second time in 1954 when he testified before a Senate Foreign Relations Committee that Communist China was the major source of illicit traffic for the entire world. This time Soviet and Polish members of the commission complained that the United States was slandering their governments and that illegal trafficking was only suspected, not proven.[7]

In responding to a question from Senator Mike Mansfield of Montana on the production of opium, Anslinger mentioned Laos as "one of the big opium-producing countries of the world." In fact, he classified Indochina (Laos, Vietnam, and Cambodia) as a potential trouble-spot for the Narcotics Bureau and stated that agents had been sent there to seize the drug from opium monopolies.[8]

During the Senate subcommittee hearings in 1955, Anslinger identified South Korea, Thailand, Burma, and Vietnam as targets of the Chinese Communists, based on reports from various governments to the United Nations, seizures, and agents' reports. Remaining anonymous, one agent testified that he was instructed by Anslinger to work undercover on special assignment in Japan under General Douglas MacArthur. The agent related that beginning in 1949 he discovered a communist trading store in North Korea that functioned as a front for the distribution of heroin. He also reported that a flood of narcotics into southeast Asia preceded a drive by communist agents whose assignment was to foment discord and create divisiveness among the people.[9]

In the dual role as a delegate to the United Nations Commission on Narcotic Drugs and in his capacity as Commissioner of the Narcotics Bureau, Anslinger was in a position to gain unique perspectives on the Cold War situation. His involvement with the international narcotics trafficking frequently put the bureau in contact with volatile areas of the world and enabled him to amass information, even if only acquired incidentally, that was valuable to government planners of American foreign policy. His charges throughout the 1950s that the communists were "spreading the debauchery of narcotic addiction among the free nations" were based not only on public discussions but on intelligence reports filed by narcotics agents.[10] Unfortunately, the information relayed to Anslinger was unsubstantiated. Thus his theory about a communist invasion was not only without basis but was also illogical.

Publicly Anslinger insisted he was right, and he also expressed great concern in his private correspondence. A series of events in 1956, no doubt including the Hungarian revolt and the Suez Canal incident, moved Anslinger to write to his friend District Judge William T. McCarthy in a letter marked "CONFIDENTIAL" that "for the first time during the Cold War I am very deeply disturbed." Especially vexing to him were the actions of the Soviet premier whom he referred to as "this drunken bum Khrushchev, who is careless with the facts as well as with the truth." Anslinger was concerned that without American superiority over him, the Russian leader might capriciously decide to launch an attack on the United States even though the Soviets at that time lacked the sophisticated long-range weaponry to carry out such an attack.

In assessing the Middle East situation, Anslinger was equally grim and feigned no optimism: "The outlook is dark indeed," he commented to his old friend as he speculated on what might happen once the Russians consolidated their gains in the Suez area. If they were not stopped soon, it might be too late to contain them. Based on a communication from "a friend of mine who conducts an underground service behind the Iron Curtain," Anslinger felt that "only the prayers of a devout Christian and calm heads could save the world from Communist subjugation."[11]

However, evidence indicates that it was not the Communists in China but the Nationalists who promoted the cultivation of opium (which can be refined into heroin) because it was profitable to their guerrilla campaign in Burma and Thailand. According to author John Helmer, evidence also exists that opium cultivation was openly encouraged in most of the southeastern Asian countries by American military and intelligence units as a hedge against the growth of popular liberation movements. Furthermore, the American resolve to stop communism in China led to an OSS and later a CIA partnership with the Corsican crime syndicates of Marseilles in the later 1940s.[12]

Anslinger appeared, however, to allow international politics to distort and greatly exaggerate his assessment of narcotics trafficking in southeast Asia. Since the creation of the People's Republic of China in 1949, officials in the United States and Taiwan frequently accused the Chinese Communists of exporting large amounts of heroin for foreign exchange. Anslinger was among the most vocal of those denouncing the People's Republic, claiming that heroin was smuggled from Chinese factories into Hong Kong where it was loaded onto freighters and airplanes. From Hong Kong it was shipped to Malaya, the Philippines, Hawaii, and the United States, where the prime target was California.[13]

The commissioner's perceptions of the Chinese as evil purveyors of narcotics may have had an impact on the American media and congressional Appropriations Committees, but no evidence supports his theory of a communist-organized heroin invasion originating in China. When asked to corroborate Anslinger's China connection, British customs and police officials in Hong Kong dismissed the charges as "ridiculous and unfounded." One of them even stated in 1971 that there had not been a "single seizure from China since 1949."[14]

Notably, since Anslinger retired in 1962, the Narcotics Bureau has changed its position with regard to the Chinese Communists and their involvement in the distribution of opium. According to Alfred W. McCoy in his book *The Politics of Heroin in Southeast Asia,* Anslinger also antagonized many of the bureau's agents who felt that they were being unfairly associated with an outrageous propaganda campaign initiated and sustained by the commissioner. In a 1971 interview, one agent went on record claiming that anytime Anslinger had the opportunity, he reiterated his story that the communists were "flooding the world with dope to corrupt the youth of America."[15] The agent also criticized Anslinger for his fantastic distortions because: "It destroyed our credibility and now nobody believes us. There was no evidence for Anslinger's accusations, but that never stopped him." Even John Warner, chief of the bureau's Strategic Intelligence Office, commented in 1971 that reports from British police officers in Hong Kong stated they had seized opium from Communist China when in reality it had come from Bangkok. Apparently narcotics agents were acting on orders from Anslinger who hoped that such propaganda would mobilize public opinion against admitting China to the United Nations.[16]

In January 1959, when Fidel Castro overthrew the Cuban dictator, Fulgencio Batista, the FBN viewed the change in leadership as an opportunity to finally shut off what the bureau claimed had become the world's largest source of cocaine. Eager to capitalize on a chance to establish closer cooperation between the United States and Cuba, Anslinger sent one of his top agents, Charles Siragusa, to meet with Castro. Siragusa never did convene with the new premier, but on 12 January, he did confer with Castro's aide, Senor De La Carrera, at the Presidential Palace in Havana.[17]

In addition to providing dossiers on gangsters Meyer Lansky, Santos Trafficante, and Paul Mondoloni, the agent also submitted an 18-page FBN report titled "Illicit Narcotics Traffic in Cuba" that was extremely critical of the Batista police. Siragusa returned to Washington confident that the Cubans would be cooperative in expelling criminals associated with the syndicate.

Unfortunately, De La Carrera never followed up on his assurances that the police would arrest any of the mobsters on Siragusa's list and turn them over to the FBN. According to Siragusa, for Castro relations with organized crime were not only profitable, but they also facilitated the communist objective of pumping cocaine into the United States to weaken and destroy the minds of Americans.[18]

Anslinger may have actually sent Siragusa or simply approved the agent's assignment to Cuba on behalf of another agency, but for any representative of the American government to have been able to operate openly there in 1959 was highly unlikely. What does seem plausible was that the CIA used the Bureau of Narcotics as a cover which involved Siragusa in a far more sensitive mission than making arrests of narcotics smugglers. Since Siragusa had close ties with the CIA, it is conceivable that he was knowledgeable about the agency's plots to assassinate Castro.[19]

That Anslinger's latest external threat to the United States shadowed the course of American foreign policy was more than coincidence. One is nearly able to follow the international crisis situations during Anslinger's career simply by charting the assignments of narcotics agents. In the 1930s, shortly after Anslinger was appointed commissioner, Japan was said to be the major source of illegal narcotics. Immediately after World War II, when it was obvious that the Yalta agreement was not holding up to expectations, Anslinger charged that the communists were the biggest producers of heroin and made accusations that the Soviets were co-conspirators. McCarthyism not only made it logical but politically expedient as well. In the early 1950s, the FBN reported exaggerated numbers of addicts among American troops in Korea. According to Anslinger, North Korean Communists supplied the GIs. When the French lost control of Vietnam in 1954, Anslinger testified in Senate hearings that the new producers of heroin and opium were Laos, Cambodia, Thailand, and Vietnam. In 1958 during the Lebanon crisis, he assigned agents to that war-torn country as well as to Syria and Turkey. Finally, three years after Castro's communist-supported takeover in Cuba, Anslinger sent American agents to that small island country presumably to make arrests.

With only 250 agents, some explanation is necessary for why Anslinger was involved in foreign affairs around the globe. The first and most apparent reason was that the FBN's policy was to concentrate on the manufacturers and distributors of narcotics. If Anslinger was serious about taking the profit out of narcotics, he had to dispatch agents, even from a small force, to international distribution points. A second justification (and it is difficult to know whether this was primary or secondary to the first) was that through his agents Anslinger gathered intelligence that he passed on to the appropriate people in Washington. His militantly anti-communist ideology provided convenient reason for his entanglement in foreign adventures, which is how Anslinger lasted through five presidential administrations representing both major political parties. The key to Anslinger's longevity seems to have been his dual role as an indispensable protector of American interests at home and abroad. The third reason Anslinger extended the Bureau internationally was his obsession with tracking down organized crime mobsters involved in narcotics. Thus, he assigned Siragusa to establish offices in Lebanon, Italy, and France in the 1950s, which coincidentally, were also CIA locations. In the Cold War period Anslinger's agents seemed to be everywhere.[20]

Because the enforcement of federal drug laws frequently involved narcotics agents in investigations of diverse criminal activities in diverse settings around the world, the bureau often came into contact with other policing agencies and organizations. Though the FBI was regarded as the preeminent law enforcement agency in the United States, it collaborated only occasionally with the Narcotics Bureau in solving a case. With the exception of the Lepke manhunt, which narcotics Agent Andy Koehn set up after a three-month investigation, the two agencies rarely engaged in a joint effort. Not only did Hoover and Anslinger disagree on whether there was a Mafia, the FBI Director also disdained involving his agents in drug enforcement, preferring to leave that area to the "narcs." But the bureau had a closer working relationship with other agencies.

Within the Treasury Department, FBN agents often worked closely with the Bureau of Customs. Despite Agent White's "dog-in-the-manger" testimony during the 1958 congressional hearings, the Narcotics Bureau frequently found it both necessary and advantageous to join forces with the Customs agents. Actually, Anslinger's men found it nearly impossible to conduct an investigation in any major port city such as New York or San Francisco without their cooperation. In fact, the Customs Bureau was as involved with drug enforcement as Anslinger's men. Customs agents conducted such extensive searches that they actually made larger seizures of illegal drugs and more arrests of traffickers from year to year than the Bureau of Narcotics.

Another Treasury agency the FBN cooperated with periodically was the Secret Service, which is responsible for the protection of the presidential family and other political officials but also enforces counterfeiting laws. Though it might not seem that the two agencies share a common jurisdiction, they occasionally did consolidate their resources. In 1951 the two agencies broke one of the biggest narcotics rings up to that time in New York City. Officials estimated that the illicit traffic, financed by a counterfeit money ring, was worth a "low figure" of $10 million a year.[21] Nine men were arrested on conspiracy charges, and warrants were issued for the arrests of nine others belonging to a ring that was reported to have smuggled fifty pounds of heroin a month into the United States. Found with counterfeit money in $20 and $50 denominations, several of those arrested had been under surveillance for two years as suspected international drug dealers. One of those who managed to elude the crackdown was Joseph Orsini, who played a major role in the "French Connection" distribution of heroin.

To complement domestic enforcement, the Narcotics Bureau had to develop international control. By setting uniform procedures and limitations on the legal production, manufacture, and importation of narcotics, each nation could more easily monitor the distribution of drugs. Cooperation with other countries through the United Nations Commission on Narcotics Drugs and other organizations was, therefore, essential. That the United States maintain a constant exchange of information with other enforcement agencies was equally important. Since the bureau's agents investigated narcotics smuggling in Europe and other parts of the world, Anslinger necessarily established ties with as many enforcement authorities as possible.

In Canada the commissioner had a staunch ally in Colonel C. H. L. Sharman, formerly a member of the Canadian Royal Mounted Police, who generally shared Anslinger's philosophy on enforcement. To reduce heroin importation into the United States, Anslinger struck an agreement with the Shah of Iran to curtail his country's opium production.[22] To insure that the poppy fields remained fallow, Anslinger sent Agent Garland H. Williams to organize and train the Iranian police, army, and customs personnel.[23] Once Anslinger dried up the source of supply for opium dens in Iran, he worked through the United Nations to halt the smuggling across the border from neighboring Afghanistan.[24] Either by direct intervention or through more discreet means, Anslinger adopted an activist approach to the international control of narcotics.

The American Commissioner of Narcotics may have been resourceful and persuasive as an individual, but he surely would have been less effective without the assistance of the intergovernmental organization known by the acronym INTERPOL. Essentially a global police network, INTERPOL originated in 1914 to facilitate the apprehension of criminals who evaded police forces that had no legal authority beyond their national borders. Through the 1930s when INTERPOL wanted to enlarge its membership, the United States approached the unique agency with cautious consideration. INTERPOL was eager to have the United States as a member, but America's premier and most domineering lawman, J. Edgar Hoover, was reluctant to join. He was about to acquiesce in 1938, after membership was authorized by Congress, but when Hitler's Nazis began storming through Europe, Hoover severed all connection with interpol.[25]

In 1946 the United States finally did join, but when Czechoslovakia demanded that INTERPOL aid it in returning ten refugees who had fled to West Germany, Hoover vehemently objected to American participation in the organization. Arguably the most powerful policeman in the world, the director considered such a request inappropriate and feared that it would encourage further political exploitation by other Soviet satellites.[26] Because INTERPOL was so potentially valuable in illicit drug trafficking, however, Anslinger continued an informal association with it until 1958, when the Attorney General designated the Treasury Department as the United States' representative. With Hoover no longer a delegate, Anslinger readily acknowledged INTERPOL as a developing but important switchboard of information. The person most involved in forging cooperation between the United States and other foreign members of INTERPOL was Charles Siragusa, who used its network to follow the movements of Chicago gangster Tony Accardo as he traveled clandestinely to London, Paris, Zurich, Milan, Rome, Barcelona, Madrid, and Lisbon. Siragusa also received assistance from INTERPOL in tracking Meyer Lansky from Paris to Rome.[27] Anslinger later recalled other occasions when the bureau received information on the movement of international traffickers that otherwise would have been impossible to obtain.

Long before the United States formally joined INTERPOL in 1958, Anslinger had been aware of the benefits of exchanging information on an international level. In 1931 he organized and coordinated for eight years a Committee of One Hundred. A highly secret panel of chief narcotics enforcement officers from London, Cairo, Ottawa (Colonel Sharman), Rotterdam, Berlin, and Paris, the committee was to function as a mini INTERPOL.[28] It operated until 1939, when World War II disrupted European and global affairs, but Anslinger always held a special interest in the concept of narcotics intelligence. For that reason, in 1958 INFORM, a private intelligence newsletter, recommended that Anslinger be appointed, along with "GENERAL Fellers, General Albert Wedemeyer and . . . that great patriot, J. Edgar Hoover," to a committee investigating problems in the chain of communication with the White House, State, and Defense."[29]

Two years later, Anslinger was again recognized for his achievement when he was praised as the "strongest, toughest, and most competent intelligence authority in the United States." In the wake of the Bay of Pigs disaster in Cuba, at least one private foundation, International Services of Information (ISI), accorded Anslinger the same distinction as President Kennedy's specially appointed investigators, Dr. James R. Killian and General Maxwell Taylor.[30] Commissioner Anslinger's appetite for foreign intrigue would stimulate more than a passing curiosity concerning the nature of covert activities.

Whether Anslinger's interest stemmed from the bureau's international investigations or whether he was influenced by the career of an old friend dating back to his days in the State Department is difficult to determine. At least since 1920, when Anslinger corresponded from the diplomatic corps at The Hague with Buffalo attorney William J. Donovan, the commissioner had an appreciation for the value of intelligence.[31]

Two decades had passed when President Roosevelt enlisted "Wild Bill" Donovan to organize an intelligence agency. Initially the agency was primarily concerned with research and analysis, espionage, and enemy propaganda. By late November 1941, when it was little publicized that Anslinger had already lost several men to Naval Intelligence, he remarked in a letter to a friend in Hollywood that Donovan's was a "rather interesting organization."[32] Three weeks later, on 15 December, Herbert Gaston of the Treasury Department reported to Secretary Morgenthau that Donovan requested that Anslinger take a job full-time in connection with some intelligence work. The commissioner was willing to offer his services but only on a part-time basis, fearing that there were too many important problems in narcotics. Apparently Morgenthau did not consider Anslinger as indispensable to the bureau and replied sardonically, "Let him [Donovan] have him."[33]

Prior to the surprise attack on Pearl Harbor, which demonstrated America's lack of preparedness, Donovan convinced the president that a new intelligence organization should be created. With the approval of Attorney General Robert H. Jackson, Secretary of State Cordell Hull, and Secretary of War Henry Stimson, the Office of the Coordinator of Information (COI) was established in June of 1941. However, by June 1942, it was clear that the COI was not operating at the efficiency level desired, and its activities were divided and re-assigned. All of the overt operations were placed in a new Office of War Information (OWI) while intelligence and covert maneuvers were transferred to the Office of Strategic Services (OSS). In the crisis of war, President Roosevelt created the nation's first spy agency.[34]

Immediately after the war, President Truman abolished the OSS in response to pressure from military intelligence services and J. Edgar Hoover, who insisted that the existence of such an agency in peacetime would be a costly duplication of functions already performed. Secretary Morgenthau was also "skeptical as to the necessity or propriety of establishing such an agency" and felt that the same purposes could be achieved by a better liaison between departments.[35] But Truman also recognized the need for a permanent organization to coordinate and analyze available intelligence and channel it to the appropriate government agencies. His "coordination of information" scheme eventually led to the creation of the Central Intelligence Agency (CIA) in 1947, which was part of the National Security Act that also created the National Security Council, the Joint Chiefs of Staff, and the United States Air Force. The intelligence agency General Donovan envisioned became a reality, though he could never have anticipated the controversy it would later provoke.[36]

Anslinger's contribution to the OSS during the war years was generally limited to instructing Naval officers and other military personnel in narcotics control. He traveled to New York; Charlottesville, Virginia; and other training sites around the country offering seminars to officers on the dangers of drug addiction among enlisted men and methods of detection.

In this context Anslinger played a relatively inconsequential role, but he and several of the bureau's agents also participated in the OSS in a very different capacity.

In a 24 November 1943 memo to Colonel G. Edward Buxton, Major John J. McDonough confirmed that:

Confidential arrangements have been made with the Narcotic Bureau of the United States Treasury Department to place X-2 [counter-intelligence] personnel in the New York office of the Narcotic Bureau so that they may gain actual investigative experience in surveillance, interrogation, search, etc.[37]

The older agents, those who had been with the bureau since its early years, had become a "breed unto themselves."[38] They were, according to John Finlator, the Deputy Director of Narcotics in the 1970s, a "swashbuckling, hard-working, tough group of men who took real delight in bringing anybody to the bar of justice." They received on-the-job training that taught them to be no less resourceful in making a buy as they were in a shoot-out or street fight. The bureau also included an ethnic cross section of Italians, Chinese, Hispanics, and blacks, often from less privileged backgrounds because Anslinger preferred agents who were streetwise and could easily intermingle with the pushers and users of narcotics.[39]

Frequently the old agents resorted to whatever means were necessary to make an arrest: using addicts as informants, employing the expediency of harassment over cordiality to break a case, and bending some laws to enforce others. For many agents, the end justified the means, and some of them were not above reinterpreting the law to accommodate the situation. Over three decades Anslinger labored to build a reputation for efficiency and strict law enforcement based on these principles. Ultimately, though, they would contribute to the bureau's ruin and a loss of public confidence in drug enforcement that has yet to be fully regained.[40]

Not only internal problems caused the bureau's image to suffer. The task of stopping the flow of narcotics into the United States is all but impossible. It is commonly estimated that DEA, Customs, and Coast Guard personnel combined manage to confiscate less than 10 percent of the drugs entering the United States. The apprehension and extradition in February 1987 of Carlos Lehder Rivas, a cocaine smuggler who headed the powerful Medellin cocaine cartel in Colombia, has helped project a more positive image of narcotics agents.

Among the thousands of agents in the employ of the Bureau of Narcotics during Anslinger's thirty-year tenure, only a handful might qualify for an FBN "Hall of Fame." Anker Bangs, who lost his life in 1950 investigating a Chinese drug ring in Minneapolis, was one of the first agents killed in the line of duty.[41] Henry "Hank" Manfredi's uncanny knowledge of the Mafia was invaluable to the Rome office as was his experience with security measures in foreign capitals, which the Secret Service used during the visits of Presidents Kennedy, Johnson, and Nixon to Europe. Agent Manfredi also served in the Army's Criminal Investigation Division; and after his death, Finlator called him an immensely "popular agent who had no enemies—except among drug dealers, of course."[42] The recipient of more awards gained in the line of duty than any other agent was James Attie, a former boxer whom Anslinger described as "our ace in the hole many times when the going got rough."[43] In addition to his appealing personal characteristics, Attie's outstanding attribute was his ability to speak several Arabic dialects, which was extremely useful to the bureau for undercover work in the Middle East. Anker Bangs, Hank Manfredi, and James Attie were honored and remembered for their distinguished service to the bureau. Their loyalty and acts of heroism as law-enforcement officials have been proudly and openly recognized by the Treasury Department. Several other bureau agents were also accomplished narcotics investigators. But this group of agents, Anslinger's triumvirate of All Stars, were as important for their intelligence work outside the FBN as they were for the drug rings they broke up.

Garland H. Williams had been involved in investigative work since 1926 when Anslinger, then chief of the Division of Foreign Control in the Treasury Department, hired him as a Customs agent stationed along the coastlines of Texas, Mississippi, and Alabama to prevent bootleggers from smuggling illegal liquor from foreign ports. Working alone on most of his cases, Williams uncovered several major smuggling rings in the South and later in Mexico, where he was sent to win the cooperation of President Lázaro Cárdenas in stopping the liquor traffic.

When Anslinger was appointed Commissioner of the new Bureau of Narcotics in 1930, Williams became one of its first agents. In the mid-1930s, while Anslinger was preoccupied with disrupting the illicit narcotics traffic from Europe through his secret international panel, Williams was promoted to district supervisor in New York where he was given the unenviable assignment of breaking up every drug ring in the city.[44] His first success came in jailing members of the Polakewitz mob. Later he was sent to Europe, where he followed the Jack Katzenburg ring's distribution route for opium from Athens to Marseilles. Back in the United States in 1935, Williams crossed paths with Lepke Buchalter and "Little Augie" Del Gracio of the 107th Street Gang in New York, who were important connections for the Eliopoulos brothers. Williams was likely the first agent to use dogs (German shepherds and fox terriers) to sniff out drugs concealed in trunks and other storage spaces, a practice long since associated with narcotics investigations.

Because Supervisor Williams had proven himself an effective administrator and because his loyalty to the bureau was unquestioned, Anslinger summoned him to Washington in late 1940 for an interview with Major General Sherman Miles, Chief of Intelligence for the Army.[45] General Miles sought someone experienced in covert operations who could organize a secret police within the Army. Williams' record in surveillance, interrogation, audits, seizures, arrests, and prosecutions qualified him as one of the FBN's most proficient personnel.

On 1 October 1940, Williams was made district coordinator of six Treasury departments and pledged "an intensification of efforts to guard against sabotage, to locate Fifth Columnists, and to push the national preparedness program." Working out of an office of 90 Church Street, Major Williams was in charge of enforcement agencies in New York state, New Jersey, and Delaware that included narcotics, customs, alcohol taxes, secret service, tax intelligence, and Coast Guard enforcement agencies—1,200 trained investigators. At the time Williams was also on the staff of the Army's Second Military Area of the Second Corps Area.[46]

Williams eventually organized and became chief of the Counter Intelligence Corps (CIC).[47] In that capacity, one of his first undertakings was to aid newly-formed nations in Africa by organizing and coordinating police and intelligence departments. After Williams's six-month tour of duty with the CIC, Anslinger recommended to his friend, General Donovan, that Williams become the director of Special Training for the OSS. Using two sites in Frederick, Maryland, and Quantico, Virginia, which were acquired from the Department of the Interior, Williams was responsible for the testing and operational training of hundreds of applicants in espionage, sabotage, and guerrilla tactics. This prospective "special forces" unit was also taught to kill "quickly and quietly" if it became necessary.[48]

By the end of the war, in addition to his OSS duties, Williams was given assignments with the Parachute Infantry and the committees of the Joint Chiefs of Staff and Combined Staff Planners. When he was discharged in 1946, Lieutenant Colonel Williams returned to the Bureau of Narcotics, where two years later—when rumors circulated that Lucky Luciano, Frank Costello, and other American Mafiosi were living in Europe in exile—he and another agent were immediately dispatched for the purpose of tracking them.

Williams did not conform to the stereotypical image of an American policeman, and his diplomatic style was not appealing to foreign enforcement officials. "Williams smacked of official Washington," Anslinger later observed, which proved to be a significant handicap for him in countries that resented American intervention.[49] But the colonel was not to remain in Europe long. When the Korean War broke out in 1950, Williams was again called to duty. This time he formed a completely new kind of intelligence organization, the 525th Military Intelligence Service Group. As its first commander, Williams trained specialists in all fields of intelligence work and formed them into combat-ready units, most of which were shipped to Korea.[50] Those that were not sent into that war zone were dispatched to other parts of Europe to lead anti-Communist activities.

After the Korean War truce in 1953, Williams left the bureau to take a position as head of Tax Frauds Investigation Division in the Internal Revenue Service. Less than a year later, however, his own returns were found to contain irregularities, and he was forced to resign.[51] The FBN offered him his former position, which he accepted, but he reported on sick leave and never returned to active duty. In a career that spanned nearly a quarter-century with the Narcotics Bureau, Williams' duties overlapped narcotics investigations, special military training operations, and the formation of intelligence organizations. Williams' activities were unusual for a narcotics agent, but they were not unique.[52]

Charles Siragusa was the agent once described in a 1957 *Saturday Evening Post* article as "a character straight out of murder-mystery fiction, the kind of shrewd, steel-nerved, and intuitive undercover agent that detective-story writers spend their lives dreaming up."[53] Of Sicilian origin, "Charlie Cigars" tired of pounding a typewriter for the United States Immigration and Naturalization Service after four years and joined the Narcotics Bureau in 1939, looking for more exciting and challenging opportunities. After a period of basic training, he reported for duty to his supervisor, Garland Williams, in New York, who assigned him to surveillance work in the investigation of Isadore Kayne and Robert Gordon, fugitives from narcotics and prostitution charges.

The turning point in Siragusa's career as an undercover investigator came in 1944 when his former boss, Colonel Williams, recruited him to join the OSS. At the age of thirty-one, he was commissioned as a naval ensign and was trained in jiu-jitsu, "dirty fighting," the handling of plastic explosives, and the use of other tools of sabotage.[54] The former narcotics agent spent seventeen months chasing Nazi spies in Italy and breaking up espionage networks. Also while he was in Italy, Siragusa's loathing of the Mafia became even more intense when he was assigned to interrogate Vito Genovese in connection with his role in the black market.

Once discharged from the OSS in 1946, Siragusa returned to the bureau and was immediately sent to Puerto Rico to clean up a narcotics ring in San Juan. In less than two months he and members of the island police force arrested forty-five persons for smuggling heroin and marijuana to the United States. From Puerto Rico he went to Athens to break up the Greek heroin ring of Marianos Bouyakis, considered to be the heir to the fragile Eliopoulos empire. Using numerous aliases and relying on an innate sense of timing, Siragusa was perhaps the bureau's best agent in tracking down dope smugglers. In Hamburg, Marseilles, Mexico City, Bangkok, Rome, and other cities around the world, his infiltration of numerous organized narcotics rings resulted in over 750 arrests. By the time he retired in 1963, he had worked in twenty-nine countries and seized five tons of heroin, opium, morphine base, hashish, and cocaine.[55]

During the 1950s, Siragusa's activities were as varied as his talents. From September to November 1951, he served as chief investigator for the Kefauver Committee and testified that Lucky Luciano was the king of the dope smugglers. He was instrumental in exposing the "French Connection" in the early 1950s and was sent to Cuba in 1959 to seek the cooperation of the new dictator, Fidel Castro, in stopping the importation of cocaine. But even Siragusa was unsuccessful in convincing the dictator to cut off relations with people like Meyer Lansky and Santos Trafficante, whom the agent suspected of killing Albert Anastasia.

In between narcotics investigations, Siragusa helped to catch a pair of monks who were stealing medieval church masterpieces from an Italian cathedral, cracked half a dozen counterfeiting gangs, and tracked a high-ranking Russian diplomat who was trading heroin for strategic materials to be used in the Soviet Union. He also participated in apprehending diamond, gold, and cigarette smugglers in the Mediterranean region; exposed a Swiss black market in penicillin; and prevented a shipment of $25 million worth of strategic American aluminum from being diverted to the Soviets.[56] For those and other exploits, including Siragusa's role as an envoy to INTERPOL, Anslinger recommended his "fabulous one-man organization" for the Exceptional Civilian Service Gold Medal, the Treasury Department's highest decoration for outstanding courage in the face of danger.

In June 1960 Agent Siragusa was made Assistant Deputy Commissioner and shortly after was promoted to Deputy Commissioner. Three years later he retired from the bureau to accept the position as executive director of the Illinois Crime Investigation Commission in Chicago. By the time Siragusa left the FBN, he complied a long and distinguished record as a narcotics agent. If ever the Federal Bureau of Narcotics produced a superspy, Charles Siragusa may have been that person.[57]

The third member of Anslinger's triumvirate, whose career closely paralleled that of Williams and Siragusa in terms of extracurricular activities, was George H. White. Like Williams, Agent White was also a loner who did not want to be responsible for a partner.[58] Initially Anslinger was inclined to fire White because he did not exhibit "enough get-up-and-go," but the agent's unusual interest in Chinese lore enabled him to infiltrate the notorious Hip Sing Tong drug syndicate and cause the deportations of many of its leaders. Having demonstrated his courage and resourcefulness, White became the top man abroad in the absence of Colonel Williams, and he remained with the bureau until 1965.

White's personality as well as his performance both awed and perplexed Anslinger. Almost as round as he was tall, the agent reminded the commissioner of Buddha, but the comparison ended with his appearance. Like Williams, White was recruited by the OSS during the war and given the rank of Lieutenant Colonel, but he saw more action than his mentor. On a mission in India he was forced to kill a Japanese spy by strangling him with his hands. As a gruesome reminder of the incident, according to Anslinger, White kept photographs on the walls of his apartment of the spy and two others he killed in self-defense.[59]

Not surprisingly, when Anslinger was vexed with a difficult case, he usually assigned "the ubiquitous White, always ready to shake hands with trouble." White's incredible success as a narcotics agent was largely attributable to his unorthodox methods and unusual ability to masquerade as one of the drug traffickers. White may have been eccentric, but he produced results, and Anslinger appreciated his dependability and respected his style.[60]

When one of Anslinger's close friends, Judge William T. McCarthy, requested the bureau's help in eradicating a growing narcotics problem in Boston, he asked for the best agent available. The commissioner sent White with his fullest assurance that "He is a very able enforcement officer, sometimes not too discreet, but he is the toughest man we have. If the traffickers get ahead of him in Boston I will be surprised."[61]

Throughout his career, White was involved in countless narcotics investigations, but he also participated in many outside projects and sensitive intelligence operations. The man Anslinger suspected of being one of the first non-scientific people to learn that the United States had discovered how to make the atom bomb also played a key role in the government's secret program of drug experimentation.[62]

Because three of the FBN's top agents were so deeply involved with the OSS during the war and because both agencies demanded similar skills and training—investigation, interrogation, and surveillance, for example—a common bond or mutuality of interest was formed. The new intelligence organization provided Agents Williams, White, and Siragusa with opportunities to develop and hone their skills in countering subversive activities such as espionage and sabotage. They also gained valuable experience that made them more capable detectives and, therefore, more valuable to the bureau.

Conversely, the primary purpose of the OSS was to produce intelligence that would facilitate the successful completion of covert military operations. The OSS, like any similar agency, was only as effective as the intelligence it acquired and interpreted. When the information could be obtained openly and willingly, the job was less arduous. Often, however, other covert, more surreptitious tactics were required to elicit potentially valuable intelligence. One method believed to be effective in withdrawing information from unwilling sources was administration of various narcotics that would lessen the individual's resistance. Consequently the task for the OSS was made easier by employing someone knowledgeable and experienced in the effects of mind-altering substances. Linking up with agents in the Bureau of Narcotics, therefore, was a marriage of convenience.

In addition to its regulatory and enforcement responsibilities, the Bureau of Narcotics also was involved in highly classified research. During the war years Anslinger not only implemented the stockpiling of opium, he also consulted with a group within the OSS that was created essentially to find a drug that would induce people to tell the truth against their will. Notations in George White's diary confirmed that he and Anslinger conducted experiments with narcotics on ways to control human behavior that would break down the psychological defenses of enemy agents when subjected to questioning by American intelligence officers.[63] "We were trying to discover a truth drug," Anslinger admitted in a 1968 interview, "by using peyote and sodium amytal."[64] But when neither of those drugs proved effective, they resorted to the "killer weed." Entries in White's early diaries stamped "SECRET" in bold red letters show that experiments with a marijuana derivative he identified as tetrahydrocannabinol acetate were begun in Washington in 1943. On at least one occasion, White volunteered to smoke a cigarette laced with the chemical when no other subjects could be found. According to the agent, the result of the test was to "knock myself out."[65]

Other experiments with the compound, which Anslinger believed were "getting pretty close," sometimes produced an unexpected outcome. To deceive unsuspecting subjects into thinking that they were being given an unbroken pack of cigarettes, American interrogators would open the bottom, insert the "T-Drug," and reseal it. But when a Naval captain and other intelligence officers were questioning a German submarine commander, the captain inadvertently picked up the wrong pack of cigarettes, and it was the captain who did all the talking.[66]

Unfortunately, not all the experiments were so amusing or inconsequential. In 1943 the OSS rented rooms at the Belmont Hotel in New York where George White administered cigarettes heavily laced with the marijuana extract to seven volunteers who were commissioned and non-commissioned Army officers. As part of the experiment, the soldiers were told they were to sail on a certain date but that they would be severely punished if they revealed that date to anyone else. Anslinger's job in the operation was to induce the men to talk. One officer was cooperative but only under hypnosis and only after he was given some uncut marijuana. The others became belligerent under the effects of the T-Drug and would not divulge any information.[67] The test proved that the secret drug was a failure, but it did not deter White from continuing to experiment with it in a different capacity during the post-war years.

One of White's most unlikely victims in a test conducted while with the OSS was Augie Del Gracio, the chief drug distributor for New York's Lower East Side who was also an associate of Lucky Luciano. Del Gracio, an opium user, was unknowingly subjected to the truth drug when he met with White as an emissary of the Mafia boss. Del Gracio tried to strike a deal for Lucky's realease from prison in return for the Mafia's cooperation in preventing acts of sabotage in the Navy's New York shipyards. According to White he informed "Little Augie" flatly that such a trade-off was out of the question, and that he would in no way intervene to help Luciano out of prison. White was no less receptive to the gangster's offer to assassinate John L. Lewis, who as president of United Mine Workers, organized several strikes that earned him public condemnation for actions harmful to the war effort.[68]

In 1954, a year after the CIA hired White as a consultant, the controversy surrounding Governor Dewey's release of Luciano became the subject of an inquiry requested by Dewey and directed by William B. Herlands, then the New York state Commissioner of Investigations. Officially White was still with the Bureau of Narcotics at that time, but he was also on the payroll of the CIA.[69]

Herlands's investigation and incisive questions about the experiments involving Del Gracio and the use of an alleged truth drug alarmed some officials in the CIA. Apparently they feared that the state inquiry might expose White's relationship with the CIA and his use of marijuana on Del Gracio, as well as the legal and moral ramifications of the agency's continued experimentation with a new, more potent substance.[70] Just prior to the Herlands investigation, White used the pseudonym "Morgan Hall" to rent an apartment on Bedford Street in Greenwich Village. In this specially outfitted safe house, the CIA gave drug-addicted prostitutes their fixes on the condition that they lure unsuspecting people to the apartment where they became subjects for experimentation with a relatively unknown chemical, lysergic acid diethylamide (LSD). Before the secret project was uncovered and the CIA was forced to abandon its interest in narcotics, however, the colonel was notified by higher-ups to stop the experiments temporarily. On 12 May 1954, five days after he received final security clearance, White recorded in his diary that Sidney Gottlieb, a biochemist and veteran CIA official who directed the agency's research into psychological warfare techniques, had telephoned him from Washington, admonishing him to "go slow on Hall Oper in view of Herlands' quiz."[71]

But the possibility that the New York state commissioner would discover the drug research that was code named "BLUEBIRD," later changed to "ARTICHOKE," soon abated, and the experiments continued in various forms and settings for the next two decades. The CIA's search for the perfect truth drug in the Cold War era, though, proved as unsuccessful as the OSS attempts during World War II.[72]

Usually the subjects of White's experiments suffered no permanent effects from the drugs. However, some victims did sustain emotional and psychological problems which occasionally required professional counseling. The worst tragedy in the CIA's experiments did not involve a victim but one of the CIA's own chemists, Dr. Franklin Olson, on a November night in 1953. A glass of liquor was spiked with about seventy micrograms of LSD (one microgram equals 1/1,000,000 of a gram; twenty-eight grams equal one ounce). The experiment proved fatal. During the next several days he was abnormally suspicious of everyone and extremely despondent. The day after Thanksgiving, Dr. Olson jumped to his death from a tenth-story window of the Statler Hotel in New York.[73] His surviving family members didn't learn the true circumstances of his death until the facts were disclosed in a government report on intelligence and drug-testing in 1975. The CIA denied Olson was an unsuspecting victim, but the government paid his family $750,000 in compensation in 1976.[74]

Two years after the Olson tragedy, White was transferred to San Francisco where he used the same pseudonym to rent and furnish another safe house. Unlike the apartment in New York, though, the one on Telegraph Hill was equipped with hidden microphones and two-way mirrors that allowed for closer observation of unsuspecting men drinking cocktails containing hallucinogenic drugs. As in New York, white and the CIA employed prostitutes in nearby night clubs to lure the victims, usually young males, back to the apartment. When investigators from the Kennedy subcommittee visited the safe house, they learned that White had been assisted by Dr. James A. Hamilton, a psychiatrist with Stanford University and friend of White since the OSS days, and Jean Pierre Lafitte (nicknamed "the pirate"), a long-time professional police informant with underworld connections.[75] Participants in White's "Operation Midnight Climax," Hamilton and Lafitte never appeared before the 1977 subcommittee for questioning.

The subcommittee never even had an opportunity to question White because he drank himself to death in 1975.[76] Even if he refused to reveal the details of his involvement in the MK-ULTRA project, interrogating a man with such personal contradictions would have been fascinating. As a narcotics agent, he was fiercely opposed to drugs, yet he experimented with everything from marijuana to LSD. Once, with himself as the subject, he wrote to Dr. Harvey Paulson in the Department of Psychiatry at the University of California at Berkeley, "So far as I was concerned, 'clear thinking' was nonexistent while under the influence of any of these drugs [marijuana or LSD], I did feel at times that I was having a mind-expanding experience, but this vanished like a dream immediately after the session."[77] He was an unorthodox law enforcement official who frequently, unhesitatingly violated the law. His willingness to exploit his authority often made it difficult for Anslinger to control the movements of a man who relished his role as a "dual agent."[78] White himself conveyed an awareness of his free-wheeling, no-holds-barred kind of lifestyle:

> I was a very minor missionary, actually a heretic, but I toiled whole-heartedly in the vineyards because it was fun, fun, fun. Where else could a red-blooded American boy lie, kill, cheat, steal, rape, and pillage with the sanction and blessing of the All-Highest?[79]

George White was an extraordinary agent and a tremendously important figure in the operations of the Narcotics Bureau. According to James J. Angleton, head of the CIA's counterintelligence division in the 1950s and 1960s, White was a "different kettle of fish," and a "maverick in narcotics enforcement."[80] As one of its oldest and most dependable agents, he fit Anslinger's image of a tough, no-nonsense law enforcer. But White's often explosive personality and unusual investigative techniques frequently caused the commissioner anguish and anxiety. White's exploits within the bureau, however, were inconsequential when compared to one of his intelligence-related activities that ultimately proved to be Anslinger's biggest problem. In a congressional inquiry scheduled to begin in early September 1977, testimony by key individuals was expected to expose White's narcotics-intelligence connection.

When Senator Edward M. Kennedy finally opened the delayed hearings on 20 September, he acknowledged that though the biological and behavioral research experiments of the CIA occurred in a different time and context, such activities could not be condoned or tolerated in a free, open society. Although projects may been carried out by properly motivated, patriotic Americans, the senator concluded that such individuals could not be permitted to violate the freedom of the nation's citizens in the name of national security.[81] Kennedy also found it inconceivable that the CIA, in a cooperative effort with the FBN, the National Institute of Health, and the Internal Revenue Service, secretly supported research on the control of human behavior at eighty institutions, including forty-four universities, hospitals, prisons, and pharmaceutical companies.

The investigators were seriously handicapped in not having access to the valuable records destroyed on orders by former CIA Director Richard Helms.[82] Still, at the outset of the hearings, the subcommittee was able to reconstruct sufficient evidence to form several conclusions, one of which named the Bureau of Narcotics as having been "heavily involved in all the drug testing projects involving unwitting witnesses." It also was concluded that "the bulk of the research led nowhere."[83]

The first witness to appear before the subcommittee was Dr. Charles F. Geshickter, a retired professor of research pathology at Georgetown University. Dr. Geshickter's testimony revealed that the Geshickter Fund, established in 1939 for research in cancer and chronic diseases, was one of the principal conduits for financing drug experiments. The professor disclosed that his fund conducted only legitimate research, but the chairman could not understand why the government's intelligence agency was involved.

Following the testimony of Dr. Geshickter, the subcommittee heard from David Rhodes and Phillip Goldman, former psychologists in the CIA, who provided operational details of MK-ULTRA from the time they were transferred to California in 1957. Rhodes testified that under the orders of Morgan Hall, George White's undercover alias, he and Goldman were given "a reasonable supply of money" and during the following week were told "to go around to a number of bars, and drink and meet people." The purpose of their bar-hopping was to establish trusting relationships with people so as not to arouse suspicion when the agents invited them to an "MK-ULTRA party" at White's safe house where the unwitting victims would be given LSD.[84]

Rhodes and Goldman also assisted White in various testing techniques. At least one experiment with LSD resembled more of a grade B comedy than a highly secretive intelligence operation. Rather than administer the drug orally, as was most common, the agents intended for their subjects to ingest it as they sprayed it from an aerosol cannister. But as Rhodes testified, they had a "singular problem." The house they were using on this particular occasion was not air conditioned, and it was too hot to keep the windows and doors closed long enough to observe the effects of the aerosol spray. Obviously conducting the experiment under these conditions was ludicrous. Out of frustration a third employee of the CIA, John Gittinger, agreed to try it on himself in the bathroom where there was no ventilation. According to Rhodes there were no effects. Senator Kennedy surely was not alone in his astonishment that "three grown men flew from the east coast to the west coast to spend a week in the bars out there, to gather people for a party." When he asked the agent to make a determination of the value of the experiment, Rhodes replied, "You cannot deliver it [LSD] by aerosol under those conditions."[85]

In conducting other experiments with drugs intended to control behavior, the safe house operatives were limited only by their imaginations. To test Gittinger's theory on the nature of personality, they attended the First National Convention of Lesbians. The value or rationalization of that project was never satisfactorily explained, but it was said to have been part of the MK-ULTRA project. The subcommittee was also puzzled as to why the CIA would be interested in a launching device for the powder "CS," until Goldman explained that the substance was a tear gas that could be used to break up demonstrations in foreign countries.

Other experiments included a powder that induced violent sneezing when released in a small room, a substance used for quieting vicious guard dogs, and a swizzle stick coated with a water- or alcohol-soluble drug that was tested in barrooms. They also used a hypodermic needle to inject drugs through the cork in wine bottles to find out if the person handling the bottle would notice that it had been penetrated. To debilitate a person without causing him physical harm, they devised a drug which brought on diarrhea.[86] All of the experiments involved unknowing subjects, and all of the test results were reported to Morgan Hall.

At least one subcommittee member suspected that MK-ULTRA involved more than experiments with bottle corks and swizzle sticks. Senator Richard S. Schweiker of Pennsylvania asked Dr. Robert Lashbrook, a CIA chemist who was in the company of Dr. Olson when he committed suicide, to discuss the CIA's projects relating to motivational studies of defectors and training techniques. Lashbrook said he was unable to recall any such projects, but Senator Schweiker continued to question the chemist about the connection between MK-ULTRA and twenty-three subprojects he believed were related to "Executive action," the CIA's term for political assassination. Lashbrook stated that he was not aware that any of the subprojects were part of Executive action, but he did not exclude that possibility either.[87]

George White was not the only agent from the Narcotics Bureau who participated in the CIA drug testing projects. In responding to Senator Kennedy's questions, Charles Siragusa testified that he, too, had been involved in the experiments, though it was difficult to ascertain from his testimony exactly what his role was. Using the alias Cal Salerno, Siragusa stated that he was not an official agent for the CIA, but that he was appointed unofficially as "liaison with the CIA."[88]

Siragusa traced the origin of his relationship with the CIA back to 1959 when Anslinger introduced him to Dr. Roy Treichler, an agency employee who worked out of the New York safe house. Treichler needed to set up an apartment as a base of operations and wanted Siragusa to help establish a front for the CIA. The two agents furnished an apartment on 13th Street off Sixth Avenue with the understanding that their respective agencies were to use it for their own purposes. Siragusa would use the facility to interview and debrief informants and to coordinate undercover operations. When the CIA wished to use the apartment, Treichler would simply notify the bureau to stay away.[89]

When asked if he knew what was going on in the safe houses, Siragusa said no, but he suspected they were being used for "some intelligence purposes." Had he known that unsuspecting witnesses were taken there for drug experiments, the narcotics agent claimed, he would have dissociated himself with the operation. Throughout his testimony Siragusa maintained that his contact with the CIA was "rather remote." But when Senator Kennedy asked him if the CIA ever approached him about setting up a safe house in Chicago, his equivocal response was, "I do not recall they ever asked me."[90] For a person with more than twenty years of training and experience in investigation and intelligence work, it was surprising that Siragusa did not respond with more conviction.

The extent of Siragusa's role became even more clouded when Senator Kennedy asked him to react to an excerpt from the record of MK-ULTRA Subproject 132 in 1964:

> This project is conducted by Mr. Cal Salerno. Mr. Salerno, a public relations consultant, has recently moved his offices from New York City to Chicago, Ill. Mr. Salerno holds a top secret agency clearance and is completely witting of the aims and goals of the project. He possesses unique facilities and personal abilities which have made him invaluable to this kind of operation.[91]

Siragusa protested that poetic license had been taken with the truth. He asserted that since he left the bureau in 1963, others had adopted his alias and used it while he was in Chicago. If he was telling the truth, which conflicted with CIA files that indicated he was "completely witting and knowledgeable about these programs, the aims and goals," then it was probable that other narcotics agents using the name "Cal Salerno" were involved. According to Marks, however, Siragusa was put in charge of a third safe house set up by the CIA in 1961.[92]

After the subcommittee heard from Siragusa, Senator Kennedy questioned former FBN supervisor George Belk about his role in the MK-ULTRA. An agent with the bureau since 1948, Belk testified that in April 1963 he was sent to New York by Commissioner Henry L. Giordano, who requested that he continue to collaborate with the CIA in a national security endeavor. Belk went to New York and took over the office from John Enright (Assistant Commissioner of Enforcement in 1964), who Belk believed was aware of the apartment. Like Siragusa, Belk emphatically denied having any knowledge of the safe house operations, even though Senator Kennedy claimed to possess agency documents referring to his involvement as "not dissimilar to the kind of characterization of Mr. Siragusa's."[93] Even though neither Siragusa nor Belk's involvement in MK-ULTRA was explicitly confirmed or denied during the hearings, Siragusa's testimony was obviously a weak attempt to cover his participation in other intelligence activities.[94]

The roles of Siragusa and Belk may not have been determined precisely, but there was no doubt about George White, according to CIA pharmacologist Dr. Sidney Gottlieb. Testifying under subpoena, Dr. Gottlieb discussed the existence of the MK-ULTRA project from 1952 to 1965 as an "arrangement set up with the Bureau of Narcotics."[95] The idea of a joint project came to him while perusing OSS research files that described an experiment into the behavior-altering possibilities of tetrohycannabinol. Aiding him in the partnership was a contact officer of the bureau (White) who had participated firsthand in the OSS investigations. Together the contact and the chemist covertly administered chemical substances to unwitting people. Gottlieb also said that the project was actively supported by the Bureau of Narcotics because of its interest in determining whether chemical materials could be used to elicit or validate information from drug informants.[96]

In his opening statement to the subcommittee, Dr. Gottlieb conveyed his impression that the Narcotics Bureau neither had no advance knowledge nor provided for the protection of the individuals concerned. In matters of national survival, Gottlieb felt, "Such a procedure and such a risk was a reasonable one to take."[97] This was also the CIA's rationale for conducting covert drug operations in safe houses through 1973.

During the thirteen years of MK-ULTRA drug testing from 1952 to 1965, the CIA made in excess of two hundred payments totaling more than $20,000 for the San Francisco safe house alone. Checks were issued in amounts of $50 or $100 by Morgan Hall, who labeled many of them "STORMY," White's code name for LSD. Thirty-two STORMY checks collected by the subcommittee indicated at least that many attempted drug administrations. Checks issued by Morgan Hall with no connotation were used, according to Gottlieb, to finance photographic equipment and the payments to prostitutes.[98]

After hearing Gottlieb's incredible testimony detailing the operations of MK-ULTRA, Senator Kennedy asked him to assess what was learned from the experiments. The doctor concluded only that predictably manipulating human behavior was very difficult but that the tests did have operational value. At this point the chairman proceeded cautiously, for he knew he was touching on extremely delicate issues relative to classified operations at the international level:

SENATOR KENNEDY: Do you know whether it led to the covert use of drugs by the Intelligence Agency?

DR. GOTTLIEB: I was advised by your staff that the area of the overseas use of these drugs was not one of your primary interests. Is that accurate?

SENATOR KENNEDY: Well, the detail of it. But if you could answer whether you know if information that was developed in these safe houses was used for covert operations overseas without getting into countries or without getting—

DR. GOTTLIEB: My answer would be yes.[99]

Gottlieb refused to clarify further, suggesting only that the senator contact the CIA for additional information.

In collaborating with the Central Intelligence Agency in MK-ULTRA—which cost American taxpayers an estimated $10 million—senior members of the Federal Bureau of Narcotics participated in the most sensitive and most despicable covert domestic operation ever conducted by the federal government.[100] Clearly, several narcotics agents had been involved in the project, but at what level in the FBN's chain of command knowledge of the project stopped, no one could determine.

The former commissioner was implicated when Dr. Gottlieb told the subcommittee that "Mr. Anslinger was knowledgeable of the safe houses that we set up and why" and that the Commissioner of Narcotics was known to have condoned and encouraged bureau agents to take an active role in the CIA's drug experiments. Gottlieb also revealed that George White's salary was paid by the CIA because "some people in high places were very angry with him and it was useful for Mr. Anslinger not to have him specifically on the Bureau of Narcotics payroll for a period of time."[101] Perhaps it was this set of circumstances that provoked White to expose the "dog-in-the-manger" arrangement with the Customs Bureau during his testimony at the hearings on juvenile delinquency in 1959.

The men who participated in MK-ULTRA may have been motivated by misguided patriotic impulses and believed that they were acting in the interest of national security, but in their zeal they perverted the most fundamental rights of the individual. The perfidious actions of the FBN and the CIA could be expected from agents of adversary countries, but not from those within the federal government who, in their roles as protectors, undermined the cherished concepts of democracy.

Though Harry Anslinger had been deceased two years when the Kennedy subcommittee opened its investigation and thus was spared the embarrassment of having to publicly explain his motives, he had to know near the time of his death that MK-ULTRA would soon be discovered. Had Anslinger testified, he might well have provided answers to lingering questions such as the precise nature of Siragusa's relationship with the CIA, why George White—who was officially still a narcotics agent—was taken off the FBN payroll, how many of his agents were involved in MK-

ULTRA, what were their roles, and how many innocent people became involuntary human guinea pigs. Anslinger could have also answered questions about the roles his agents played in other CIA-related "extracurricular activities."

More significantly, the extent of Anslinger's own participation—not only in MK-ULTRA, but in other intelligence activities in which the bureau was involved—remains largely unknown. This chapter established that several agents (Williams, White, Siragusa, Chappell, and Manfredi) worked for the OSS during the war years, and that Anslinger himself trained OSS personnel. Those acts of patriotism are well documented; but what part Anslinger played a few years later when Sidney Gottlieb approached him about borrowing George White (and probably Charles Siragusa) to conduct CIA drug experiments is not so clear. Moreover, if Anslinger really sent Siragusa to Cuba in 1959 just after Castro had overthrown Fulgencio Batista, it is difficult to believe it was solely for the purpose of arresting drug traffickers. On the contrary, these two instances are evidence that the Bureau of Narcotics was likely involved in several clandestine operations. Little doubt exists that during the Cold War years, Anslinger's agents functioned as important intelligence gatherers.

What remains unknown is why and under what circumstances Anslinger decided to expand the bureau's sphere of influence. Over a thirty-year tenure, the commissioner quite naturally amassed a formidable degree of power, but it was virtually limited to the FBN. He did not have the kind of power necessary to manipulate other federal law enforcement agencies (like Hoover at the FBI), much less covert intelligence operations. A more plausible explanation is that by the mid-1950s, Anslinger was still setting narcotics policies and controlling domestic enforcement activities, but agents like White and Siragusa had been working independently for so long with the CIA directly or tangentially, that they had become the bureau's de facto leadership. Since White was on the CIA payroll, it is also likely that Anslinger simply gave his approval for his agents' involvement in intelligence-related activities, if he was informed at all.[102]

Also, one theory purports that by the mid-1960s no one individual was in control at the Bureau of Narcotics or dominated it the way Anslinger did. Support for this hypothesis rests on the rapid turnover of high-level personnel in the 1960s and 1970s. In a three-year period (1962–1965) Anslinger, Siragusa, and White retired. Having begun their careers in the 1930s, they represented a combined eighty-six years experience. Their records may have been controversial, but they brought stability to the upper level of the Bureau. Henry Giordano, appointed commissioner in 1962, held that position only six years. By 1968, when the FBN was completely dismantled, the Bureau's dominant people were gone, rendering it extremely vulnerable to internal power struggles and external political whims.

That the Federal Bureau of Narcotics was deeply involved in certain CIA affairs is beyond dispute. The activities of Agents Williams and in particular White and Sirgusa in clandestine operations from the early years of the OSS in the 1940s through the 1960s amply justify suspicions about their roles in numerous covert projects. Unfortunately, because so many documents containing details about their links to these operations and their association with other agencies were destroyed or are inaccessible, determining their precise roles is difficult, if not impossible. Still, such material must be presented for consideration because it is evident that the Narcotics Bureau played a multifaceted part in our government's sensitive endeavors to preserve national security. It is a role that the bureau's agents have played in various contexts continuously through the 1980s.

8
Coda, 1962–1975

The inauguration of John Kennedy in January 1961 represented not only a change in administrations but a change of presidential style and image as well. In contrast to the grandfatherly Eisenhower, the youthful Kennedy brought to the White House a renewed vitality and pioneering spirit as he challenged America to accept its responsibility as a world leader. It was a time for a new beginning and a new direction.

"The torch has been passed to a new generation of Americans," Kennedy emphasized in his inaugural address, and to translate his vision into reality, the president lured intellectuals from the nation's universities to fill the two hundred most important posts in the government. "To get America moving again," he appointed his thirty-five-year-old brother, Bobby, as the new attorney general. As president and the government's chief law enforcer, the Kennedy brothers personified a sharp break from the old-line style of politics.

The Kennedy administration's emphasis on youth and innovation would seem to have necessitated replacing the aging and conservative Commissioner of Narcotics. Surprisingly, the president did not ask for Anslinger's resignation but reappointed him the same day Bobby was named to head the Department of Justice. Even the commissioner was shocked that he had been rehired, commenting to an attorney friend in February 1961 that he "wasn't expecting this so it came as quite a surprise."[1]

Of the five presidents Anslinger served, he held the greatest admiration for Harry Truman because he was "crisp, a man of decision," but he also had tremendous respect for the Kennedys and in particular the Attorney General.[2] Despite the incompatibility of their political ideologies, Anslinger had been impressed with Bobby Kennedy since the two met during the McClellan Committee hearings. Initially, Kennedy's determination to reverse the increasing crime rates most appealed to Anslinger. But the commissioner also extolled what he perceived as the Attorney General's fearlessness in going after the big criminals or untouchable members of the Mafia.[3]

Anslinger sharply criticized past attorneys general with whom he had worked (Tom Clark in the Truman Administration was the lone exception) because they occasionally "let loose a blast against the underworld" but never followed their words with actions. Compared to these men "who only went half way in their efforts," the commissioner reflected, "Kennedy would go the distance." The alliance between Anslinger and the attorney general may have been a strange one, but the commissioner attributed the conviction of Vito Genovese, John Ormento, Joe Valachi, and Carmine Galente to the resoluteness of Bobby Kennedy, who encouraged the Narcotics Bureau to apprehend them. "One of these days," Anslinger prophesized, "the country will realize what it owes Bobby Kennedy for trying to free the public from the claws and tentacles of these gangsters, racketeers, and hoodlums."[4]

The cooperation he received from Attorney General Kennedy in fighting his old Mafia nemesis was one of the few bright spots for Anslinger during his last years in office. Just prior to Anslinger's retirement, several different institutions attacked the bureau's long-held advocacy of lengthy prison sentences for narcotics addicts. The New York Academy of Medicine, which sponsored the controversial ABA-AMA Report published in 1961, continued to urge the Narcotics Bureau to abandon its punitive approach to drug addiction. It publicly criticized the bureau's policies in general and specifically denounced its policy of immediate and complete withdrawal of drugs for all addicts. In a 21,000-word report that was eventually released in 1963, the Academy argued that not only were those policies ineffective, they could actually result in the deaths of some addicts and jeopardize the mental balance of others. Because the FBN's continued role in its withdrawal therapy was so potentially risky, the Academy recommended that narcotics agents should " 'gracefully' bow out of the practice of medicine and let M.D.'s decide how to treat addicts."[5]

While the bureau was still reeling from the attack by the medical profession, in late June 1962 the Supreme Court ruled unconstitutional a California law making it a crime to be addicted to narcotics or to use them without a prescription. In delivering the 6-2 decision, Justice Potter Stewart wrote, "A state imprisoning a person as a criminal, even though he had never touched any narcotic drug within the State or been guilty of any irregular behavior there, inflicts a cruel and unusual punishment in violation of the 14th Amendment."[6] In a concurring opinion William O. Douglas commented, "Addiction, like insanity, is a disease. . . . An addict must be treated as a sick person."[7]

Anslinger's position was shaken, but he weathered the challenge to his authority from the medical community. The doctors could dispute and debunk the bureau's policies on the treatment of addicts with scientific research, but Anslinger responded with studies of his own proving his methods were effective. It was simply a matter of out-maneuvering the opposition. A Supreme Court decision, however, posed a different kind of problem. The repression of federal drug policies terminated the bureau's thirty-year practice of enforcing extraordinarily stringent narcotics laws. Anslinger, deprived of one of his most formidable weapons, was incensed at the court's 1962 decision, which culminated a protracted feud between the FBN and the judicial system. Only a year earlier, New York District Supervisor George Gaffney stated that when a judge intervened in a narcotics case because he regarded the mandatory sentence as being too harsh, "He is putting himself above the law . . . and should be impeached."[8] Though Anslinger withstood the medical and judicial assaults and personally remained invulnerable in Congress, he had yet to face his most serious challenge.

President Kennedy's election was similar to other elections in that it was won to a great extent on the basis of endorsements from influential politicians. One of Kennedy's most important supporters in 1960 was California Governor Edmund (Pat) Brown, who two years earlier won the statehouse in an election that centered around the issue of drug enforcement. His opponent in 1962 was former U.S. Senator William Knowland, who accused Brown of being too soft on drug offenders during his eight years as the state attorney general.[9] To neutralize the impact of Knowland's anti-drug campaign and because Brown was fearful of defeat, the governor pressured Kennedy to sponsor a White House Conference on Drugs.

Recognizing his political obligation to the governor, President Kennedy wanted to make a commitment to Brown for the conference, but two factors deterred him from pushing it beyond the talking stage. First, though a drug abuse problem existed in California, it had not yet become a serious national concern. With only regional support, Kennedy felt he had little justification for organizing a national conference. The other reason for Kennedy's reluctance was Anslinger's vociferous opposition. Testifying before a subcommittee of the House Judiciary Committee in March 1960, the commissioner angrily protested the proposal of the White House Conference primarily because he feared that it might result in modifications to his own program for suppressing narcotics traffic.[10] He also did not want to direct unnecessary attention to the claims of California's state politicians that 75 percent of the heroin distributed in their state was smuggled across the border from Mexico. Anslinger discredited that statistic, but was still viewed as a reluctant enforcer of the laws who, according to a *Los Angeles Times* editorial, did not wish to become "involved in an international negotiation . . . affecting one state."[11]

For nearly two years, Anslinger was able to forestall a national conference on narcotics. Had Governor Brown's opponent not been one of Kennedy's biggest political adversaries, such a conference would probably not have taken place. But when Richard Nixon decided to run for governor in his home state and renewed the attacks against Brown as a sympathizer with drug dealers (which were reminiscent of the scurrilous accusations he made against Jerry Vorhees and Helen Gahagan Douglas in the 1940s for their alleged communist connections), the president was too incensed to remain a casual observer. In the spring of 1962, he personally campaigned in California on the governor's behalf, and in May he announced that the proposal for a White House Conference was under study. Four months later Kennedy's formal announcement of the conference was strategically planned to coincide with the gubernatorial elections. [12]

The White Houuse Conference on Narcotic and Drug Abuse convened on September 27 and 28. In his address to the opening session in the State Department Auditorium, President Kennedy observed that this administration has recognized the need to protect our society from the unfortunate results of the misery of dangerous drugs and narcotics," and he challenged the participants to evaluate existing drug policies with objectivity. [13]

The two-day drug conference, chaired by the attorney general, included representatives from the departments of Justice; Treasury; Defense; State; and Health, Education, and Welfare. In an effort to entertain a wide range of viewpoints, the White House extended invitations to approximately four hundred authorities in various fields related to the problem—including law enforcement, corrections, the judiciary, law, medicine, legislation, sociology, and education—as well as to representatives from the mass media and pharmaceutical manufacturers. [14]

The topics identified for panel discussions focused on controls, research, sentencing, and legislation. By confining themselves to topics relevant to their disciplines, the experts hoped to offer different perspectives on the overall problems of how to deal with the "new dangerous drugs," amphetamines and barbiturates, and to debate rehabilitation as an effective form of treatment. While the conferees endeavored to compile an up-to-date appraisal of the magnitude and nature of the drug problem, they stated explicitly that their objective was not to arrive at specific solutions but rather to highlight various aspects of the problem.

Politically the conference was a success. Pat Brown was reelected Governor, and Richard Nixon promised he would not run again for public office. On the matter of narcotics use in the United States, the general consensus of the conference was that misinformation and inadequte factual data contributed substantially to the problem. The conferees also concluded that previous efforts to treat and rehabilitate drug addicts had proven unsuccessful. In a direct repudiation of Anslinger's punitive approach, they determined that a recovering addict was less of a financial burden in mainstream society than he was to keep in prison.[15] The impact of the conference, however, was minimal; and, by the time the findings were made public in late 1962, the Bureau of Narcotics was under the direction of its second commissioner.

Anslinger had to experience mixed emotions as he anticipated the celebration of his birthday in 1962. On May 20 one of the most controversial men in Washington was seventy years old, the mandatory retirement age for federal government employees. The commissioner submitted his resignation to President Kennedy at that time, but since no successor was immediately decided upon, Anslinger agreed to stay in his $18,500-a-year post until one could be named.[16] Whether the "narcotics czar"—as some journalists referred to him—of thirty-two years retired voluntarily or was pressured by the White House to step down is also uncertain. Even a comparison of documented statements made by Anslinger himself fails to clear the controversy.

In early May 1962 Anslinger said he had given no thought to retiring and cited a number of instances in which other agency heads had remained in office past age seventy. Two months later the *New York Times* reported that he wanted to stay in office past his seventieth birthday. On other occasions, however, he complained of "burnout," leaving the reader of his personal correspondence with the impression that he wished to retire.[17]

The White House also issued conflicting reports regarding the circumstances of Anslinger's retirement. Rufus King, a member of the ABA-AMA Joint Committee, implied that Anslinger's fondness for Bobby Kennedy was not reciprocated, that the Kennedys detested the commissioner's hardline approach to law enforcement and wanted him out.[18] But because they suspected Anslinger would vigorously protest being replaced in 1960, the president and his attorney general decided to wait for him to reach the mandatory age for retirement. Privately that may well have been the case, but publicly Pierre Salinger, the White House press secretary, insisted, "It was Mr. Anslinger's wish to retire."[19] The reaction of Dave Powers, one of Kennedy's top White House aides, was especially puzzling. In response to this writer's inquiry about the circumstances surrounding the association between the commissioner and the administration, Powers stated, "I was with John F. Kennedy from 1946 until that tragic day in Dallas, and I can recall no 'relationship between President Kennedy and Harry Anslinger.' "[20]

Whether Anslinger retired voluntarily or was forced out by the Kennedys remains unclear; however, there is no question that by 1962 it had become increasingly more difficult for him to endure growing criticism of his policies. The outspoken commissioner still enjoyed the support of those who shared his view that drug addiction was chiefly a problem of law enforcement and that stiff criminal sentences should be used to punish those involved in narcotics trafficking. But ranged against him were a number of highly respected members of the medical and legal professions who saw addiction primarily as a medical problem and who preferred more humane, enlightened methods of dealing with victims of narcotics abuse. Since the president maintained such a close alliance with the intellectual community and encouraged new ideas, Anslinger would not likely find defenders in the White House.

If Anslinger's reitrement was not a surprise, President Kennedy's choice for his successor was. During the summer months of 1962, while Anslinger remained as acting commissioner, most observers anticipated that Kennedy would fill the post with a physician or at least a person who did not approach the problem of illicit narcotics use with the viewpoint of a cop.[21] Instead of appointing someone outside the Bureau, however, President Kennedy named forty-eight-year-old Deputy Commissioner Henry L. Giordano, a veteran of twenty-one years in the bureau. Although Giordano, previously a pharmacist, had served as Anslinger's closest aide, often running the bureau during the chief's absences, he was regarded by Treasury officials as a more flexible executive. At least he appeared to be more willing than Anslinger to entertain new ideas. Giordano might have been more receptive to different thinking, but he stood with his former boss in believing that stiff prison sentences were the strongest deterrent to the illegal traffic in drugs.

Adherents of the medical approach who awaited an overhauling of existing policies in the Narcotics Bureau were tremendously disappointed. Philosophically the contrast between Giordano and his mentor was negligible. Shortly after his swearing in, the new head of narcotics pledged that he would make no changes in the bureau policies set by the retired Commissioner Harry J. Anslinger.[22] Giordano was faithful to his promise. During his six-year tenure, his most significant accomplishment was enlarging the bureau's training school. He supported no reform measures of any importance and continued to defend incredibly out-dated policies adopted by Anslinger thirty years earlier. As late as 1967, Giordano was still testifying before congressional committees that marijuana caused temporary psychoses, led to the use of heroin, and had dangerous effects on the user—long after scientific research had repeatedly and conclusively refuted these assertions.[23]

Giordano fumed at even the suggestion that the weed should be legalized and strongly condemned the movement to decriminalize it. If marijuana were legalized, he pondered, "What would be next?" To Giordano the legalization of marijuana was "just another effort to break down our whole American system." If the drug were to become widely available, the commissioner could only "imagine all of our youth spending the rest of their days high on marijuana, and I do not know what our society would come to if that were the case."[24] Frequently in contact with Anslinger during his retirement in Hollidaysburg, Giordano never deviated markedly from the ideological pattern established by his predecessor.[25]

Commissioner Giordano proved almost as effective at deflecting challenges to bureau policies as Anslinger. When the National Institute of Mental Health (NIMH), which was known to support theories opposite those of Giordano, wanted to conduct research on marijuana, it took months to obtain an occupational tax stamp to purchase the drug. NIMH officials complained that their applications kept getting lost at the bureau and that they were constantly asked why they wanted to experiment with marijuana.[26] Eventually NIMH was allocated a suitable amount of the drug for testing, but the criticisms within the government against the FBN continued to mount. In 1966 Dr. James Goddard, head of the Food and Drug Administration (FDA), which also housed the Bureau of Drug Abuse Control (BDAC), recommended that the bureau be abolished and its responsibilities transferred to the FDA. Goddard's reorganization plan received little consideration primarily because of his liberal views on the legalization of marijuana; thus he remained a vocal minority. By 1968, though, it was clear that the semi-independent Federal Bureau of Narcotics was on the brink of extinction.

Challenges from individuals in the academic and scientific disciplines, government agencies, and President Johnson's Commission on Law Enforcement and Administration of Justice, which all questioned the validity of the Marijuana Tax Act, overwhelmed the new commissioner. Anslinger's retirement, external pressures, ineffective enforcement policies, and a scandal of major proportions collectively contributed to the bureau's demise. Anslinger left the FBN just as it was to become mired in a miasma of diversionary issues and internal power struggles.

Two events occurring in early 1968 added to Giordano's problems and virtually doomed the bureau. The first was a Supreme Court decision in January that made it unconstitutional to require gamblers to buy a gambling stamp, thus incriminating themselves in violation of the Fifth Amendment. Other federal laws, including the Marijuana Tax Act, which required individuals to register for the purchase of the illegal weed, seemed likely to be declared invalid.[27] The second setback for Giordano was President Johnson's decision in February to dismantle the Bureau of Narcotics. By early 1968 the fate of the FBN was no longer open to debate. The only questions looming at that time had to do with how to carve up and redistribute its responsibilities.

Influenced by the recommendations of his Commission of Law Enforcement, which had just completed an extensive study of the entire federal government's drug enforcement effort, Johnson had become concerned about its lack of effectiveness "to stop the sale of slavery to the young," as he remarked in his 1968 State of the Union speech. Though the President's Commission did not make specific recommendations, Johnson submitted a reorganization plan to Congress on February 7 that would abolish the Bureau of Narcotics in the Department of Treasury, including the office of Commissioner of Narcotics. Unless Congress voted against the president's proposal within sixty days, the bureau's activities would be reassigned. On 8 April 1968, both the Bureau of Narcotics and the foundering Bureau of Drug Abuse Control (BDAC) were merged into a newly created federal agency, the Bureau of Narcotics and Dangerous Drugs (BNDD), in the Department of Justice. The agents of both bureaus were consolidated into what was to be a most inharmonious organization, since both former bureau chiefs jockeyed for power as subordinates under a new head in the BNDD who was directly responsible to Attorney General Ramsey Clark.[28]

Johnson's Reorganization Plan Number One, as it was officially known, appeared to be a move by the president to achieve greater efficiency. By placing narcotics enforcement in the Justice Department, investigative and prosecuting attorneys could coordinate their activities more expeditiously. However, some observers, felt that since the reorganization was rushed through in an election year, the move was politically motivated. Eugene Rossides, who was responsible for all law enforcement activities in the Treasury Department, believed that "Johnson's main reason for moving the Bureau [of Narcotics] from Treasury was to strengthen the crime-busting image of Ramsey Clark."[29]

Perhaps even more stressful for the bureau in the 1960s than a Supreme Court decision or bureaucratic reorganization was the internal bickering and clamoring for positions of power that followed immediately on the heels of Anslinger's retirement and continued until it was merged with BNDD in 1968. With Anslinger's resignation, the number one position in the Bureau of Narcotics was open for the first time since its inception in 1930. Despite the Commissioner's legacy, Giordano was unable to exert the tyrannical leadership over bureau personnel that Anslinger had. Consequently his vulnerability set the stage for a chaotic Machiavellian power struggle.

Following the new commissioner in descending order of authority was Wayland L. Speer, an outsider whose enforcement experience was with the Military Police during the American occupation of Japan; Charles Siragusa, who became deputy commissioner; and George Gaffney, the district supervisor of New York City, which was generally the stepping-stone to a higher administrative position in Washington.[30] Because Speer did not rise to his position from the ranks, his appointment elicited antagonism from field personnel and resentment from a handful of administrators at the top who felt that they had been unfairly passed over. In time Speer was set up by several agents, which resulted in administrative complaints and his eventual reassignment as the inspector west of the Mississippi River, in reality a form of banishment.

According to senior agent Thomas Tripodi, Giordano and Gaffney then joined forces to push Siragusa out, and he became the Director of the Illinois Crime Commission. The two surviving contestants subsequently went after each other like gladiators battling it out in an arena of politics and power. They filed civil service charges against one another, and Giordano won, but it was essentially a Pyrrhic victory since he was too weak to survive the massive reorganization that occurred in 1968.

To head the new narcotics agency, Attorney General Clark appointed John Ingersoll, who at thirty-nine possessed an extensive background in law enforcement. One of Ingersoll's first projects was to formally appraise the BNDD's capabilities in policy-making and particularly enforcement activities. In probing the records of the old Bureau of Narcotics, Ingersoll found an investigative agency abysmally weak in organizing information and lacking the techniques for detecting major channels of narcotics distribution in the United States. Occasionally, Ingersoll concluded, the Bureau's agents could make arrests that were good for headlines but were generally ineffective for enforcement. The other half of the merger, he discovered, was even worse. BDAC had fewer trained agents, almost no informants, and inadequate experience.[31] Though it was depressing for Ingersoll to realize deficiencies of the Narcotics Bureau, he had yet to uncover the most serious problem.

Historically New York City had always been a trouble spot for the honest and impartial enforcement of narcotics laws. Since Levi Nutt was charged with falsifying arrest reports in 1930 (a practice that has been repeated several times since), the New York district had experienced problems of corruption. In February 1968 an intensive investigation by four different agencies of the city's narcotics bureau resulted in the removal of the top three commanders of the police department. In what was the most dramatic shake-up in the world's largest narcotics enforcement agency (350 agents), the chief inspector and his two top assistants were transferred out of the department for selling narcotics to peddlers.[32]

In that same year John Ingersoll also learned that federal agents left over from the old Bureau of Narcotics were deeply involved in their own drug scandal. To root out the corrupt agents, Ingersoll assigned nine of his special inspectors to aid an investigation already under way by the Internal Revenue Service. In only a few weeks, the special team uncovered enough evidence to prove that several federal agents in the New York office were also selling heroin or protecting known drug dealers.[33] Furthermore, the bureau itself was actually the major source of supply and protector of heroin in the United States.[34]

Not only were narcotics agents selling heroin; many of them admitted to being "owned" by dealers in what Edward J. Epstein described as a "nefarious working relationship" between agents and traffickers. Obviously this arrangement realized tremendous profits, but the agents also maintained a constant number of arrests every year; which, of course, reflected on their record of performance. In a system where promotion and tenure largely depended on reaching a quota of arrests, pressure to perform was enhanced by the always existing temptation of illegal monetary gain. Without the cooperation of narcotics traffickers, meeting the quota was difficult. Since the selling of narcotics is a victimless crime, that is, no complainant notifies the police, both the buyer and the seller are willing participants in the offense.[35]

The partnership between agents and traffickers was mutually beneficial. The agents supplemented their income and met their monthly quota of arrests. The traffickers, usually dealers, needed the protection of the Narcotics Bureau to stay in operation. Eventually the agents found it more convenient and profitable simply to go into business with the heroin dealers.

The findings of this extensive investigation—in which nearly fifty agents were fired, transferred, or resigned—were compiled in what has been commonly referred to as the Wurms Report, which has not been released by the government.[36] Epstein claims the report that touched off the biggest shake-up in the bureau's history remains inaccessible in government files was named for Ivan Wurms, a federal narcotics investigator. Wurms was a participant, but the investigation was led by Andrew C. Tartaglino, who was in BNDD's internal security unit. Most of the narcotics agents involved in the investigation came from outside the New York office, including Special Agent Tom Tripodi who was the wireman. It is worth noting that Tripodi transferred to BNDD from the CIA where his specialty was counterintelligence.[37]

Harry Anslinger was no longer the dominant force at the Bureau of Narcotics after his retirement in 1962, but he remained active in current affairs as the United States representative on the Commission on Narcotic Drugs of the United Nations Economic and Social Council. In that capacity he continued to attend annual conferences on international narcotics control in Geneva and other European cities until he retired from the post in 1970. In 1969 he was appointed as an "expert at the various training schools operated by the Bureau of Narcotics and Dangerous Drugs."[38] His successor, Giordano, kept him informed of news from the Washington Bureau, and he followed the evolution of the FBN to the BNDD and finally the DEA in 1973 with great personal interest. With the exception of an occasional trip abroad, however, Anslinger spent his retirement years as a widower in his hometown of Hollidaysburg because, he reasoned, "I was born and raised here, these are good people, nice people to talk to in a pleasant town."[39] There he enjoyed a less active but more languid lifestyle as a member of a small town community—quite different from the frantic pace he maintained in Washington.

The commissioner was far removed from the seat of the federal government, but he was not forgotten by friends and neighbors who had followed his activities in the newspapers over the years. On 8 August 1962 his hometown observed Harry Anslinger Day in honor of its most famous citizen. In homage to the commissioner, the townspeople held a picnic at the American Legion Park followed by a testimonial. Several public officials joined in the tribute to Anslinger including Henry Giordano; Charles Siragusa; George Gaffney, Assistant Commissioner of Narcotics; Nicholas Katzenbach, Deputy U.S. Attorney General; Congressman J. Von Gary, a ranking member of the House Appropriations Committee; and Congressman Jimmy Van Zandt, a personal friend of Anslinger who represented his district. As a demonstration of the town's appreciation for "an outstanding record of achievement . . . skill, perseverance and ingenuity," the people presented him with a plaque which hangs as a permanent fixture on the wall in the main corridor of the Blair County Courthouse.[40]

Neither honors nor retirement, however, tempered Anslinger's outspokeness or influenced his views on the drug problem. In a 1968 interview, he continued to categorize marijuana as a deadly drug and castigated those people wanting to legalize the drug or at least reduce the criminal sanctions against it. "To legalize marijuana would be to legalize slaughter on the highway," he argued. When asked to justify the penalties for marijuana when alcohol, a legal drug, also contributed to traffic fatalities, Anslinger countered laconically with, "Why condone a second hazard?"[41]

In conjunction with the marijuana menace as a problem among young people, Anslinger put the blame squarely on "permissive parents, college administrators, pusillanimous judiciary officials, do-gooder bleeding hearts and new-breed sociologists with their fluid notions of morality." He also cautioned the American public to be on guard against drug addicts and dealers and an impending drug revolution which he believed was "nothing less than an assualt on the foundation of Western civilization."[42] For that reason he once claimed, "The only persons who frighten me are the hippies."[43]

Anslinger's last years brought ill health and gnawing anxieties. His Federal Bureau of Narcotics had been dismantled completely and absorbed with another agency. Worse, many of the agents implicated in the Wurms Report in 1968 had been hired while Anslinger was still commissioner. He could not have been personally responsible for their activities, but they reflected poorly on top-level administrators in the FBN. His private life was nearly as disconsolate. The slow, agonizing death of his wife who suffered heart failure less than a year before he left office exacted tremendous emotional and mental anguish. No doubt that personal trauma accounted for his ambivalence about retirement in 1962.

In Hollidaysburg he found time to take advantage of the surrounding woods to do some hunting. He also renewed old acquaintances and formed new friendships through his daily routine that consisted of a three-block walk downtown to pick up his mail at the post office and a stop at Lusardi's Luncheonette for a cup of coffee and idle conversation with other regular patrons. He often spent Monday nights at the Blairmont Country Club where a weekly stag night consisted of a leisurely game of poker with several friends he had maintained contact with since his youth. One of those closest to Anslinger, Abe Cobus of Altoona, who was also Anslinger's lawyer, remembered the commissioner as a "compassionate and generous man with a wonderful sense of humor."[44]

Harry Anslinger displayed a side of his personality in Hollidaysburg that few people outside the small town had an opportunity to know. In his official capacity, Anslinger was subjected to harsh criticism from his enemies, who were always more vocal than his allies. Among his detractors he was scorned and resented for his repressive enforcement policies. To the people who resided in the tranquil county seat of Hollidaysburg, a world far removed from Washington, Harry Anslinger counted many friends who delighted in his presence and conversation.

Anslinger's step-son, Joe, and daughter-in-law, Bea (who currently lives in Anslinger's house), were also in Hollidaysburg. But relations between them were always strained. Joe went to Dickinson College in Carlisle, Pennsylvania, but he did not graduate. Eventually, Anslinger used his influence to get Joe a position as a pharmaceutical salesman with the DuPont Chemical Company.

By 1973 Anslinger began to experience serious physical problems. He had become totally blind and suffered from an enlarged prostate gland that severely restricted his mobility. He was also plagued with angina for which he took morphine to dull the pain, an incredible irony for the man who devoted his adult life to the enforcement and control of such narcotics.[45] By the fall of 1975, his health had deteriorated rapidly, and after several days of prolonged discomfort, he was admitted to Hollidaysburg Mercy Hospital in early November. Under close medical supervision he was assured of good care and prompt attention, but the debilitation was irreversible. At approximately 1:00 on Friday afternoon, 14 November 1975, the eighty-three-year-old commissioner succumbed to heart failure. At his request the funeral at the Hollidaysburg Presbyterian church was closed to the public.[46]

Epilogue

From 1930, when he was appointed Commissioner of the Federal Bureau of Narcotics, to his death in 1975, Harry Anslinger was credited with oppressive anti-marijuana laws based on his activities in the 1930s and his international participation against narcotics trafficking in the United States. That he played a major role in shaping American drug enforcement policies is beyond dispute. But Anslinger was a multidimensional figure whose peripheral activities have been skimmed over or totally neglected by recent authors who have limited their studies to him as Commissioner of the Federal Bureau of Narcotics.

Anslinger must not be misunderstood or misinterpreted. His policies were oppressive and overly simplistic. He was tyrannical and inflexible; even though longer prison sentences failed to deter traffickers or reduce addiction rates, he steadfastly refused to consider alternative approaches to solving a growing problem. His insistence on severe penalties, lack of empathy for addicts, and faulty conception of drug enforcement likely prevented the government from dealing more effectively with drug abuse.

However, Anslinger was a more complex individual with a talent for bureaucratic survival whose interests were not limited to narcotics legislation. He could not and did not function independently. Throughout his three decades as commissioner, he not only established working relationships with other federal agencies, but was instrumental in forging associations with international organizations such as INTERPOL. The bureau's involvement in the CIA's MK-ULTRA project, as odious as it was, and his relentless pursuit of world-wide narcotics smugglers exemplify Anslinger's extracurricular activities, usually overshadowed by the Marijuana Tax Act and other drug-related controversies.

In his study of deviancy titled *Outsiders,* sociologist Howard S. Becker argued that Anslinger adhered to what the author called his model of "moral entrepeneurship" that theorized that the Marijuana Tax Act was passed in 1937, not because there was a need or demand for it, but because Anslinger wanted it to justify the bureau's existence.[1] A reassessment of this thesis, however, would show that Anslinger did support the legislation but that Becker overstated the commissioner's ability to exploit the marijuana scare by manipulating the public through the media. To do so it would have been necessary for Anslinger to enlist newspapers with huge circulations such as the Hearst chain to undertake a nationwide campaign. Nor was it necessary for him to feed bizarre marijuana-related tales of lurid and perverse behavior to the weekly magazines. Many of the publications were tabloids that relished sensational stories about the Chinaman seducing opium-addicted white women into prostitution rings, the pusher sentenced to a hard prison term in San Francisco, or a man gone berserk killing two people in Baltimore. These headlines sold copies, and publishers welcomed them, thriving on this kind of story as did their readers. Anslinger furnished bureau episodes of the agents' derring-do to the media during the period 1935–1937, and he unequivocally supported federal legislation—at this point he had established himself as the "narcotics czar"—but he only fueled the marijuana myth; he did not ignite it.

Notwithstanding Roosevelt's proclamation that the narcotics commissioner should not be a political appointee, Anslinger's position was tenuous in the early years of his career. His bureaucratic instinct for self-preservation was hardly unprecedented. As John F. Galliher and Allynn Walker have pointed out, Anslinger "promised no budget increase and indicated an unwillingness to allow his agents to spend great amounts on marijuana cases."[2] Throughout his career, he consistently requested only moderate increases in appropriations, once commenting, "We have enough funds and men."[3] Nor was Anslinger an expansionist. At no time during his three decades as Narcotics Commissioner did the Bureau ever have a force exceeding four hundred agents or a budget greater than $4 million. Clearly these were characteristics of a bureaucrat, not an empire-builder in the traditional sense who sought huge appropriations to employ thousands of agents.

Anslinger responded to congressmen because it was politically prudent; 1936 was an election year, and Southwestern politicians wanted some action against the marijuana problem. In 1937 Anslinger acted as an efficient and competent bureaucrat. By supporting the Marijuana Tax Act, he was protecting his and the bureau's interests as any resourceful bureaucrat would under similar circumstances. He also supported legislation that would outlaw what he and other trained professionals—physicians, botanists, chemists, and jurists—perceived to be a threatening and dangerous drug.

But in a different context, Anslinger greatly expanded the Narcotics Bueau's powers well beyond its official responsibilities. At least since the end of World War II, when Anslinger propagandized and greatly exaggerated the threat of a communist invasion of narcotics in the same style that he capitalized and promoted the marijuana scare in the 1930s, the FBN was involved in numerous sensitive operations shrouded in secrecy. When the bureau began to branch out into so many diverse activities—tracking mobsters, moving into Cuba in the early 1960s, and collaborating with the CIA in drug experiments—an empire of a different sort was being established. In the process of expanding his domain Anslinger was not above resorting to such tactics as entrapment, legal harassment, threatening suspects with indictments, and generally intimidating those who opposed bureau policies (Alfred Lindesmith of the University of Indiana and Circuit Attorney Thomas Eagleton in Missouri, for example).

As a preservationist, Anslinger manipulated annual addiction figures (higher reates to show that there was a problem and thereby a need for the bureau, or lower rates to demonstrate its effectiveness), distorted the problem of drug use among the juvenile population, and advanced unproven links between drugs (especially marijuana) and crime. As a figure of both national homage and controversy, he gained passionate support from those who viewed his advocacy of repressive sanctions as a deterrent. They saw him as a dedicated opponent of the insidious drug traffic that threatened to weaken the character of the American people. His ardent belief in strong legislation and vigorous enforcement won their approval, as did his opposition to people they considered to be high-minded theorists and bleeding-heart humanitarians who advocated leniency and rehabilitation for drug users.

His opponents bitterly criticized him as tyrannical and ineffective, denouncing him as a vengeful persecutor of hapless addicts who stubbornly ignored enlightened medical and psychological approaches to treating those who had become enslaved by drug addiction. An extensive examination of his papers clearly reveals that at least in the 1930s Anslinger actually believed that marijuana was a "killer weed" and that the United States was vulnerable in the Cold War era to an invasion of communists armed with narcotics. Still, the commissioner was not above capitalizing on opportunities by which he could advance himself in the media or in the eyes of Washington politicians whose support was vital to his existence. Anslinger was quite willing to exploit these fears to enhance his performance and public image. To silence his critics, or at least neutralize them, he cultivated the media, manipulated citizen groups who opposed narcotics, and maintained strong ties with Congress, in particular those who held positions on House Appropriations Committee. He also allied himself with state and local law-enforcement officials whom he relied on to disseminate his pronouncements on narcotics-related issues.[4]

Anslinger and his agents exerted considerable influence on drug enforcement as public policy.[5] In the 1930s, the FBN promoted a marijuana scare that resulted in federal legislation which created a new class of criminals and opened the door for later narcotics laws that were more severe and less effective. That was a pre-determined and coordinated bureaucratic campaign involving Treasury Department officials at the highest level.

Investigation procedures and reporting techniques by the bureau's field agents could also affect the public's perception of the narcotics problem. One example occurred in the 1950s when Vice President Alben Barkley pressured the FBN to clean up the drug problem in Memphis. Unconvinced that there was a problem in that city, the district supervisor responsible for making Memphis drug-free imported drugs from New Orleans and had his agents make buys until it appeared that what was perceived as a problem was under control.

As commissioner, Harry Anslinger was the dominant figure in shaping federal narcotics legislation for the thirty-two years he headed the Federal Bureau of Narcotics. He endured attempts to merge and reorganize the FBN with other enforcement agencies in the Treasury Department and survived repeated efforts by vexed detractors to oust him from office. Though volatile international relations, domestic politics, economic conditions, and public opinion had at varying times adversely affected his anti-drug policies, Anslinger not only remained in power but continually broadened his sphere of influence and affirmed his autonomy.

Harry Anslinger will, of course, be most remembered as the nation's primary force in formulating federal drug laws. But because of the nature of his agents' clandestine activities, Anslinger's bureau established an international network of intelligence gathering that stretched around the world—a veritable prototype for the American intelligence community. Often the information amassed by bureau agents in these strategic locations was beneficial to other American interests, and there is little doubt that Anslinger relayed valuable intelligence to Presidents Truman, Eisenhower, and Kennedy.[6]

His determination to disrupt the apparatus of international criminal conspiracies required bureau agents to thwart smuggling rings from remote field offices in Asian, Middle Eastern, European, and Latin American countries—global hot spots where "Anslinger's army" worked undercover to break up the web of distribution points of opium, heroin, cocaine, and marijuana. These strategic locations were also vital to American interests during the Cold War era that developed in the aftermath of World War II and continued through the early 1960s.

In particular the activities and abstruse roles of Agents Charles Siragusa and George White, who also worked for the Central Intelligence Agency, clearly indicate that the Narcotics Bureau was involved in more than the enforcement of drug laws. Unfortunately, the records pertaining to sensitive intelligence operations are not easily accessible; however, the FBN's functioning as a nonpolitical guise for highly sensitive CIA-related activities becomes obvious when recalling White's close association with the CIA and Siragusa's appearance in Cuba in 1959, for example.

The assertion that Anslinger and his agents were involved in postwar foreign policy missions is not unprecedented.[7] Anslinger was a surprisingly powerful figure who collected and leaked confidential information to his own bureaucratic advantage. Usually, Anslinger and his drug policies are the focal point of such studies, but in concentrating on narcotics legislation, bureau agents have been almost totally ignored. George White and Charles Siragusa, who have been most widely discussed are not unknown to scholars who have investigated the FBN, OSS, or CIA. Perhaps the key, unsung member of the triumvirate, though, was Garland Williams who brought to the bureau in its formative years administrative acumen and a penchant for developing competent investigative techniques. Along with Malachi Harney (formerly Eliot Ness's boss) and Alfred L. Tennyson, who were the bureau's legal and policy experts, Williams' skills were instrumental in training agents in fundamental investigative techniques. Anslinger could not have claimed accomplishments either in narcotics enforcement or outside intelligence work without the former prohibition agent. Williams also brought White into the bureau and later into the OSS, along with Siragusa and Hank Manfredi, where they gained valuable experience on the international level. Williams implemented policies and trained intelligence personnel, White chased Japanese spies in India, Siragusa and Manfredi aided the Allied cause in Italy, which is why when Anslinger opened the bureau's first permanent foreign office in 1950, he sent Siragusa to Rome. To place Harry Anslinger and the Federal Bureau of Narcotics in their proper context, the versatility of his agents must be recognized.

Historically the Bureau of Narcotics has existed as a comparatively little known and unsung agency in federal law enforcement. The American public easily identifies the Internal Revenue Service and Secret Service; people commonly associate Customs with huge drug busts; and the FBI, the Bureau's closest rival, has always enjoyed greater publicity.[8] Yet with a fraction of the agents, the FBN has been consistently responsible for more arrests.[9] In its assault on organized crime, the Narcotics Bureau has been especially effective (regardless of Anslinger's views about a national commission) in apprehending high-level leaders, as demonstrated during the McClellan hearings in 1963 when a list of eighty-four organized crime arrests was published, including Saul Gelb, Vito Genovese, John Ormento, Nig Rosen, and Joe Valachi.[10]

Why the Bureau has existed in relative obscurity has as much to do with the personality of Anslinger as it does with the kind of work mandated in the Porter bill that created it in 1930. First, Anslinger's intelligence background began early in his career in covert operations when he worked for the State Department in Europe and developed an appreciation for being able to function secretly. Anslinger was never concerned that the FBN was not getting the same degree of publicity as the FBI; on the contrary, he felt quite comfortable with his small agency tucked away in Washington. This made perfect sense: the smaller the number of personnel, the easier it was to exert control, especially when considering how extensively the bureau was involved in outside intelligence activities.

The second reason for the bureau's non-glamorous image has to do with the nature of the work it performs. Making an arrest for selling narcotics usually requires the use of an informant, who may or may not be furnishing reliable information; long hours of surveillance; and often times undercover work, which according to one agent is perceived as being only one step above that of an informant. Almost without exception, cultivation of the informant, the surveillance, and the actual arrest occur in seedy bars or inner city slum areas, and because until recently drug use had been predominantly a ghetto problem, the FBI has been reluctant to get involved in drug enforcement.[11]

No other federal law enforcement agency has an area of jurisdiction as vast as the Narcotics Bureau. Customs agents work abroad and patrol national border points, the Secret Service conducts investigations throughout the United States and travels to other countries to accompany an official political entourage, and the IRS and FBI are primarily domestic agencies. But by contrast, narcotics agents operate in all fifty states and forty-one countries.[12] This immense network creates innumerable opportunities for intelligence gathering that can be conducted less conspicuously by narcotics agents than by CIA operatives, for example.[13] It is and has been possible for these agents to enforce domestic or international narcotics legislation without becoming involved as protectors of national interests.

For forty years very little happened in the world of drugs or foreign affairs that Anslinger did not know about. At times it appeared that Anslinger was virtually omnipresent. Whether chasing Mafiosi across Europe, condemning communist aggession in testimony at congressional hearings, or coordinating a nationwide bust of pushers and peddlers, he always took an active role above and beyond bureau affairs. His policies may have been controversial, and to many unpopular, but he made a distinct, indelible impression on the history of federal narcotics legislation.

Notes

Introduction

1. See particularly an in-depth discussion of Anslinger's testimony before House Appropriations Committees in chap. 8 of Richard B. Fenno's *The Power of the Purse: Appropriations Politics in Congress* (Boston: Little, Brown, and Company, 1966), 350–413.

2. U.S. Department of Treasury, *Traffic in Opium and Other Dangerous Drugs For the Year Ended December 31, 1932* (Washington, D.C.: Government Printing Office, 1933), 44.

3. Martin A. Lee and Bruce Shlain, *Acid Dreams: The CIA, LSD and the Sixties Rebellion* (New York: Grove Press, Inc., 1985), 246.

4. The Anslinger collection is currently held by the Special Collections Department of Pattee Library at The Pennsylvania State University. Initially Anslinger offered only his published papers to the University, but in 1959, after he was made an honorary alumnus, he donated his private correspondence. The documents were received in shipments and sorted topically and chronologically. There are no restrictions on the use of the papers, and researchers are permitted to quote freely. Hereafter Anslinger Papers are referred to as AP.

5. Howard S. Becker, *Outsiders: Studies in the Sociology of Deviance* (New York: The Free Press, 1963), 147–63.

6. Joseph R. Gusfield, *Symbolic Crusade: Status Politics and The American Temperance Movement* (Urbana: University of Illinois Press, 1972), 7.

7. Undated narcotics speech, AP, box 1, file "Speeches by Harry Anslinger (undated)."

8. Edwin Meese in a speech before the Knights of Columbus in Washington, D.C. *New York Times,* 8 August 1985. 6.

9. "A Real All-Out War on Drugs," *Family Weekly,* 25 August 1985, 14.

10. Remarks of Gordon C. Canfield, 8 July 1950, *Congressional Record,* 81st Cong., 2d sess., 96: A1521.

11. Remarks of John J. Cochran, 10 February 1943, *Congressional Record,* 78th Cong., 1st sess., 89: A523.

12. Letter from Ralph Hayes to R. W. Woodruff, 4 December 1952. AP, box 2, file "Correspondence 1952."

13. Paul H. Douglas, "Help Wanted in Washington," *American Magazine* 152 (July 1951): 127.

14. Sensational or tabloid magazines like *True Detective Story, Official Detective* ("Lucky Luciano's Own Story"), *True, True Crime, Actual Romance* ("I Joined A Teen-age Sex and Dope Gang"), *Woman's Home Companion* ("How That 'Nice Girl Next Door' Became A Dope Addict"), all of which are contained in Anslinger's archives, were quick to exploit and exaggerate drug busts, addiction in

school yards, or underworld trafficking. Dozens of scandal sheet articles are contained in box 12 of Anslinger papers.

15. Letter from Ralph Hayes to R. W. Woodruff, undated, AP, box 2, file "Correspondence 1954–1956."

16. Larry Sloman, *Reefer Madness: Marijuana in America* (New York: Grove Press, Inc. 1979), 245.

17. Reverend John Martin, interview with author, Hollidaysburg, Pennsylvania, 23 January 1985.

18. Clarification of a few technical errors in *Reefer Madness* should be noted. Granted they are minor and do not detract seriously from the narrative, but it is annoying to see "Julietta" College rather than Juniata located in "Huntington" not Huntingdon (page 246). Sloman also writes on page 31 that Anslinger was of "sturdy Dutch parentage." Perhaps Sloman assumed that because Anslinger was fluent in Dutch and German that the family resided in Holland. According to an anonymous interviewee who knew the commissioner intimately, Anslinger's father, Robert, brought his family to the United States from Switzerland in 1881. Also see Harry J. Anslinger's Official Personnel File, United States Office of Personnel Management, Philadelphia, hereafter referred to as Anslinger OPM File.

Chapter 1. Getting Started: From Consul to Commissioner, 1915–1930

1. His father, Robert J. Anslinger, was born in Bern, Switzerland, and his mother, formerly Rosa Christiana Fladt, was born in Baden, Germany. Documents in Anslinger's OPM File. Interestingly, Anslinger indicated his ethnicity on a Data Card he completed for the civil service as "Franco-Swiss." Anslinger OPM File.

2. The story of Robert Anslinger's decision to leave Switzerland and Harry's early years is taken from two sources, a retirement notice appearing in the *Altoona Mirror,* 30 November 1926, and an interview by the author with a close acquaintance of Anslinger, Hollidaysburg, 13 January 1985, who requested anonymity. According to the acquaintance, Harry related to her with reasonable certainty that his father did not want to get involved with the Swiss army. It is also probable that he had a wealthy grandmother in Switzerland who operated a tobacco monopoly. Robert Anslinger, however, came to America a poor man and remained a man of moderate means throughout his life.

3. Education and employment information pertaining to Anslinger's early years (1892–1917) is taken from a résumé he composed for application in the federal civil service. See AP, box 1, file "Counsel for the Traveler in Europe." From 1919 to 1921 he studied at the School of International Relations at the Hague. In 1930 he received an L.L.B. from Washington College of Law, currently part of American University in Washington, D.C. Documents in Anslinger OPM File. Curiously, Anslinger also listed on some of his résumés that he earned an L.L.D. from the University of Maryland Law School. However, an extensive check by the registrar of that institution's records failed to produce any evidence that Anslinger was ever enrolled there, or that he was conferred with an honorary degree.

4. Application for employment, 2 May 1918, Anslinger OPM File.

5. "Native Altoonan Handles Big Job Combatting Dope," *Altoona Mirror* 26 June 1939. Also found in AP, box 5, file "Scrapbook 1-B, 1930–1944."

6. Harry J. Anslinger and Will Oursler, *The Murderers: The Story of the Narcotics Gangs* (New York: Farrar, Straus and Cudahy, 1960), 8.

7. Anslinger, *The Murderers,* 9–10. For a more recent scholarly study of the

Black Hand, *see* Humbert S. Nelli, *The Business of Crime: Italians and Syndicate Crime in the United States* (Chicago: University of Chicago Press, 1976), 70–100.

8. Additional information pertaining to Anslinger's account of the Black Hand was related to the writer by the aforementioned Hollidaysburg acquaintance. There is considerable controversy over the existence of the Black Hand and its connection with the Mafia, if any. For example, Burton B. Turkus and Sid Feder, in *Murder, Inc.* (Garden City, New York: Permabooks, 1952), 87–8, are critical of the Kefauver Committee for referring to Mafia, Black Hand, and Unione Sciliano, as one and the same organization. Frederick Sondern, however, in *Brotherhood of Evil* (New York: Bantam Books, 1960), 3, holds that in reality the Black Hand did not even exist as a society of any kind. For an excellent historiographic study of syndicate crime and its origins, see chap. 1, "Syndicate Crime: A Prelude to Its Conceptualization" in Joseph L. Albini's *The American Mafia: Genesis of A Legend* (New York: Irvington Publisher Inc., 1979), 1–17; and chap. 1, "Myth and Reality," in Alan Block's *East Side-West Side: Organizing Crime in New York, 1930–1950* (Swansea, Wales: University College Cardiff Press, 1980).

9. Anslinger, *The Murderers,* 10.

10. AP, box 1, file "Counsel For the Traveler in Europe."

11. When he was seventeen, "Inky" Anslinger was involved in horseplay with several friends one summer afternoon when he was accidentally struck in the left eye by a thrown pear. He suffered a detached retina and never regained sight in that eye. Consequently, he was not considered to be physically fit by Army doctors examining prospective inductees. Interview with anonymous source.

12. Letter from Captain Erskine Barins to Major L. H. Van Dusen, 8 May 1918, AP, box 3, file "Correspondence 1921." The high salary offered to Anslinger by ACF was $3,500. Memo from Major L. H. Van Deusen to Captain James Moffitt, 3 May 1918, Anslinger OPM File.

13. Anslinger, *The Murderers,* p. 13.

14. Order from Secretary of State Robert Lansing to Harry J. Anslinger, AP, box 3, file "Correspondence 1921."

15. In *The Murderers,* 14–16, and in numerous pieces of correspondence in his papers, Anslinger tells how he obtained the field utility kit and "certain other minor personal possessions of His Imperial Highness, Kaiser Wilhelm II." Throughout his life, though, he would not divulge how it happened, stating only that it "must remain a state secret."

16. Letter from the Director of the Consular Service (unsigned) to Harry J. Anslinger, 24 August 1921. In November 1921 Anslinger was appointed "Vice Counsul de carriere of Class Three," Anslinger OPM file.

17. He also supervised all activities relative to the extension of American trade, American shipping, immigration, and "other matters of importance to the United States government." "Statement of Training and Experience of Harry J. Anslinger, AP, box 3, file "Correspondence 1929."

18. Letter from Arvardo Chaves to Harry Anslinger, AP, box 3, file "Correspondence 1923."

19. "Obituary of Martha Anslinger," *Altoona Mirror,* 10 September 1961. The Anslingers' only child, Joseph, was born in 1911 to Martha Anslinger during a previous marriage. Though Harry never adopted him as his legal son, Joseph Leet took the Anslinger name for the benefit of political connections. It seems Anslinger resisted adoption because of personality conflicts with his wife's son.

20. Letter from William Reills to Harry Anslinger, 25 January 1924. AP, box 3, file "Correspondence 1924."

21. Letter to Franklin M. Gunther, Department of State, 2 May 1924, AP, box 3, file "Correspondence 1924."

22. Letter to Charles B. Dyar, American Vice-Consul, Hamburg, 10 June 1924, AP, box 3, file "Correspondence 1924."

23. Letter to B. S. Rairden, 30 June 1924, AP, box 3, file "Correspondence 1924."

24. Secretary of Treasury Andrew Mellon asked Secretary of State that Anslinger be "detailed to the Treasury Department for a temporary period commencing July 3, 1926, in order that he might accompany Hon. L. C. Andrews, Assistant Secretary of the Treasury in charge of Customs, Coast Guard, and Prohibition, to England." Letter to Secretary of State from A. W. Mellon, 6 July 1926, AP, box 3, file "Correspondence 1926."

25. Laurence F. Schmeckbier, *The Bureau of Prohibition: Its History, Activities, and Organization* (Washington, DC: The Brookings Institution, 1979), 26.

26. "Prize Committee on the Eighteenth Amendment," 19 November 1928, AP, box 3, file "Correspondence 1928."

27. An Act of 9 February 1909 limited the importation of opium to medicinal use only but contained no enforcement measures. For a more comprehensive account of federal drug legislation in this period as it related to international affairs, see Arnold H. Taylor's *American Diplomacy and the Narcotics Traffic, 1900–1939* (Durham, N.C.: Duke University Press, 1969).

28. See chap. 3, "That Harrison Act," in David Musto's *The American Disease* and Rufus King's "The Narcotics Bureau and the Harrison Act: Jailing the Healers and the Sick," *Yale Law Journal* 62 (April 1953): 736–49 for discussions of circumstances surrounding the passage of the act and ensuing controversy.

29. Earlier Supreme Court cases involving the Harrison Act include *Jin Fuey Moy* (1916), *U.S. v. Doremus* (1918), *Webb, et al.* (1918), and *Linder v. U.S.* (1928).

30. Musto, *The American Disease,* 135. Secretary of the Treasury William McAdoo appointed a special committee in March 1918 to study the future of narcotics enforcement. Committee members were Democratic Congressman Henry T. Rainey of Illinois; Dr. Reid Hunt, professor of pharmacology at Harvard; B. C. Keith, deputy commissioner of the Internal Revenue Bureau; and A. G. DuMez, of the Public Health Service.

31. Musto, *The American Disease,* 135. Wayne B. Wheeler, general counsel for the Anti-Saloon League, also criticized the Prohibition Bureau because "under the present system, prohibition agents are chosen in most places because of their political qualifications rather than their fitness for the position. Schmeckbier, *Bureau,* 47.

32. Schmeckbier, *Bureau,* 53.

33. Schmeckbier, *Bureau,* 52.

34. *Establishment of Two Federal Narcotics Farms, Hearings before the Committee on the Judiciary on H.R. 12781,* 70th Cong., 1st sess., 1928, 12.

35. *Establishment of Two Federal Narcotics Farms, Hearings,* 12.

36. *Establishment of Two Federal Narcotics Farms, Hearings,* 12–13.

37. *Establishment of Two Federal Narcotics Farms, Hearings,* 45.

38. *Establishment of Two Federal Narcotics Farms, Hearings,* 48.

39. "Work to Begin Saturday on First Narcotic Farm," *Washington Herald,* 27 July 1933, AP, box 8, file 16 "Addiction"; John F. Landis, "U.S. Narcotic Farm," *Federal Probation* 1 (April 1937): 25.

40. *Bureau of Narcotics Hearings before the Committee on Ways and Means on H.R. 10561,* 71st Cong., 2d sess., 1930, 3–6.

41. *Bureau of Narcotics, Hearings*, 19.

42. *Bureau of Narcotics, Hearings*, 31.

43. *Bureau of Narcotics, Hearings*, 32.

44. Congressman Porter introducing H.R. 9054, 23 January 1930, *Congressional Record*, 71st Cong., 2d sess., 72:1784.

45. Congressman Porter introducing H.R. 11143, 26 March 1930, *Congressional Record*, 71st Cong., 2nd sess., 72:4892.

46. Senator Royal S. Copeland's remarks on H.R. 11143, 22 April 1930, *Congressional Record*, 71st Cong., 2nd sess., 72:7392.

47. *Congressional Record* 72:7292–93.

48. "Narcotics Official Suspected Addict," undated; "Nutt Out As Head of Narcotic Unit," 28 February 1930; and "Agents Who Aided Nutt Quiz Shifted," all *New York World*, AP, box 6, file "Scrapbook 6-B, March–December 1930."

49. *Bureau of Narcotics, Hearings*, 73–77; and Stanley Meisler, "Federal Narcotics Czar," *Nation* 190 (January–June 1960): 160.

50. Leo Katcher, *The Big Bankroll: The Life and Times of Arnold Rothstein* (New York: Harper & Brothers, 1958), 290–99.

51. *Bureau of Narcotics, Hearings*, pp. 75–77.

52. Letter from Secretary of the Treasury A. W. Mellon to Harry J. Anslinger, 1 July 1930, Anslinger OPM File.

53. "Urge Altoonan as Narcotics Chief," *Altoona Mirror*, 8 May 1930.

54. Letter to Harry J. Anslinger from A. R. Royner, 19 June 1930, AP, box 3, file "Correspondence 1930."

55. Letter to President Hoover from Sanborn Young, 6 July 1930, in Herbert Hoover Presidential Library, box 416; and 11 July 1930, AP, box 3, file "Correspondence 1930."

56. Letter to Anslinger from H. H. W., 4 September 1930, AP, Box 3, File "Correspondence 1930." This was the same Bill Donovan Anslinger had corresponded with since the early 1920s and who would later be appointed by President Roosevelt to organize American intelligence during World War II.

57. Letter to Anslinger from Harry Smith, 8 September 1930, AP, box 3, file "Correspondence 1930."

58. Letter to Anslinger from Harry Smith, 30 September 1930, AP,a box 3, file "Correspondence 1930."

59. The discussion of candidates for Commissioner of Narcotics is taken from the *Altoona Mirror;* Herbert Hoover Library, boxes 54A and 416; AP, box 3, file "Correspondence 1930"; and H. Wayne Morgan, *Drugs in America: A Social History, 1800–1980* (Syracuse, NY: Syracuse University Press, 1981), 122–24.

60. "President Announces Two Appointments," White House press release, 24 September 1930, Herbert Hoover Presidential Library, box 54A.

61. Remarks of Congressman Fiorello H. LaGuardia, 5 December 1930, *Congressional Record*, 71st Cong. 3d sess., 74:274.

62. "Senate Confirms Harry Anslinger," *Altoona Mirror*, 20 December 1930; Senator Royal S. Copeland on the confirmation of Harry J. Anslinger, 18 December 1930, *Congressional Record*, 71st Cong., 3rd sess., 74:1043.

Chapter 2. Anslinger at the Helm, 1930–1937

1. Department of Treasury, *Annual Report of the Commissioner of Narcotics For the Fiscal Year Ended June 30, 1931* (Washington, D.C.: Government Printing Office, 1932), 9–11.

2. "Narcotic Agent Lectures Here," from *The Dickinsonian*, 15 December 1932, AP, box 6, file "Scrapbook 11-B, March 1930–December 1933."

3. James Sterba, "The Politics of Pot," *Esquire,* August 1968, 59.

4. A. E. Fossier, "The Marihuana Menace," *New Orleans Medical and Surgical Journal* 84 (1931): 247. Several versions of the Assassin myth are found throughout the Anslinger collection, and Sloman, *Reefer Madness,* 41–42.

5. Eugene Stanley, "Marihuana As A Developer of Criminals," *American Journal of Police Science* 2 (1931): 256; and Dan Wakefield, "The Prodigal Powers of Pot," *Playboy,* August 1967, 58.

6. "Use of New Narcotics Reported Spreading," March 1931, AP, box 6, file "Scrapbook 9-B, January-December 1931."

7. Untitled correspondence, AP, box 3, file "Correspondence 1936."

8. The title of the Harry J. Anslinger and Courtney Riley Cooper article, "Marihuana: Assassin of Youth," *American Magazine,* July 1937, 18–19, 150–53, was taken from *Assassin of Youth,* a low-budget movie produced in the 1930s. See also Wayne Gard, "Youth Gone Loco," *Christian Century,* June 1938, 812–13; Henry G. Leach, "One More Peril For Youth," *Forum,* January 1939, 1–2; and "Danger," *Survey,* April 1938, 221.

9. William Wolf, "Uncle Sam Fights A New Drug Menace . . . Marihuana," *Popular Science Monthly,* May 1936, 119.

10. Speech made at the Women's National Exposition of Arts and Industry, March 1935, AP, box 1, file "Speeches by Harry Anslinger, 1930–1938."

11. *Treasury Department Appropriations Bill For 1936, before a subcommittee of the House Committee on Appropriations,* 74th Cong., 1st sess., 1934, 210.

12. "Marihuana Reports 1926–1948," AP, box 9, file 41.

13. "Arrests and Convictions," AP, box 8, file 10.

14. Letter to Anslinger from Floyd Baskette, 4 September 1936, AP, box 6, file "Clippings 1934–1939."

15. Wooster Taylor, "Economy Cut Ties Hands of 'Dope' Agents," *Washington Herald,* 7 November 1933, AP, box 1, file "Articles on Narcotics 1930–1937."

16. Summary of Victor Licata case, 17 October 1933, AP, box 5, file "Scrapbook, vol. 7, 1931–1949."

17. Department of Treasury, *Traffic in Opium and Other Dangerous Drugs For the Year Ended December 31, 1931* (Washington D.C.: Government Printing Office, 1932).

18. Richard J. Bonnie and Charles Whitebread II, *The Marihuana Conviction: A History of Marijuana Prohibition in the United States* (Charlottesville: University Press of Virginia, 1974) 97.

19. Treasury, *Traffic in Opium,* 13.

20. *Uniform Narcotic Drug Act Drafted by the National Conference of Commissioners on Uniform State Laws, 4–12 October 1932.* (Washington D.C.: Government Printing Office, 1933), 9.

21. "Memorandum for Acting Assistant Secretary," 6 April 1933, AP, box 3 file "Correspondence 1930."

22. "Memorandum for Acting Assistant Secretary."

23. *Treasury Department Appropriations Bill for 1936,* 211.

24. "Uniform Dope Laws Is Plea of Roosevelt," *Washington Herald,* 22 March 1935, AP, box 5, file "Scrapbook 3-B, 1935–1937."

25. Speech to the World Narcotics Defense Association, 13 April 1936, AP, box 1, file "Speeches by Harry Anslinger, 1930–1938."

26. Speech to the World Narcotics Defense Association.

27. Senator Carl Hatch introducing S. 1615, 4 February 1935, *Congressional Record* 74th Cong., 1st sess., 79:1419; Representative John Dempsey introducing H.R. 6145, 25 February 1935, *Congressional Record,* 74th Cong., 1st sess., 79:2600.

28. Committee on Immigration, *Deportation of Aliens Convicted of A Violation*

of Narcotic Law, Hearings, Senate, on H.R. 3394, 71st Cong., 3d sess., 1931, 1–2.

29. Representative William H. Stafford speaking on H.R. 3394, 2 July 1930, *Congressional Record,* 71st Cong., 1st sess., 74:12367.

30. Representative Stafford speaking on H.R. 3394.

31. Pascall Brotteaux, "Hashish—Weed of Folly and Dream," AP, box 9, file 12.

32. Brotteaux, "Hashish."

33. Letter from Michael V. Ball, M.D., to Will S. Wood, 7 October 1936, AP, box 9, file 17, "Marihuana."

34. Letter from Harry J. Anslinger to Dr. Michael V. Ball, 18 October 1936, AP, box 9, file 17, "Marihuana."

35. "Undue Alarm About Narcotics," *New York Sun,* 23 February 1932; AP, box 6, file 8, "Clippings, 1924–1933."

Chapter 3. The Second Prohibition: Outlawing Marijuana, 1933–1937

1. Leslie Dowell, "U.S. Narcotic Law Enforcement Breaking Down From Lack of Funds," *Washington Herald,* 4 November 1933, AP, box 6, file "Scrapbook 6-B, September–December 1933."

2. *Treasury Department Appropriation Bill for 1936,* Hearings before the subcommittee of House Committee on Appropriations, 74th Cong., 1st sess., 1934, 206; "Memorandum for Louis B. Howe," from Louis B. Ruppel, 27 November 1933, Franklin D. Roosevelt Presidential Library, box 19, file OF 21-X.

3. *Treasury Department Appropriation Bill for 1936,* 216–17.

4. *Treasury Department Appropriation Bill for 1936,* 217–18.

5. Letter from Senator William McAdoo to President Roosevelt, 27 October 1933, Franklin D. Roosevelt Presidential Library, box 79, file OF 21-X.

6. "Memorandum For Assistant Secretary Gibbons," 5 February 1936, AP, box 3, file "Correspondence 1936."

7. "Memorandum for Assistant Secretary Gibbons."

8. Senator Carl Hatch introducing S. 325, 6 January 1937; Representative Fish introducing H.R. 229, 5 January 1937; and Representative Thomas C. Hennings introducing H.R. 3873, 28 January 1937, *Congressional Record* 75th Cong., 1st sess., 81:70, 29, 541.

9. "Conference on 'Cannabis Sativa,'" 14 January 1937, AP, box 6, file "Clippings 1934–1939."

10. Representative Robert L. Doughton introducing H.R. 6385, 14 April 1937, *Congressional Record,* 75th Cong., 1st sess., 81:8545.

11. Committee on Ways and Means, *Taxation of Marihuana, Hearings,* House of Representatives, on H.R. 6385, 75th Cong., 1st sess., 1937, 6.

12. *Taxation of Marijuana, Hearings,* 20.

13. *Taxation of Marijuana, Hearings,* 21.

14. *Taxation of Marijuana, Hearings,* 24.

15. *Taxation of Marijuana, Hearings,* 29–39.

16. *Taxation of Marijuana, Hearings,* 73–74.

17. *Taxation of Marijuana, Hearings,* 87.

18. *Taxation of Marijuana, Hearings,* 92.

19. *Taxation of Marijuana, Hearings,* 94.

20. *Taxation of Marijuana, Hearings,* 108–13.

21. *Taxation of Marijuana, Hearings,* 118–21; Sloman, *Reefer Madness,* 79.

22. Occupational Excise Tax on Marihuana, H.R. 6906, 10 June 1937, *Congressional Record,* 75th Cong., 1st sess., 81:5575.

23. Tax on Marihuana, H.R. 6906, 26 July 1937, *Congressional Record,* 75th Cong., 1st sess., 81:7624.

24. "Marihuana: New Federal Tax Hits Dealings in Potent Weed," *Newsweek,* 14 August 1937, 22–3.

25. "Denver Court Imposes First U.S. Marihuana Law Penalties," *The Denver Post,* 8 October 1937, AP, Box 6, File "Clippings 1934–1939."

26. "Denver Court Imposes First U.S. Marihuana Law Penalties.

27. "Obituary of Harry Anslinger," *Newsweek,* 20 November 1975, 47.

28. "Marihuana Research," 1938, AP, box 1, file "Articles on Dope, 1933–1961."

29. Roger Smith, "U.S. Marijuana Legislation and the Creation of A Social Problem," *Journal of Psychedelic Drugs* 1–2 (1967–1969): 97.

30. Donald E. Miller, "Narcotic Drug and Marihuana Controls," *Journal of Psychedelic Drugs* 1–2 (1967–1969): 29.

31. Treasury, *Traffic in Opium,* 1939, 17–19.

Chapter 4. Storms and Stress, 1930–1950

1. Two U.S. Agents Found Guilty of Drug Bribe Plot," *New York Herald Tribune,* 16 June 1931, AP, box 6, file "Scrapbook 9-B, January–December 1931." See also 1931 *New York Times,* 4 April, 12; 10 June, 3; 16 June, 29; 26 June, 4; and 30 June, 6.

2. "Congressman Says Federal Men Protected Diamond," *New York Times,* 11 February 1932, 3.

3. "Morgenthau Favors Tapping of Wires in Treasury Agents War on Narcotics," *New York Times,* 16 October 1934, 1.

4. Representative Loring M. Black introducing H. Res. 98, 9 January 1932, *Congressional Record,* 72nd Cong., 1st sess., 75:1645.

5. "Walker Admits Dope Charge Propaganda," *San Francisco News,* 11 November 1933, AP, box 6, file "Scrapbook 6-B, September–December 1933."

6. Letter from H. J. Anslinger to Sanborn Young, 6 July 1933, AP, box 3, file "Correspondence 1933."

7. Unsigned letter to James A. Farley, Assistant Secretary of the Treasury, 19 December 1934, AP, box 6, file "Correspondence 1934."

8. Circular Letter No. 324 from H. J. Anslinger, 4 December 1934, Franklin D. Roosevelt Presidential Library, box 19, file OF 21-X.

9. Sloman, *Reefer Madness,* 46.

10. Letter from Robert L. Vann to Louis M. Howe, 17 December 1934, Franklin D. Roosevelt Presidential Library, box 19, file OF 21-X.

11. "Expect Altoonan Will Be Retained," *Altoona Mirror,* 28 March 1933.

12. "See Patronage Appointments At Early Date," *Charlotte News,* 8 July 1933, AP, box 6, file "Clippings 1924–1933."

13. "Memorandum for the President," 28 November 1933, Franklin D. Roosevelt Presidential Library, box 19, file OF 21-X.

14. Letter to Louis Howe from Walter F. Enfield, M.D., 15 May 1934, AP, box 3, file "Correspondence 1934."

15. Treasury, *Traffic in Opium,* 1936, 65.

16. Drew Person, "The Daily Washington Merry-Go-Round," *Washington Herald,* 5 September 1933, AP, box 6, file "Scrapbook 11-B, 1930–1933."

17. Letter to William Randolph Hearst from H. J. Anslinger, 23 November 1933, AP, box 3, file "Correspondence 1933."

18. Letter from Elsie S. Bellows to Harry J. Anslinger, 4 February 1960, AP, box 2, file "Correspondence 1960."

19. See, for example, Frank G. Menke, "Hopping Horses," *Esquire,* April 1936, 37, 206–07; Bradford Wells, "A Landis for Racing," *Post Time,* July 1935, 6–7, 39; G. F. T. Ryall, "A Year of Racing," *Polo,* January 1934, 13–14; and Dayton Stoddart, "Race Tracks: A Billion-Dollar Racket With Murder on the Side," *Liberty,* January 1936, 22–26.

20. He did more than just survive. In 1936 Roosevelt appointed him as the American delegate to a League of Nations Conference to suppress the illicit traffic in narcotics.

21. William O. Walker, *Drug Control in the Americas* (Albuquerque: University of New Mexico Press, 1981), 78.

22. "Cummings Favors Merging 2 Bureaus," *The Washington Post,* 14 April 1933, AP, box 3, file "Correspondence 1933. More than saving money, Cummings was enthusiastic in his support of what he hoped would result in the creation of a "super police force" to lead his "war on crime." On 10 June 1933, President Roosevelt did sign an Executive Order that combined the bureaus of Prohibition, Identification, and Investigation to form a new Division of Investigation in the Department of Justice headed by J. Edgar Hoover, who like Anslinger was initially opposed to the merger. See Richard Gid Powers, *Secrecy and Power: The Life of J. Edgar Hoover* (New York: The Free Press, 1987), 181–86.

23. Harry J. Anslinger, "Peddling of Narcotic Drugs," *Journal of Criminal Law and Criminology* 24 (September–October 1933): 637, 651.

24. Letter from H. J. Anslinger to F. W. Russe, 5 April 1933, AP, box 3, file "Correspondence 1933."

25. "Roosevelt Opposes Merger Plan," *New York Times,* 20 April 1933, 12.

26. Thomas A. Reppetto, *The Blue Parade* (New York: The Free Press, 1978), 286–88.

27. Representative Robert L. Doughton introducing H.R. 10585, 24 January 1936, 74th Cong., 2nd sess., *Congressional Record,* 80:1002.

28. "Memorandum in Respect to H. R. 10586," 1 February 1936, AP, box 3, file "Correspondence 1936."

29. Committee on Ways and Means, *Secret Service Reorganization Act, Hearings,* House of Representatives, on H.R. 11452, 74th Cong., 2nd sess., 1936, 40–44.

30. "Merger Plan Shifts to Bar 'Ogpu' in U.S.," undated article, AP, Box 3, File "Correspondence 1936."

31. Repetto, *Parade* 287.

32. "Memorandum of conference," 18 August 1936, Morgenthau diary, book 30, 3–5, Franklin D. Roosevelt Presidential Library.

33. "Memorandum of conference."

34. Representative John M. Coffee introducing H.J. Res. 642, 17 April 1938, *Congressional Record,* 75th Cong., 3rd sess., 83:5026.

35. "The Narcotic Law Called A Failure—Will A Suggestion," *St. Louis Post-Dispatch,* 22 March 1934, AP, box 5, file "Scrapbook 5-B, 1934."

36. Extension of Remarks of Hon. John M. Coffee, 14 June 1938, *Congressional Record,* 75th Cong., 3rd sess., 83:A2706; King, *The Drug Hang-up,* 63–68.

37. Remarks of John M. Coffee, A2706–07.

38. Remarks of John M. Coffee, A2707.

39. Remarks of John M. Coffee, A2707.

40. Remarks of John M. Coffee, A2708.

41. Remarks of John M. Coffee, A2709.

42. Letter from Sanborn Young to Harry J. Anslinger, 14 October 1939, AP, box 3, file "Correspondence 1939.

43. Meeting in Secretary Morgenthau's office, 22 November 1935, Morgenthau diary, book 12, 137, Franklin D. Roosevelt Presidential Library.

44. Committee on Appropriations, *Treasury Department Appropriations Report For 1943, Hearings,* 77th Cong., 2nd sess., 1943, 160.

45. According to former agent and Assistant Director of International Affairs George Belk, some of the opium still remains in those vaults. Interview with author, 7 January 1987, Washington, D.C.

46. "Narcotics Traffic Is Curbed By War," *New York Times,* 27 September 1942, 51.

47. "The Marihuana Bugaboo," *Military Medicine* 93 (July 1943): 94–95.

48. Eli Marcovitz and Henry J. Myers, "The Marihuana Addict in the Army," *War Medicine* 6 (December 1944): 382–91.

49. "Marijuana Camp Sales Fought," *New York Times,* 5 February 1944, 19.

50. Letter from Harry Anslinger to Charles B. Dyar, 1 April 1947, AP, box 2, file "Correspondence 1946–1947."

51. Treasury, Traffic in Opium, 1942, 6–7.

52. Anslinger interviewed on radio station WFBR, Baltimore, 28 February 1947, AP, box 1, file "Speeches by Harry Anslinger 1939–1969."

53. Harry J. Anslinger and Will Oursler, *The Murderers* (New York: Farrar and Straus, 1961), 181–82. In an undated newspaper clipping in the Anslinger collection entitled "Witness For Reform," Anslinger was sharply criticized for his inconsistent position in ambulatory treatment for addicts. Described as the "darling of the 'treat-em-tough' school of narcotics suppression," Anslinger was berated for admitting that he arranged a continuous supply of drugs—the "feeding station" technique—for a "morphine-addicted Congressman who was not prosecuted and in fact was permitted to continue functioning as a lawmaker."

54. Interview with John T. Cusack, 7 January 1987, Washington, D.C. Based on existing evidence, it is highly plausible that McCarthy used morphine, at least for medicinal purposes, and that Cusack knew about it. Also see Maxine Cheshire, "Drugs and Washington, D.C.," *Ladies Home Journal,* December 1978, 180–82. Cheshire confirmed the Anslinger-McCarthy incident with two retired narcotics agents and Will Oursler, who concurred with the agents on McCarthy's addiction, "Yes, I'm sure that is correct." David M. Oshinsky discusses McCarthy's alcoholism in *A Conspiracy So Immense: The World of Joe McCarthy* (New York: The Free Press, 1983), 503–4.

55. Anslinger, *The Murderers,* 182; and Thomas C. Reeves, *The Life and Times of Joe McCarthy: A Biography* (New York: Stein and Day Publishers, 1982), 671.

56. Anslinger and Oursler, *Murderers,* 182.

57. Wakefield, "The Prodigal Powers of Pot," 58.

58. "Marihuana Users—Musicians, 1933–1937," AP, box 9.

59. Wakefield, "Powers" 58. For a fuller discussion of Mezzrow's career see Sloman, *Reefer Madness,* 84–101; and Milton "Mezz" Mezzrow and Bernard Wolfe, *Really the Blues* (New York: Random House, 1946), pp. 85–86.

60. "Gene Krupa is Arrested," 21 January 1943, 23; "Krupa Sentenced in Drug

Case," 19 May 1943, 21; and "Krupa Gets 1 to 6 Years," 3 July 1943, 15, all from *New York Times.*

61. "The Weed," *Time,* 19 July 1943, 54.

62. "Crisis in Hollywood," *Time,* 13 September 1948, 100–01; *New York Times,* 8 September 1948, 22; 11 January 1949, 31; and 1 February 1951, 65. Howard W. Chappell, an FBN agent from 1947 to 1961 and supervisor of the Houston and Los Angeles offices, claimed that Mitchum was set up because he would serve as a good example. Actually, according to Chappell, the actor was suffering from a back problem and took demerol to alleviate the pain. It was when he tried to renew his prescription at a drugstore on a verbal order from his doctor that the pharmacist became suspicious and alerted the authorities. Interview with author, 17 January 1987, Paso Robles, California.

63. Anslinger and Oursler, *Murderers,* 200; letter from H. J. Anslinger to Louis B. Mayer, 25 August 1948, AP, box 2, file "Correspondence 1948."

64. "Memorandum For Discussion With Mr. Mayer," undated, Anslinger Papers, box 2, file "Correspondence 1948."

65. " 'Drug Addict' Ban Puzzles Director," *New York Times,* 10 May 1949, 48.

66. "U.S. Narcotics Commr. Rues 'H'wood Hokum' in Dope Film's Happy Ending," *Variety,* 19 October 1955, 1, 15; "U.S. Aide's Attack on Film Assailed," *New York Times,* 25 October 1955, 38.

67. "T-Man Powell Pursues Poppy," *Washington Post,* 16 April 1948, AP, box 5, file "Scrapbook 2-B, 1940–1948"; letter from Tom Gries to H. J. Anslinger, 9 October 1958, AP, box 2, file "Correspondence 1958.

68. Lester Grinspoon, *Marihuana Reconsidered* (Cambridge: Harvard University Press, 1971), 26. *See also* Mayor LaGuardia's Committee on Marihuana, *The Marihuana Problem in the City of New York* (Lancaster, PA: Jacque Cattell Press, 1944); reprint Metuchen, New Jersey: Scarecrow Reprint Corporation, 1973.

69. David Soloman, *The Marihuana Papers* (New York: The Bobbs-Merrill Company, 1966), 228.

70. LaGuardia Committee, *Marihuana Problem,* 10.

71. These conclusions are summarized in the LaGuardia Committee, *Marihuana Problem,* 24–25.

72. Samual Allentuck, and Karl R. Bowman, "The Psychiatric Aspects of Marihuana Intoxication," *American Journal of Psychiatry* 99 (1942): 248–50; Harry J. Anslinger, "The Psychiatric Aspects of Marihuana Intoxication," *Journal of the American Medical Association* 101 (1943): 212–13. Hereafter the *Journal* is referred to as *JAMA.*

73. Anslinger, "Psychiatric Effects of Marihuana Intoxication," 213.

74. See, for example, J. Bouquet, "Marihuana Intoxication," letter to the editor, *JAMA* 124 (1944): 1010; J. D. Reichard, "The Marihuana Problem," *JAMA* 125 (1944): 594; "Marihuana Problems," *JAMA* 127 (1945): 1129; Robert P. Walton, "Marihuana Problems," letter to the editor, *JAMA* 128 (1945): 283; Karl R. Bowman, "Marihuana Problems," letter to the editor, *JAMA* 128 (1945): 889–90; and Eli Markovitz, "Marihuana Problems," letter to the editor, *JAMA* 129 (1945): 378. For additional reactions to the LaGuardia Report, see "Marihuana Found Useful in Certain Mental Ills," *Science News Letter* 41–42 (1942): 341–42; George B. Wallace, "The Marihuana Problem in New York City," *American Journal of Correction* 5–6 (1943–1944): 7, 24–26; "What Happens to Marihuana Smokers," *Science Digest* 17 (January–June 1940): 35–40; Arnold E. Esrati, "How Mild Is Marihuana?" *Magazine Digest* (June 1945): 80–86; "The Marihuana Problem," *Federal Probation* 9–10 (1945–1946): 15–22; and "Marijuana and Mentality," *Newsweek,* 18 November 1946, 70–71.

75. George Belk, interview with author.

76. Unsigned letter, 12 November 1952, AP, box 3, file "Correspondence Reginald Kaufman."

77. Letter from William T. McCarthy to H. J. Anslinger, 26 June 1952, AP, box 3, file "Correspondence William T. McCarthy, 1937–1963."

78. Undated *Washington Star* article, AP, box 6, file 9, "Clippings, 1950–1959." Unfortunately, neither documents in the Anslinger collection nor the Dwight D. Eisenhower Presidential Library pertaining to Anslinger's "candidacy" in 1952 provide any clues as to why President-elect Eisenhower considered replacing Anslinger.

79. Letter from Margaret Chase Smith to General Dwight D. Eisenhower, 24 November 1952, AP, box 3, file "Correspondence Reginald Kaufman."

Chapter 5. Retreat into the Future, 1945–1961

1. Appropriations figures are taken from Anslinger's annual reports, *Traffic in Opium and Other Dangerous Drugs.*

2. " 'Fugitive' Label on Addicts Urged," *New York Times,* 20 September 1951, 33.

3. *Control of Narcotics, Marihuana, and Barbiturates, Hearings,* before a subcommittee of the Committee on Ways and Means, House of Representatives, on H.R. 3490, 82nd Cong., 1st sess., 1951, 1–2.

4. Congressman Victor L. Anfuso commenting on H.R. 3490, 21 June 1951, *Congressional Record,* 82d Cong., 1st sess., 97:6931.

5. Congressman Hale Boggs introducing H.R. 3490, 3 April 1951, *Congressional Record,* 82d Cong., 1st sess., 97:3306.

6. Helmer, *Drugs and Minority Oppression,* 99–100.

7. *Control of Narcotics, Marihuana, and Barbiturates, Hearings,* 1–2.

8. *Control of Narcotics, Marihuana, and Barbiturates, Hearings,* 206.

9. *Control of Narcotics, Marihuana, and Barbiturates, Hearings,* 208; *New York Times,* 15 April 1955, 59.

10. Congressman Emanuel Celler debating H.R. 3490, 16 July 1951, *Congressional Record,* 82d Cong., 1st sess., 97:8205.

11. "Narcotics Drop Reported," *New York Times,* 21 January 1952, 22.

12. Congressman Fred E. Busbey commenting on H.R. 8700, 2 April 1954, *Congressional Record,* 83rd Cong., 2nd sess., 100:4540–41.

13. Richard J. Bonnie and Charles H. Whitebread II, *The Marijuana Conviction: A History of Marijuana Prohibition in the United States* (Charlottesville: University Press of Virginia, 1974), 215–17.

14. "Bill Sinks Teeth in Narcotics Code," *New York Times,* 15 January 1955, 9.

15. Senator Price Daniel introducing S. Res. 67, 18 March 1955, *Congressional Record,* 84th Cong., 1st sess., 101:6875.

16. "Texas Roundup Time," *Time,* 6 August 1955, 18.

17. *Illicit Narcotics Traffic, Hearings,* before the subcommittee on Improvements in the Federal Criminal Code of the Committee of the Judiciary, Senate, on S. Res. 67, 84th Cong., 1st sess., Part I, 1955, 173, 230.

18. *Illicit Narcotics Traffic, Hearings,* 17.

19. *Illicit Narcotics Traffic, Hearings,* 18.

20. *Illicit Narcotics Traffic, Hearings,* 45. An article Anslinger referred to specifically in the hearings was Herbert Berger and Andrew A. Eggston, "Should We Legalize Narcotics?" *Coronet,* June 1955, 30–35.

21. *Illicit Narcotics Traffic, Hearings,* 59–61; and "Narcotics Users Are Put at 60,000," *New York Times,* 3 June 1955, 25.

22. *Illicit Narcotics Traffic, Hearings,* 89.

23. *Illicit Narcotics Traffic, Hearings,* 940.

24. *Traffic in, and Control of, Narcotics, Barbiturates, and Amphetamines, Hearings,* before a subcommittee of the Committee on Ways and Means, 84th Cong., 1st sess., 1955, 1010.

25. The Control of the Illicit Drug Traffic, 30 April 1956, *Congressional Record,* 84th Cong., 2d sess., 102:7283.

26. Alfred R. Lindesmith, *The Addict and the Law* (Bloomington: Indiana University Press, 1965), 26–7.

27. The Control of Illicit Drug Traffic, *Congressional Record,* 102:7283–84.

28. Senator Frederick G. Payne commenting on the Control of Narcotic Drugs, 25 May 1956, *Congressional Record,* 84th Cong., 2d sess., 102:9031.

29. Senator Lehman commenting on the Control of Narcotic Drugs, 9033.

30. Senator O'Mahoney commenting on the Control of Narcotic Drugs, 9035.

31. Marshall McNeil, "U.S. Starts New War on Traffic in Narcotics," *News Digest,* 27 August 1956, 7.

32. "Bar Urges Reform," *New York Times,* 19 February 1955, 17.

33. Rufus King, *The Drug Hang-up,* 162–63; William Butler Eldridge, *Narcotics and the Law: A Critique of the American Experiment in Narcotic Drug Control* (New York: New York University Press, 1962), 35–37; Benjamin DeMott, "The Great Narcotics Muddle," *Harper's Magazine,* March 1962, 46.

34. *Drug Addiction: Crime or Disease? Interim and Final Reports of the Joint Committee of the American Bar Association and the American Medical Association on Narcotic Drugs* (Bloomington, Indiana University Press, 1961), 10–115.

35. *Comments on Narcotic Drugs. Interim Report of the Joint Committee of the American Bar Association and the American Medical Association on Narcotic Drugs* (Washington, D.C.: Government Printing Office, 1959), vii.

36. *Comments on Narcotic Drugs,* vii.

37. Eldrige, *Narcotics and the Law,* pp. 79–80; and Lindesmith, *Addict and the Law,* 246–47.

38. Interview with Henry L. Giordano, 25 March 1985, Silver Spring, Maryland.

39. *Comments on Narcotic Drugs,* 51–54.

40. Department of Health, Education, and Welfare, Public Health Service, *Narcotic Drug Addiction Problems: Proceedings of the Symposium on the History of Narcotic Drug Addiction Problems, March 27 and 28, 1958, Bethesda, Maryland* (Washington, D.C.: Government Printing Office).

41. *Comments on Narcotics Drugs,* 53.

42. James Sterba, "The Politics of Pot," *Esquire,* August 1968, 60.

43. "Narcotic Aide Bars Criticism of Court," *New York Times,* 19 March 1960, 12.

44. Letter from Harry Anslinger to William T. McCarthy, 2 March 1961, AP, box 3, file "Correspondence William T. McCarthy, 1937–1961."

45. Stanley Meisler, "Federal Narcotics Czar," *The Nation,* 20 February 1960, 161; and King, *The Drug Hang-up,* 171.

46. "New York Physician Scores Anslinger," *New York Times,* 8 February 1959, 55.

47. John M. Murtagh and Sara Harris, *Who Live in Shadow* (New York: McGraw Hill, 1959), 74.

48. "Murtagh Sees U.S. Lax in Enforcing Narcotic Act Here," *New York Times,* 9 August 1959, 1.

49. "Murtagh Scores Narcotics Chief," *New York Times,* 25 May 1959, 30; and "Judge Urges Ax for Dope Chief," *Philadelphia Inquirer,* 24 May 1959.

50. Meisler, "Federal Narcotics Czar," 160.

51. Letter from St. Louis attorney James J. Murphy to Jon M. Austin (Press Secretary for Senator Thomas F. Eagleton) 1 July 1985, in response to author's inquiry; Meisler, "Federal Narcotics Czar," 161.

52. James J. Murphy letter.

53. "Anslinger's Sit-Down Strike," *St. Louis Globe-Democrat,* 23 September 1959, 2.

54. Thomas A. Wadden, Jr., "We Put the Heat on Washington Dope Peddlers," *Saturday Evening Post,* 3 October 1953, 20.

55. Wadden, "We Put the Heat," 134.

56. Wadden, "We Put the Heat," 134.

57. Wadden, "We Put the Heat," 134.

58. *Juvenile Delinquency, Hearings,* before a subcommittee to Investigate Juvenile Delinquency of the Committee on the Judiciary, Senate, on S. Res. 54, 86th Cong., 1st sess., Part 5, 1959, 689–90. White borrowed the "dog-in-the-manger" phrase from Aesop's fables.

59. *Juvenile Delinquency, Hearings,* 692.

60. *Juvenile Delinquency, Hearings,* 693.

61. *Juvenile Delinquency, Hearings,* 692.

62. *Juvenile Delinquency, Hearings,* Part 7, 86th Cong. 2d sess., 1960, 1287.

63. *Juvenile Delinquency, Hearings,* 1290.

64. *Juvenile Delinquency, Hearings,* 1292.

65. *Juvenile Delinquency, Hearings,* 1314.

66. George Belk, interview with author.

Chapter 6. Anslinger Goes After the Mob, 1930–1962

1. "A Godfather's Fall: Mob Under Fire," *Newsweek,* 30 December 1985, 20–21.

2. See Albini's *The American Mafia,* 2–7, for a brief but useful historiographical examination of interpretations offered on the origins of "Mafia;" Annelise G. Anderson's *The Business of Organized Crime: A Cosa Nostra Family* (Stanford, Calif.: Hoover Institution Press, 1979), pp. 9–17; and Peter Reuter's *Disorganized Crime: The Economics of the Visible Hand* (Cambridge, Mass.: The MIT Press, 1983), pp. 1–10.

3. There is considerable debate on the nomenclature referring to types of organized crime. Burton B. Turkus and Sid Feder, as cited in chapter 2, maintain that "Mafia," "Black Hand," and "Unione Siciliano," are different terms describing different organizations. Anslinger consistently used them interchangeably. It should be noted that the Mafia, a part of organized crime, traditionally implied Sicilian or Italian membership, but has become more generic in recent years with the discovery of Black, Hispanic, Jewish, and Vietnamese "mafias." The common characteristic shared by each is its ethnicity.

4. "Narcotics Commissioner Pegged Mafia Year Ago," *Hollidaysburg Blair Press,* 2 October 1963.

5. J. Edgar Hoover, *Law Enforcement Bulletin,* 31 (January 1962), 3–6.

6. Hoover was well aware that nothing succeeds like success and understood, as columnist George Will observed that "when gangsters were dramatized, gang-

busters were glamorized." "A Grim Monument to U.S. Penology," *Philadelphia Inquirer,* 21 July 1987, 11-A.

7. Fred J. Cook, "Organized Crime: The Strange Reluctance," in *Investigating the FBI,* ed., Pat Watters and Stephen Gillers (Garden City, New York: Doubleday, Inc., 1973), 161–62. For Hoover's views on the nature of organized crime, see Richard Gid Powers, *Secrecy and Power: The Life of J. Edgar Hoover* (New York: The Free Press, 1987), 198–99, 332–35.

8. Donald R. Cressey, *Theft of the Nation: The Structure and Operations of Organized Crime in America* (New York: Harper & Row, Publishers, 1969), 21–23.

9. See especially a letter from Hoover to Anslinger, 1 August 1933, AP, box 3, file "Correspondence 1933"; and a letter from Hoover to Anslinger, 3 June 1970, AP, box 2, file "Correspondence 1967–70."

10. Anslinger claimed credit for this discovery in *The Murderers,* page 79. "I am proud," he wrote, "that it was the Bureau of Narcotics which led the way in exposing the activities of this organization." Certainly he had to know, as Nelli has pointed out (page 124), that narcotics was more lucrative during and after prohibition than prostitution, counterfeiting, or even bootlegging.

11. Hubert S. Nelli, *The Business of Crime: Italians and Syndicate Crime in the United States* (Chicago: University of Chicago Press, 1976), 234–35; "Lonnie Affronti Report," AP, box 4, file "Mafia."

12. "Lonnie Affronti Report."

13. Nelli, *Business of Crime,* 236.

14. "Lonnie Affronti Report."

15. "Lonnie Affronti Report."

16. "Lonnie Affronti Report."

17. "Speech to International Association of Chiefs of Police," 13 October 1931, AP, box 1, file "Speeches by Harry Anslinger, 1930–1938."

18. "Memorandum for Mr. Anslinger from H. T. Nugent," 25 March 1937, AP, box 3, file "Correspondence 1937."

19. Hank Messick, *John Edgar Hoover* (New York: David McKay Company, Inc., 1972), 78–79. Annenberg was the American ambassador to St. James' Court from 1969 to 1974. Also see *Current Biography,* 1970, 9-12; and "Annenberg to pay $8,000,000 on Tax," *New York Times,* 1 June 1940, 17."

20. "The Ice House Gang," 1938, AP, box 4, file "Illicit Drug Traffic, 1929–1952."

21. "Nicolo Impostato," 1943, AP, box 4, file "Mafia."

22. "Gagliano Narcotic Case," March 1947, AP, box 4, file "Mafia."

23. "Untitled Report," AP, box 4, file "Illicit Drug Traffic, 1929–1952."

24. "Untitled Report," 3–4.

25. "Drug Barons of Europe," undated, AP, box 4, file "Drug Barons of Europe, 1956–1932." Anslinger's pursuit of the Eliopoulos brothers is also detailed in Will Oursler and Laurence Dwight Smith's *Narcotics: America's Peril* (Garden City, NY: Doubleday Company, 1952), 113–31.

26. "Drug Barons of Europe," 3.

27. Harry J. Anslinger and Dennis Gregory, *The Protectors: Narcotics Agents, Citizens, and Officials Against Organized Crime n America* (New York: Farrar, Strauss and Company, 1964), 147.

28. "Louis Buchalter Case," AP, box 4, file "Illicit Drug Traffic, 1929–1952."

29. "Louis Buchalter Case," 1.

30. Messick, *Hoover,* 80.

31. "Louis Buchalter Case," 5.

32. Messick, *Hoover,* 80. According to Powers, the reason Buchalter surren-

dered to the FBI was because President Roosevelt was "using Hoover to dim Dewey's reputation as the nation's leading racket buster" before the 1940 presidential election was held, Powers, *Secrecy and Power,* 209.

33. "Danger! Columnist At Large," undated, AP, box 6, file "Clippings 1960–1966."

34. "Louis Buchalter Case," 11.

35. "Louis Buchalter Case," 13.

36. "Louis Buchalter Case," 13.

37. Messick, *Hoover,* 81.

38. "The Boss," AP, box 4, file "Draft of Book."

39. Luciano came to New York with his family in 1907 and settled on First Avenue near Fourteenth Street, on the Lower East Side of Manhattan, a predominantly Jewish neighborhood. At the age of eighteen he was sentenced to six months in a reformatory for the unlawful possession of narcotics. Nelli, *Business of Crime,* 105–06.

40. These two murders are commonly referred to as "purge day" when supposedly between thirty and forty "greaseballs" or Mustache Petes," as the oldtimers were called, were assassinated. Both Nelli (pages 179–80) and Albini (pages 243–47) dispute this, however. According to them, no evidence has ever been produced that supports the purge. Consequently, the theory (attributed to the testimony of Joe Valachi during the McClellan hearings) that Luciano became the head of a national commission that coordinated Mafia activities, has been grossly exaggerated.

41. Anslinger, *The Protectors,* 74–75.

42. Sid Feder and Joachim Joesten, *The Luciano Story* (New York: David McKay Company, Inc., 1954), 213.

43. "Luciano War Aid Called Ordinary," *New York Times,* 27 February 1947, 46.

44. "Luciano Not So Lucky," undated, AP, box 5, file "Scrapbook 8, 1951–1961."

45. Drew Pearson, "Luciano Talked Freely But Revealed Little," *Washington Post,* 15 March 1962.

46. "Memorandum Report," 16 August 1951, AP, box 2, file "Correspondence 1952."

47. "Confidential Report," 24 July 1952, AP, box 2, file "Correspondence 1952;" and Michael Stern, *No Innocence Abroad* (New York: Random House, 1953), 27–62.

48. "Confidential Report."

49. Joachim Joesten, "A Statement Concerning the book *The Luciano Story,*" 7 January 1955, AP, box 4, file "Draft of Book." Succumbing to political pressure from New York State Democrats Owen McGivern and later Walter R. Lynch, who were suspicious of Dewey's motives, the governor ordered an investigation of the affair. Headed by New York State Commissioner of Investigations, William B. Herlands, the 1954 inquiry included unpublicized testimony from FBN agents George White and Charles Siragusa. Thomas E. Dewey Papers, University of Rochester Library, Rochester, New York.

50. The first reporter to find Luciano in Cuba was Walter Winchell who noted it in his column on 11 February 1947. Robert C. Ruark of the New York *World Telegram* and the Scripps-Howard organization also wrote in detail about Luciano's Cuban holiday.

51. "U.S. Ends Narcotics Sales to Cuba While Luciano Is Resident There," *New York Times,* 22 February 1947, 4; "Cuba Puts Luciano in Detention, Seeks

End of U.S. Narcotics Ban," *New York Times,* 23 February 1947, 9; "Luciano to Leave Cuba in 48 Hours," *New York Times,* 24 February 1947, 1; "Cuba Will Deport Luciano to Italy," *New York Times,* 25 February 1947, 19.

52. Feder and Joesten, *The Luciano Story,* 272.

53. Control of Narcotics, Marihuana, Barbiturates, Hearings, 59–60.

54. Feder and Joesten, *The Luciano Story,* 319; "In Re: Salvatore LUCIANA," 9 February 1960, AP, box 4, file "Draft of Book."

55. Drew Pearson, "Luciano Talked."

56. *Investigation of Organized Crime in Interstate, Commerce, Hearings,* before a Special Committee To Investigate Organized Crime on Interstate Commerce, pursuant to S. Res. 202 and S. Res. 129, 82nd Cong., 1st sess., 1951.

57. Kefauver Committee, *Final Report.*

58. Kefauver Committee, *Final Report.* While Anslinger was often accused of exaggerating the numbers of addicts or drug-related crimes, he was understating the 20 percent share of the narcotics market to "Murder, Inc."

59. This theory contradicts what Anslinger later wrote in *The Murderers* (1962) when he defined "syndicate" as "nationally it refers to what others call the 'organization,' a term that takes in not only Mafia itself but other related groups," (page 88).

60. That senior narcotics agents George White and Charles Siragusa worked for the committee as investigators is significant, in March 1951, White was questioned as a witness. Whatever the official views of the bureau were, they could be conveniently conveyed through these agents. In *The American Mafia,* (page 8), Albini argues that the Kefauver Committee failed to prove that there was any Mafia in operation, much less one on a national level. Senator Kefauver "merely assumed its existence and then set out to offer proofs to reinforce this assumption." Sociologist Daniel Bell also disputed the validity of the Committee's findings, stating that they "revealed no real evidence of the existence of the Mafia"; *The End of Ideology* (New York: Collier Books, 1962), 139. For a more comprehensive study of the Kefauver investigation, see William Howard Moore's *The Kefauver Committee and the Politics of Crime* (Columbia: University of Missouri Press, 1974).

61. Details of the Mario Lanza incidents in Los Angeles and Italy are taken from "Letter to George H. White from Howard W. Chappell," 27 November 1956, AP, box 4, file "Mafia"; and "Memorandum Report" from Charles Siragusa, 12 November 1957, AP, box 4, file "Mafia;" and Howard Chappell, interview with author, 17 January 1987, Paso Robles, California. Agent Chappell first acquired experience in undercover work during World War II as a captain in the OSS when he parachuted into German-held northern Italy to organize resistance forces among the Italian partisans. For his efforts he was awarded the Silver Star and Purple Heart.

62. Howard Chappell, interview with author.

63. Agent Chappell recalled the weekly figure as $25,000.

64. Dwight C. Smith, *The Mafia Mystique* (New York: Basic Books, Inc., Publishers, 1975), 153–54.

65. *Investigation of Improper Activities is the Labor Management Field, Hearings,* before the Senate Select Committee on Investigation of Improper Activities in the Labor Management Field, Part 32, 85th Cong., 2nd sess., 1958, 12201–19. Hereafter referred to as *Organized Crime and Illicit Traffic in Narcotics, Hearings.*

66. Not only is the total number of "guests" impossible to calculate, no one is in agreement on how many were actually apprehended. Sergeant Crosswell, the arresting officer, reported a total of sixty-two, but that number varied depending on

the source. Cressey in *Theft of A Nation,* (page 57) and Gerard L. Goettel in "Why the Crime Syndicate Can't Be Touched," *Harper's Magazine,* November 1960, 33, cited the figure of seventy-five; Watters and Gillers, *Investigating the FBI,* 149, prefer sixty; Chairman McClellan in *Crime Without Punishment* (New York: Duell, Sloan and Pearce, 1964), 113, asserted that fifty-eight men were picked up; *Newsweek,* 25 November 1957, 37, and Murtagh, *Who Live in Shadow,* 108, reported sixty-five; Salerno and Thompkins, *The Crime Confederation,* 298, counted sixty-three; and Schiavo, *The Truth About the Mafia,* 118, quoted "58 or 60."

67. *Improper Activities in the Labor Management Field, Hearings,* 12222–27.

68. "Memorandum to H. J. Anslinger from George H. Gaffney," 6 January 1960, AP, box 2, file "Correspondence 1960"; "Gang Strife Linked to Apalachin Edict Against Narcotics," *New York Times,* 28 February 1960, 1; Gay Talese, *Honor Thy Father* (New York: Dell Publishing Company, 1971), 89.

69. Letter from Richard B. Ogilvie to Milton R. Wessel, 12 November 1959, AP, box 4, file "Mafia."

70. Ogilvie letter.

71. See Albini, 247–50, where he analyzes the significance of Apalachin as the alleged meeting of the Mafia Grand Council, and other meetings held by syndicate leaders.

72. Siragusa was the first agent in charge of the bureau's first permanent foreign office established in Rome in 1951. He was able to break up the ring primarily because he organized an extensive network of informants throughout Europe; John Cusack, former FBN agent, interview with author, Washington, D.C., 6 January 1987. Cusack might well be regarded as the unofficial historian of the Federal Bureau of Narcotics. In the three-hour interview, he displayed an incredibly accurate recall of names, dates, places, and the nature of events. In the Narcotics Bureau (much of the time in Europe) from 1947 to 1978, he was the chief of staff for New York Congressman Charles Rangel's Select Committee on Narcotics Abuse and Control from 1983 to 1987.

73. *Organized Crime and Illicit Traffic in Narcotics, Hearings,* 787–88, 922; "6 Imprisoned by U.S. in Narcotics Ring; Stromberg, Leader Gets 5 Years and Fine," *New York Times,* 24 April 1958, 27; "Letter to H. J. Anslinger from James C. Ryan," 26 July 1957, AP, box 2, file "Correspondence 1956–1957." See also "The Rosen Era: 1929–1959," in Philip Jenkins and Gary Potter, *The City and the Syndicate: Organizing Crime in Philadelphia* (Lexington, Mass.: Ginn Publishing, 1985), 13–23.

74. There were, of course, powerful Jewish gangsters who continued to profit from the lucrative narcotics trade, but after Apalachin the FBN, like most law enforcement agencies, focused on Italian criminals. "Commissioner Sued For Libel," *Altoona Mirror,* 29 January 1965. According to Anslinger, the top ten bosses in descending order of importance were (1) Vito Genovese, (2) Guiseppe "Joe" Profaci, (3) Gaetano "Thomas" Lucchese, (4) Carmine Galente, (5) Santo Sorge, (6) Joseph "Little Rabbit" Biondi, (7) Joseph Bonanno, (8) Vincenzo Gutroni, (9) Salvatore Mannarino, and (10) Santos Trafficante.

75. "Commissioner Sued For Libel"; "Ex-Narcotics Commissioner Sued For Libel," *Altoona Mirror,* 30 January 1965; "Anslinger Suit Trial Shifted to Pittsburgh," *Altoona Mirror,* 14 May 1965; and "Anslinger Suit Figure Sought in Mafia Probe," *Altoona Mirror,* 4 August 1965.

Chapter 7. Tentacles, 1943–1965

1. "Jap 'Secret Weapon' Dope," *Los Angeles Examiner,* undated, AP, box 5, file "Scrapbook 7, 1931–1949."

2. Untitled correspondence, AP, box 5, file "Scrapbook V. 1-B, 1930–1944." No doubt Anslinger was as affected as the general public when the China Lobby bombarded Americans through 1949 with fake information. By the end of that year, Chiang Kai-shek and the Nationalists were forced to flee Mainland China for Formosa (now Taiwan) by Mao Tse-tung and the Communists. Until then most Americans thought that Chiang was winning the war.

3. "Soviet Retorts on Heroin," *New York Times,* 3 May 1952, 5; "Anslinger Replies to Zakusov Charges," *New York Times,* 6 May 1952, 4.

4. Committee on the Judiciary, *Juvenile Delinquency, Hearings,* before a subcommittee to Investigate Juvenile Delinquency, Senate, on S. Res. 89, 83rd Cong., 1st sess., 1953, 160–61.

5. Untitled article, AP, box 5, file "Scrapbook 7, 1931–1949." Anslinger had been appointed the American delegate to the UN Commission in 1946 by President Harry S. Truman. Letter from Harry J. Anslinger to President Harry S. Truman, 11 June 1946, Anslinger OPM File.

6. The eight were Senator Alexander Wiley, Wisconsin; Congressman Samuel W. Yorty, California; Norris Poulson, California; Gordon L. McDonough, California; Gordon Canfield, New Jersey; Homer Angell, Oregon; James E Van Zandt, Pennsylvania; and Peter Rodino, New Jersey.

7. "U.S. Charges China Spurs Drug Habit," *New York Times,* 5 May 1954, 8; *International Opium Protocol, Hearing,* before a subcommittee of the Senate Foreign Relations Committee, Senate, 83d Cong., 2nd sess., 1954, 7.

8. *International Opium Protocol, Hearing,* p. 17.

9. Committee on the Judiciary, *Communist China and Illicit Narcotic Traffic, Hearings,* before the subcommittee to Investigate the Administration of the Internal Security Act and Other Internal Security Laws, Senate, 84th Cong., 1st sess., 1955, 14–17.

10. "Taxpayers Trim U.S. at $116 A Clip," *New York Times,* 5 May 1955, 5.

11. Letter from H. J. Anslinger to William T. McCarthy, 6 December 1956, AP, box 3, file "Correspondence William T. McCarthy, 1937–1963."

12. John Helmer, *Drugs and Minority Oppression* (New York: Seabury Press, 1975), 103–04. In *The Politics of Heroin in Southeast Asia* (New York: Harper & Row Publishers, 1972), 7–8, Alfred W. McCoy states that in the 1940s, "Marseilles became a major battleground between the CIA and the French Communist party. To tip the balance of power in its favor, the CIA recruited Corsican gangsters to battle Communist strikers and backed leading figures in the city's Corsican underworld who were at odds with the local Communists."

13. Anslinger, *The Murderers,* 230.

14. McCoy, *The Politics of Heroin in Southeast Asia,* 145–46.

15. McCoy, *The Politics of Heroin,* 147.

16. McCoy, *The Politics of Heroin,* 147–48.

17. Charles Siragusa, *The Trail of the Poppy: Behind the Mask of the Mafia* (Englewood Cliffs, NJ: Prentice-Hall, Inc., 1966), 185–99.

18. Siragusa, *Trail,* 185–99.

19. Jack Anderson, "Castro Has A New Weapon: Dope," *Washington Post,* 29 July 1962, 1–2. For a more comprehensive account of Cuba's role in narcotics trafficking see Warren Hinckle and William W. Turner, *The Fish Is Red: The Story of the Secret War Against Castro* (New York, Harper & Row, Publishers, 1981). On page 91 the authors link Siragusa with highly secretive CIA operations.

20. The author has interviewed agents who were stationed in Rome, Trieste, Beirut, Marseilles, and throughout the Far East in the 1950s.

21. "Narcotics-Counterfeit Ring Broken With Seizure of 9 in Federal Trap," *New York Times*, 28 July 1951, 28.

22. Anslinger, *The Murderers*, 222.

ı23. Anslinger, *The Murderers*, 222. Anslinger's reconstruction of the chronology here is interesting since Williams retired from the bureau in 1953. Officially, he may not have been a narcotics agent, but it is likely that he was in Iran or had knowledge of the CIA-backed coup that overthrew Prime Minister Moosadegh and put the shah in power.

24. Anslinger, *The Murderers*, 222. The commissioner claimed that because of Williams' efforts, the opium market in Singapore, Hong Kong, and other Far Eastern ports virtually disappeared. In Iran addiction rates "went on the greatest toboggan ride in history . . . plunging from 2,000,000 to approximately 50,000."

25. Department of Justice, *A Guide to Interpol: The International Criminal Police Organization in the United States*, National Institute of Justice, Washington, D.C., August 1985, 19.

26. *A Guide to Interpol*, 19; Tom Tullet, *Inside Interpol* (New York: Walker and Company, 1965), 60.

27. Anslinger, *The Murderers*, 224–25.

28. "Committee on One Hundred," 1931, AP, box 1, file "Initiation, Awards, Articles by Anslinger."

29. Newsletter from J. Edward Johnston, Jr. to INFORM subscribers, 19 July 1958, AP, box 2, file "Correspondence 1958."

30. Special letter to ICI trustees and Supporters, 10 May 1961, AP, box 2, file "Correspondence 1961."

31. Letter from William J. Donovan to Harry Anslinger, 11 August 1920, AP, Box 3, File "Correspondence 1920."

32. Letter from H. J. Anslinger to Keith Weeks, 24 November 1941, AP, box 2, file "Correspondence 1940–1941."

33. Treasury Department Conference, 15 December 1941, Morgenthau Diary, Box 473, 36–37, Franklin D. Roosevelt Presidential Library.

34. The OSS was created by presidential order on 13 July 1942. Two excellent studies of the OSS in its formative years are Richard Harris Smith, *The OSS: The Secret History of America's First Central Intelligence Agency* (Berkeley: University of California Press, 1972) 1–35; and John Ranelagh, *The Agency: The Rise and Fall of the CIA* (New York: Simon and Schuster, 1986), 37–56.

35. Letter from H. Morgenthau, Jr. to General Donovan, 12 April 1945, Morgenthau Diary, Book 836, 222, Franklin D. Roosevelt Presidential Library.

36. For additional information of the evolution of the OSS to the CIA, *see* Roger Hillsman, *Strategic Intelligence and National Decisions* (Glencoe, Ill.: The Free Press, 1956), 28–32; Andrew Tully, *CIA: The Inside Story* (New York: William Morrow and Company, 1962), 8–11; Lyman B. Kirkpatrick, Jr., *The Real CIA* (New York: The Macmillan Company, 1968), 14–17, 74–6; Victor Marchetti and John D. Marks, *The CIA and the Cult of Intelligence* (New York: Alfred A. Knopf, 1978), 21–23; and Anthony Cave Brown, *The Last Hero: Wild Bill Donovan* (New York: Random House, 1982).

37. Memorandum for W. N. Thompson from H. J. Anslinger, 17 October 1942; Memorandum for W. N. Thompson from H. J. Anslinger, 15 December 1942; Letter from H. J. Anslinger to Rudyard Boulton, 12 March 1942; Letter from Stanley P. Lovell to Harry J. Anslinger, 24 August 1943, all in AP, box 2 file "Correspondence, 1942–1943." Lovell was General Donovan's chief scientist in charge of research and development. William L. Cassidy, ed., *History of the Schools and Training Branch Office of Strategic Services* (San Francisco: King-

fisher Press, 1983), 199.

38. John Finlator, *The Drugged Nation: A Narc's Story* (New York: Simon and Schuster, 1973), 57–59; Howard Chappell, interview with author.

39. Former Agent Howard Chappell confirmed that "The bureau pretty much had a policy of hiring Italians and blacks" but also felt that "when they didn't have any undercover use, they didn't have a use for them in the bureau . . . which is why a lot of agents only lasted five, six, or seven years."

40. "The Fall of A Cocaine Kingpin," *Time,* 16 February 1987, 37; "Snaring the King of Coke," *Newsweek,* 16 February 1987, 16–18; "Arrest Has Only Nicked A Rich and Ruthless Cocaine Cartel," *Philadelphia Inquirer,* 15 February 1987, 1; Alan Riding, "Cocaine Billionaires: The Men Who Hold Colombia Hostage," *The New York Times Magazine,* 8 March 1987, 27–36.

41. During Anslinger's tenure, five agents were killed in the line of duty, all in the United States. Jerry N. Rice, *Drug Enforcement: The Early Years* (Washington, D.C.: Drug Enforcement Administration, 1980), 67.

42. Finlator, *Drugged Nation,* 64.

43. Anslinger, *The Protectors,* 67–68. There were other agents with colorful personalities and competence in investigative work whose activities should not be overlooked. Regrettably, they are too numerous to mention.

44. Anslinger, *The Protectors,* 46.

45. Anslinger, *The Protectors,* 76.

46. "Assumes New Duties As Treasury Aide," *New York Times,* 2 October 1940, 38.

47. Williams was called to Washington in November 1940 to submit recommendations for a "plain clothes investigative unit to combat possible enemy espionage and sabotage." He prepared organizational plans, as well as the curriculum for a training school, and in January 1941, he became the first chief and then commandant of what was then named the Counter Intelligence Police. Williams later served as Director of Training for the OSS as Assistant Commandant of the Parachute School. See documents held by the United States AINSCOM, Dr. Jack P. Finnegan, IAOPS Historian, Arlington Hall Station, Virginia. Hereafter referred to as AINSCOM.

48. Anslinger, *The Protectors,* 78.

49. Anslinger, *The Protectors,* 107.

50. Anslinger, *The Protectors,* 107.

51. "Tax Aide Resigns: Own Returns Eyed," *New York Times,* 27 November 1949, 36.

52. Former Agent Cusack referred to Williams as a brilliant administrator who was the "modern developer of the Federal Bureau of Narcotics." The training program Williams directed included instruction in demolitions, weapons, close combat, silent killing, sabotage, undercover work in a foreign country, conduct of passive resistance, parachute jumps, and guerilla warfare. The training school curriculum also provided for landing from submarine and surface craft on hostile shores in darkness, and the social control of the local population. See Kermit Roosevelt, *War Report of the OSS* (New York: Walker and Company, 1975), 81.

53. Toni Howard, "Dope Is His Business," *Saturday Evening Post,* 27 April 1957, 38–39, 146–48.

54. Siragusa completed his OSS training at an indoctrination school for new officers at Ft. Schyuler in the Bronx. His official tour of duty in the OSS lasted seventeen months. Siragusa, *The Trail of the Poppy,* 58.

55. Siragusa, *The Trail of the Poppy,* 219.

56. Howard, "Dope Is His Business," 38–39.

57. Though Siragusa enjoyed an extensive career in the FBN and was instrumental in bureau affairs both home and abroad, several agents interviewed by the author who worked for "Charlie Cigars" felt that some of his exploits have been exaggerated. At the same time there is compelling evidence that Siragusa did play an important part in more clandestine activities. The testimony he provided in secrecy during the Herlands Commission investigation in 1954, for example, indicates that he was very well informed about the parties involved on both sides of the Dewey-Luciano affair. In 1960 when the CIA was plotting the assassinations of Third World leaders and was allegedly seeking to organize a Mafia hit squad to carry out the executions, the agency approached Siragusa. Since he was the FBN's liaison with the CIA during the wars years and was assumed to know more about the Mafia than anyone, he was a logical candidate. He refused the job, commenting, "in wartime it's one thing, but in peacetime, it's something different." Hinckle and Turner, *The Fish is Red,* 31.

58. In July 1935, White transferred from the Immigration and Naturalization Service and was trained by Garland Williams. Prior to joining the FBN, White was a private investigator and a newspaper correspondent for the *San Francisco Bulletin* and *Los Angeles Herald Express.* Documents are in George H. White's Official Personnel Folder, United States Office of Personnel Management, Philadelphia. Hereafter referred to as White OPM File.

59. Anslinger, *The Protectors,* 67–68. Former chief of the CIA's counterintelligence, James J. Angleton, remembered White as "not known to people . . . a different kettle of fish." James J. Angleton, telephone interviews with the author, December 1986–May 1987, Falls Church, Virginia.

60. Cusack felt that White was "the kind of agent Harry Anslinger loved . . . incorruptible, brilliant, tough." Unfortunately, because he drank too much, White could be the "bull in the China shop . . . he could be a little over flamboyant."

61. Letter from H. J. Anslinger to William T. McCarthy, 28 September 1951, AP, box 3, file "Correspondence William T. McCarthy, 1937–1963."

62. Anslinger, *The Protectors,* 79. Anslinger's suspicions about White's knowledge of the atom bomb were also shared by John Marks, who mentioned the narcotics agent in connection with a "Manhattan Project counterintelligence man" in *The CIA and Mind Control: The Search For the "Manchurian Candidate"* (New York: McGraw-Hill Book Company, 1980), 7.

63. John M. Crewdson, "File Show Tests For Truth Drugs Began in O.S.S.," *New York Times,* 5 September 1977, 1.

64. Sterba, "The Politics of Pot," 60; Anslinger, *The Protectors,* 79.

65. George White's Diaries, Perham Electronics Museum, Los Altos, California, 24 May 1943. Notations referring to drug experiments continue through August. Hereafter referred to as White Diaries; Crewdson, "File," 1.

66. Sterba, "The Politics of Pot," 60.

67. Crewdson, "Files Show Tests For Truth Drugs," 1; Sterba, "The Politics of Pot," 60; and Brown, *The Last Hero,* 747.

68. Anslinger, *The Protectors,* 104; and Testimony of George White before the Herlands Investigation, 1 April 1954, New York City, 41. This commission was ordered by New York Governor Thomas E. Dewey to investigate his role in the release of Lucky Luciano. For a discussion of White, Del Gracio, and John L. Lewis, see Brown, *The Last Hero,* 749–50; and David Stafford, *Camp X* (New York: Dodd, Mead, and Company, 1986), 81–82.

69. On 9 June 1952 White made a notation in his diary that "Gottlieb proposes

I be a CIA consultant and I agree." Nearly a year later, on 30 April 1953 he wrote: "CIA—got final clearance and sign contract as a 'consultant'—met Gottlieb . . . lunch Napoleon's—met Anslinger." Gottlieb was Dr. Sidney Gottlieb, who headed the CIA's Chemical Division of the Technical Services Staff and was responsible for MK ULTRA. Although Anslinger was not as actively involved in MK ULTRA as White, there is little doubt that the commissioner was aware of his agent's affiliation with the CIA. Given Anslinger's penchant for clandestine operations, White likely worked for the CIA with his knowledge and support. Another entry in White's diary on 20 July 1953 infers Anslinger's knowledge: "arrive Wash.—confer Anslinger and Gottlieb re CIA reimbursement for 3 men's services."

70. On the second day of the Herlands investigation, a bitter exchange took place between Herlands and White over White's references to Del Grazio in the agent's diaries. White was extraordinarily defensive about the diaries—which Herlands wanted to examine—because they contained remarks about his relationship with the CIA and clandestine operations. See White's testimony of 2 April 1954, 97–142.

71. White Diaries, 12 May 1954. Though Herlands could not have known it at the time, in investigating the Dewey-Luciano affair, he came close to exposing an even more sensational operation.

72. For background material on BLUEBIRD and ARTICHOKE, see Marks, *Search For the Manchurian Candidate,* 26–33; and Martin A. Lee and Bruce Schlain, *Acid Dreams: The CIA, LSD and the Sixties Rebellion* (New York: Grove Press, Inc., 1985), 9–11.

73. As a frame of reference, twenty-five micrograms produces noticeable psychological effects in some people; 100 micrograms brings on LSD hallucinations in most people. An amount of LSD weighing as little as the aspirin in a five-grain tablet is enough to produce effects in 3,000 people. See Edward M. Brecher, *Licit and Illicit Drugs* (Boston: Little, Brown and Company, 1972), 346–48. White also seems to have been connected with Olson's suicide. At the time Olson was unknowingly given the LSD, at Camp Detrick in Maryland, Dr. Robert V. Lashbrook, a CIA chemist, was in the room. After Olson jumped to his death, Lashbrook contacted his supervisor, Gottlieb, and went to the police station to identify the body. In Olson's pocket he found a slip of paper with the initials "G. W." and "M. H."—George White and Morgan Hall, White's code name. The note also had the address 81 Bedford Street, White's New York safehouse. John Jacobs, "The Diaries of a CIA Operative," *Washington Post,* 4 September 1977, 1.

74. Anthony Marro, "Drug Tests By CIA Held More Extensive Than Reported in '75," *New York Times,* 16 July 1977," 1. Marks provides a comprehensive account of the Olson incident in chapter 5, "Concerning the Case of Frank Olson," 73–86.

75. John C. Crewdson, "Ex-C.I.A. Aide Asks Immunity to Testify," *New York Times,* 7 September 1977, 11; White Diaries, 9 June–17 October 1952.

76. None of the several agents interviewed by the author who knew White had difficulty recalling a story about White's drinking, which had become legendary by the time he left the bureau in 1965.

77. White Diaries, letter to Dr. Harvey Paulson, 30 September 1970.

78. In 1951, he was assigned to Boston as District Supervisor but got no closer than New York where he stayed for two years. He was then made "Supervisor At Large." Former District Supervisor Michael G. Picini, interview with author, 28 July 1987, Alexandria, Virginia; and White OPM File.

79. Marks, 101.

80. James J. Angleton, telephone interviews with author, December 1986–May 1987, Falls Church, Virginia.

81. *Human Drug Testing By the CIA, 1977, Hearings,* before the subcommittee on Health and Scientific Research of the Committee on Human Resources, on S. 1893, 95th Cong., 1st sess., 1977, 1–2.

82. See Thomas Powers, *The Man Who Kept the Secrets: Richard Helms and the CIA* (New York: Simon & Schuster, 1979), 378–82.

83. *Human Drug Testing, Hearings,* 2.

84. *Human Drug Testing, Hearings,* 100.

85. *Human Drug Testing, Hearings,* 100–01.

86. *Human Drug Testing, Hearings,* 106–08. See Marks, *Search for the "Manchurian Candidate,"* 87–104 for a detailed account of George White's role in MK-ULTRA.

87. *Human Drug Testing, Hearings,* 116.

88. *Human Drug Testing, Hearings,* 117.

89. *Human Drug Testing, Hearings,* 117.

90. *Human Drug Testing, Hearings,* 117–18.

91. *Human Drug Testing, Hearings,* 117–18.

92. Marks, *Search for the Manchurian Candidate,* 99.

93. *Human Drug Testing, Hearings,* 119–120.

94. When the subject of MK-ULTRA was raised during a recent interview, Belk was adamant about his non-involvement in the project. He confirmed that George White was working for the CIA. He could not be as certain about Charles Siragusa but was sure that he had the commissioner's approval. If, however, Belk is correct that "Siragusa got White involved in the thing [safehouse] on the West Coast and in New York," obviously Siragusa was well connected with the CIA.

95. *Human Drug Testing, Hearings,* 170.

96. *Human Drug Testing, Hearings,* 170–71.

97. *Human Drug Testing, Hearings,* 174.

98. White used this money for such expenses as household supplies, installation of special equipment, surveillance and photographic equipment, and replacement of woodwork and plaster. See Memorandum: For the Record, "Discussion with Morgan Hall Concerning Past and Future Accounting For Funds," 1 August 1955, CIA Freedom of Information File.

99. *Human Drug Testing, Hearings,* 190.

100. Marks, *Search For the "Manchurian Candidate",* 197–99.

101. *Human Drug Testing, Hearings,* 201–02. Anslinger's successor, Henry Giordano, also knew about the FBN's involvement in MK-ULTRA. During a 1967 Senate committee's investigation of illegal wiretapping by government agencies chaired by Senator Edward Long, Giordano told a senior Technical Services staff man that the "most helpful thing [the CIA] could do would be to turn the Long Committee off." Marks, *Search for the Manchurian Candidate,* 199.

102. Though it is possible that White and Siragusa might have been contacted directly by the CIA without going through Anslinger first, it is not likely, given his own extensive background in intelligence work and his more than twenty years in Washington where he had important allies in Congress and the State Department.

Chapter 8. Coda, 1962–1975

1. Letter to William P. Smith from H. J. Anslinger, 8 February 1961, AP, box 2, file "Correspondence 1961." Anslinger recalled in *The Protectors* (page 214) that

when he received a special citation at his retirement in 1962, the president remarked that the commissioner was the first appointment he made. But in 1961 Kennedy referred to Anslinger as "one of the first persons I reappointed." Letter to William T. McCarthy from John F. Kennedy, file ME 1-3/M, John F. Kennedy Presidential Library.

2. Anslinger, *The Protectors*, 87.

3. Anslinger, *The Protectors*, 214–15.

4. Anslinger, *The Protectors*, 216.

5. "New Approach," *Newsweek*, 16 April 1963, 94.

6. "Court Says It's No Crime To Be Narcotics Addict," *Washington Star*, 25 June 1962, AP, box 2, file "Correspondence January–July 1962."

7. "Court Says It's No Crime To Be Narcotics Addict."

8. "Narcotics Agent Scores Leniency," *New York Times*, 22 June 1961, 18.

9. For a more detailed account of the drug issue in the Brown-Knowland 1962 gubernatorial race, see Rufus King, *The Drug Hang-up*, "The White House Conference, 1962–63," 229–39.

10. "How to Qualify as 'Crackpot,'" *Los Angeles Times*, 4 March 1970, AP, box 6, file "Clippings, 1960–1966, 1972, 1975."

11. "How to Qualify as a 'Crackpot."

12. Rufus King, "'The American System': Legal Sanctions To Repress Drug Abuse," in James A. Inciardi and Carl D. Chambers, *Drugs and the Criminal Justice System* (Beverly Hills, Calif.: SAGE Publications, 1974), 27–29.

13. "White House conference on Narcotic Drug Abuse," 20 November 1962, AP, box 8, file "Articles on Drug Addiction."

14. "White House Conference on Narcotic Drug Abuse."

15. "White House Conference on Narcotic Drug Abuse."

16. "Narcotics Bureau Head Retiring," *New York Times*, 2 July 1962, 2.

17. Letter to H. J. Anslinger from Judge Twain Michelsen, 20 July 1962, Papers of Harry J. Anslinger in the Harry S. Truman Presidential Library; Frank Cormier, "Narcotics Chief Is Quitting His Post," *DuBois Courier Express*, 9 July 1967.

18. King, *The Drug Hang-up*, 70.

19. "Narcotics Commissioner Named," *New York Times*, 5 July 1962, p. 2.

20. Letter to the author from Dave Powers, 11 September 1985.

21. "Narcotics Policy Divides Officials," *New York Times*, 9 July 1962, 21.

22. Senator John M. Butler speaking on the appointment of Henry L. Giordano, U.S. Commissioner of Narcotics, 23 August 1962, *Congressional Record*, 87th Cong., 2d sess., 108:17359.

23. *Treasury-Post Office Departments and Executive Office Appropriations, Hearings*, before a subcommittee of the Committee on Appropriations, 90th Cong., 1st sess., 1967, 404–85.

24. *Treasury-Post Appropriations, Hearings*, 405.

25. According to the interviewee who requested anonymity, Giordano was overwhelmed by the pressures of the job and was constantly calling Anslinger at his Hollidaysburg home seeking advice, 13 January 1985.

26. Sterba, "The Politics of Pot," 118.

27. Sterba, "The Politics of Pot," 119.

28. Sterba, "The Politics of Pot," 119.

29. Edward Jay Epstein, *Agency of Fear: Opiates and Political Power in America* (New York: Putnam's Sons, 1977), 105.

30. Information on the internal power struggle is taken from an interview by the author with Thomas Tripodi, an agent with the FBN and CIA from 1960–1985, 30 July 1987, Alexandria, Virginia.

31. Epstein, *Agency of Fear,* 105.

32. David Burnham, "Police Shake-Up Shifts 3 Top Aides in Narcotics Unit," *New York Times,* 17 January 1968, 1.

33. Ironically, one of the agents involved was Frankie Waters, who had worked with Eddie Egan of the New York City Police, in exposing the French Connection, Interview by the author with Thomas Tripodi, one of the special investigators, and Thomas Byrne, currently director of DEA's Intelligence Division, 30 December 1987. Byrne was one of 50 agents indicted in the 1968 scandal.

34. Epstein, *Agency of Fear,* 105.

35. Epstein, *Agency of Fear,* 106. Byrne recalled that "The rule was you had to make two [arrests] a month. It was called an F-58-N. This was the arrest syndrome that if you made two arrests or more, you were good."

36. In response to an FOI request for DEA documents pertaining to its internal security investigation of the New York City office in 1968, the author was informed that all such "records are destroyed after 5 years of closing." Letter from John H. Langer, Chief, Freedom of Information Section, DEA, 17 August 1987. In the first six months of the investigation, thirty agents were fired, six prosecuted. Former Agent Tripodi asserts that Attorney General Clark threatened to put drug enforcement in the FBI if the BNDD was incapable of cleaning up its own operations.

37. Tripodi worked for the CIA from 1962 to 1968.

38. Letter from N. E. Bentsen, Chief, Personnel Management Division to Harry J. Anslinger, 5 August 1969, Anslinger OPM File.

39. Ted Humes, "The Crisis in Drugs," pamphlet, Saint Francis College (Summer, 1969), 8–9. Anslinger's wife, Martha, died of a heart attack at her Pine Street home in Hollidaysburg on 8 October 1961, *Altoona Mirror,* 9 October 1961. Prior to her death, she suffered from multiple sclerosis and since late 1960 had been confined to her room. Letter to William McCarthy from H. J. Anslinger, 26 January 1961, AP, box 2, file "Correspondence 1961."

40. "Hollidaysburg Community Picnic," *Blair Press,* 7 August 1963, 8; "H. J. Anslinger Honored at Hollidaysburg Picnic," *Altoona Mirror,* 9 August 1963?; and "H. J. Anslinger Plaque Placed in Courthouse," *Altoona Mirror,* 16 August 1963,?

41. Humes, "The Crisis in Drugs," 9.

42. Humes, "The Crisis in Drugs," 9.

43. Carol Parks, "Harry Jacob Anslinger: Distinguished Citizen," *Town and Gown,* September 1968, 47.

44. Abe Cobus, interview with author, 16 January 1985, Altoona, Pennsylvania.

45. Interviewee who furnished the author with information about Anslinger's personal life requested anonymity, 13 January 1985. According to the interviewee, "Morphine was the only thing that would relieve it [the pain]."

46. "Obituary of Harry J. Anslinger," *Altoona Mirror,* 15 November 1975; the Rev. John Martin, minister of Hollidaysburg Presbyterian Church, interview with author, 28 January 1985. Anslinger is buried in the Presbyterian cemetery just a few blocks from his Hollidaysburg home.

Epilogue

1. Howard S. Becker, *Outsiders: Studies in the Sociology of Deviance* (New York: The Free Press, 1963), pp. 135–62.

Narcotics in general, since the Marijuana Tax Act, has been perceived as a problem, currently one of staggering epidemic proportion. The greatest controversy lay in who should bear the responsibility for handling it and how it should be categorized. The states, federal government, and the legal and medical professions each have held different views and advocated various approaches to the problem.

See James A. Inciardi, *The War on Drugs: Heroin, Cocaine, Crime, and Public Policy* (Palo Alto, Calif. Mayfield Publishing, 1986), pp. 18–21 and 207–9.

2. Galliher, John F. and Walker, Allynn, "The Puzzle of the Social Origins of the Marihuana Tax Act of 1937," *Journal of Social Problems* 24 (February 1977): 367–76.

3. DeMott, "The Great Narcotics Muddle," p. 47.

4. Lynn White, chief of police of Los Angeles, was a case in point. According to former agent and Los Angeles District Supervisor Howard Chappell, White "got himself well acquainted with Anslinger so he was able to get copies of our national lists [of syndicate crimes] which . . . were strictly in-house books." The chief used these files to write speeches that he delivered before various professional groups in the Los Angeles area. It was an effective way to publicize Anslinger's views on the Mafia.

5. With regard to contemporary public policy and for all the current anti-drug rhetoric from the White House, Inciardi argues that the government's approach to controlling drug abuse "lacks a true commitment" because "federal funding for the prevention and treatment of drug abuse was reduced by the Reagan administration, and in the area of interdiction, many efforts appear to be halfhearted." *War on Drugs*, pp. 209–15.

6. Interviews with both drug enforcement and CIA personnel confirmed that the two agencies routinely exchange information.

7. See, for example, Douglas Kinder and William O. Walker, "Stable Force in a Storm: Harry J. Anslinger and United States Narcotic Foreign Policy, 1930–1962," *Journal of American History* 72 (March 1986): 908–27.

8. The rivalry between the two agencies, however intense it may be, will likely disappear within the next few years if, as rumor has it, they will merge into the FBI. The current top two DEA administrators, John Lawn and Tom Kelly, are former FBI agents.

9. The DEA currently has approximately 2,600 agents, the FBI 9,200.

10. *Organized Crime and Illicit Traffic in Narcotics, Hearing*, pp. 772–89.

11. Beginning in 1982 the DEA began training FBI agents in the nature and characteristics of drug enforcement. Currently all FBI basic agents are given sixteen hours in the fundamentals of drug enforcement. The FBI also conducts familiarization courses for DEA agents. *Drug Enforcement Administration: A Profile* (Washington, D.C.: United States Government Printing Office, March 1986).

12. This includes nineteen field divisions, five district offices, and ninety-six resident offices in the United States. Agents are stationed in sixty offices in the forty-one countries. *Drug Enforcement Administration.*

13. In testifying before the Iran-*Contra* hearings in 1987, Gen. Richard Secord mentioned DEA agents in connection with delivering money in Lebanon to be used for the release of American hostages. Because the DEA pursues drug traffickers, its agents have a legitimate "cover" that allows them to travel inside some Communist bloc countries.

Bibliography

Articles

Allentuck, Samuel, and Karl M. Bowman. "The Psychiatric Aspects of Marihuana Intoxication." *American Journal of Psychiatry* 99 (1942): 248–50.

"Another Problem for the Big Cities." *U.S. News & World Report,* 6 April 1959, 74–78, 80.

Anslinger, Harry J. "A Comparison of Some Important National Narcotic-Control Policies of the United States and Canada." *Food, Drug, Cosmetic Law Journal* 10 (September 1955): 597–603.

————. "Cooperation in Narcotic-Law Enforcement." *Food, Drug, Cosmetic Law Journal* 12 (February 1957): 88–92.

————. "Crime and Narcotics." *The National Sheriff* 3 (January 1951): 3–4.

————. "Criminal and Psychiatric Aspects Associated with Marihuana." *The Union Signal,* 5 February 1944, 77–78.

————. "Drug Addiction." *Journal of the American Medical Association* 144 (September–October 1950): 333.

————. "Federal Legislation: The Reason For Uniform State Narcotic Legislation." *Georgetown Law Journal* 21 (1932–33): 52–61.

————. "The Federal Narcotics Laws." *Food, Drug, Cosmetic Law Journal* 6 (October 1951): 743–48.

————. "Marihuana . . . the Assassin of the Human Mind." *Law Enforcement* 1 (October 1941): 7–10.

————. "Narcotic Addiction as Seen by the Law-Enforcement Officer." *Federal Probation* 21–22 (1957–58): 34–41.

————. "Narcotic-Drug Legislation and Its Further Protective Extension." *Food, Drug, Cosmetic Law Journal* 10 (March 1955): 133–39.

————. "Opium After the War." *American Journal of Correction* 5–6 (1943–44): 10, 28–29.

————. "Organized Protection Against Organized Predatory Crime: Peddling of Narcotic Drugs." *Journal of the American Institute of Criminal Law and Criminology* 24, no. 1 (May–October 1933): 636–55.

————. "Peddling of Narcotic Drugs." *Journal of Criminal Law and Criminology* 24 (September–October 1933): 637–51.

————. "The Psychiatric Aspects of Marihuana Intoxication." Letter to the Editor. *Journal of the American Medical Association* 121 (January–February 1943): 212–13.

————. "Relationship Between Addiction to Narcotic Drugs and Crime." *Bulletin on Narcotics* 3 (April 1951): 1–3.

———. "The Treatment of Drug Addiction." *Food, Drug, Cosmetic Law Journal* 14 (April 1959): 240–47.

Anslinger, Harry J., and Courtney Riley Cooper. "Marihuana: Assassin of Youth." *American Magazine,* July 1937, 18–19, 150–53.

Armstrong, William D., and John Parascandola. "American Concern Over Marihuana in the 1930s." *Pharmacy in History* 14 (1972): 25–35.

"Army Study of Marihuana Smokers Points to Better Ways of Treatment." *Newsweek,* 15 January 1945, 72–73.

Ausubel, David P. "An Evaluation of Recent Adolescent Drug Addiction." *Mental Hygiene* 36 (1952): 373–82.

Barzini, Luigi. "The Real Mafia." *Harper's Magazine,* June 1954, 38–46.

Beck, Clarence W. "Marihuana Menace." *Literary Digest,* January 1938, 26.

Berger, Herbert, and Andrew A. Eggston. "Should We Legalize Narcotics?" *Coronet,* June 1955, 30–35.

Berliner, Arthur K. "The Drug Addict—Criminal or Victim?" *Focus* 33 (May 1954): 78–84.

Bloomquist, Edward R. "Marihuana: Social Benefit or Social Deterrent?" *California Medicine* 106, no. 5 (January 1967): 346–53.

"Blowing Up A Joint." Time, 24 April 1952, 50–51.

Bouquet, J. "Marihuana Intoxication." Letter to the Editor. *Journal of the American Medical Association* 124 (March–April 1944): 1010–11.

Bowman, Karl M. "The Problem of Drug Addiction." *American Journal of Psychiatry* 108 (July 1951–June 1952): 791–92.

———. "Marihuana Problems." Letter to the Editor. *Journal of the American Medical Association* 128 (January–June 1945): 889–90.

Bowrey, L. E., and M. H. Hayes. "Marihuana." *Journal of Criminal Law and Criminology* 23 (March 1933): 1086–98.

Brean, Herbert. "Crooked, Cruel Traffic in Drugs." *Life,* 25 January 1960, 87–98.

———. "Men of Mafia's Infamous Web." *Life,* 1 February 1969, 59–70.

Bromberg, Walter. "Marihuana: A Psychiatric Study." *Journal of the American Medical Association* 113 (July–December 1939): 4–12.

———. "Marihuana Intoxication." *American Journal of Psychiatry* 91 (September 1934): 303–30.

Brown, Clair A. "Marihuana." *Nature Magazine,* July 1938, 271–72.

Caputo, Rudolph R. "The Federal Narcotic Agent." *Law & Order* 6 (December 1958): 6–16.

Charen, Sol. "Facts About Marihuana: A Survey of the Literature." *American Journal of Pharmacy* 117 (1945): 422–30.

Chein, Isidor, and Eva Rosenfeld. "Juvenile Narcotics Use." *Law and Contemporary Problems* 22 (1957): 52–68.

Cheshire, Maxine. "Drugs and Washington, D.C." *Ladies Home Journal,* December 1962, 62, 176–81.

Clausen, John A. "Social and Psychological Factors in Narcotics Addiction." *Law and Contemporary Problems* 22 (1957): 34–51.

Connery, George E. "Control of Narcotic Addiction." *Journal of the American Medical Association* 147 (November–December 1951): 1162–65.

Connolly, Vera. "The Dope Menace." *Good Housekeeping,* 20 January 1955, 90–100.

"Crisis in Hollywood." *Time,* 28 August 1948, 100–101.

"Danger." *Survey Graphic,* April 1938, 221.

DeMott, Benjamin. "The Great Narcotics Muddle." *Harper's Magazine,* March 1962, 46–54.

Dickson, Donald T. "Bureaucracy and Morality: An Organizational Perspective on a Moral Crusade." *Social Problems* 16 (Summer 1968): 143–56.

Douglas, Paul H. "Help Wanted in Washington." *American Magazine,* July 1951, 21, 124–28.

Dowd, Lee George. "Seek Drug to Save Dope Fiends." *Popular Science,* May 1931, 21–22, 134.

"Drug Addicts in America." *Outlook,* 25 June 1919, 315.

"Drugs For Addicts?" *Time,* 12 May 1961, 74–75.

Eddy, Clyde Langston. "One Million Drug Addicts in the United States." *Current History Magazine,* July 1923, 637–43.

"End of the Illicit Drug Traffic Now in Sight." *Literary Digest,* July–September 1938, 19.

"Enforcement of Narcotics Laws." *Nation,* January–June 1930, 284.

Esrati, Arnold E. "How Mild Is Marihuana?" *Magazine Digest,* June 1945, 80–86.

"Facts and Fancies About Marihuana." *Literary Digest,* 24 October 1936, 7–8.

"Federal Regulation of the Medical Use of Cannabis." *Journal of the American Medical Association* 108 (January–June 1937): 1543–44.

Finestone, Harold. "Narcotics and Criminality." *Law and Contemporary Problems* 22 (1957): 69–87.

Fisher, Eunice, C. "Cocaine, Hashish, Marijuana." *Police and Peace Officers Journal* 12 (June 1934): 25–26.

Fossier, A. E. "The Marihuana Menace." *New Orleans Medical and Surgical Journal* 84 (1931): 245–52.

Foulger, John H. "The Marihuana Problem." *Delaware State Medical Journal* 16 (February 1944): 24–28.

Freedman, Estelle B. "'Uncontrolled Desires': The Response to the Sexual Psychopath, 1920–1960." *Journal of American History* 74 (June 1987): 83–106.

Galliher, John F. and Allynn Walker. "The Puzzle of the Social Origins of the Marihuana Tax Act of 1937." *Journal of Social Problems* 24 (February 1977): 367–76.

Gard, Wayne. "Youth Gone Loco." *The Christian Century,* June 1938, 812–13.

Gaskill, Herbert S. "Marihuana: An Intoxicant." *American Journal of Psychiatry* 102 (July 1945–May 1946): 202–4.

Gerrity, John. "The Truth About the 'Drug Menace.'" *Harper's Magazine,* June 1952, 27–31.

Gilbert, Rodney. "Why Dope Clinics Won't Work." *American Mercury,* March 1957, 7–17.

"A Godfather's Fall: Mob Under Fire." *Newsweek,* 30 December 1985, 20–21.

Goettel, Gerard L. "Why the Crime Syndicate Can't Be Touched." *Harper's Magazine,* November 1960, 33–38.

"Green Light For Daniel." *Time,* 27 May 1956, 36.

Grinspoon, Lester. "The Campaign Against Marijuana." *International Journal of Psychiatry* 9 (1970–71): 488–516.

———. "Marihuana." *International Journal of Psychiatry* 9 (1970–71): 488–516.

Hagan, John. "The Legislation of Crime and Delinquency: A Review of Theory, Method, and Research." *Law and Society Review* 14 (Spring 1980): 603–28.

Harney, Malachi L. "The 'New Look' at Narcotics Is Just the Same Old Sack." *Police* 1 (March–April 1959): 28–29.

Himmelstein, Jerome L. "Drug Politics Theory: Analysis and Critique." *Journal of Drug Issues* 8 (1978): 37–52.

"The History of Marihuana." *Newsweek,* 28 November 1938, 29.

Holmes, Raymond. "Marihuana: Our Domestic Narcotic Menace." *The Pacific Coast Journal of Nursing* 38 (January 1942): 12–14.

Howard, Toni. "Dope Is His Business." *Saturday Evening Post,* 27 April 1957, 146–48.

Hughes, James E. "Dope." *State Government* 6–7 (1933–34): 11–14.

Humes, Ted. "The Crisis in Drugs." Saint Francis College, Summer 1969, 8–9.

Jarvis, C. S. "Hashish Smuggling in Egypt." *Living Age,* January 1938, 442–47.

Kinder, Douglas, and William O. Walker. "Stable Force in a Storm: Harry J. Anslinger and United States Narcotic Foreign Policy, 1930–1962." *Journal of American History* 72 (March 1986): 908–27.

King, Rufus. "Narcotic Drug Laws and Enforcement Policies." *Law and Contemporary Problems* 22 (Winter 1957): 113–31.

———. "The Narcotics Bureau and the Harrison Act: Jailing the Healers and the Sick." *Yale Law Journal* 62 (April 1953): 736–49.

———. "Narcotics Regulation." *The Yale Law Journal* 62 (April 1953): 751–87.

Kobler, John. "The Narcotics Dilemma: Crime or Disease?" *Saturday Evening Post,* 8 September 1962, 64–70.

Koeves, Tibor. "Lucky Luciano vs The United Nations." *United Nations World* 3 (1949): 34–38.

Kolb, Lawrence. "Marihuana." *Federal Probation* 2 (July 1938): 22–25.

Landis, John F. "U.S. Narcotic Farm." *Federal Probation* 1 (April 1937): 25–29.

Leach, Henry G. "One More Peril For Youth." *Forum,* January 1939, 1–2.

Lewis, Alfred H. "Marihuana." *Cosmopolitan,* October 1913, 645–55.

Lindesmith, Alfred R. "DOPE: Congress Encourages Traffic." *Nation,* March 1957, 228–31.

———. " 'Dope Fiend' Mythology." *Journal of Criminal Law and Criminology* 31 (May 1940–April 1941): 199–208.

———. "Federal Law and Drug Addiction." *Social Problems* 7 (Summer 1959–Spring 1960): 48–57.

———. "60,000 New Candidates For Jail." *Nation,* January–June 1956, 464.

Lodge, John E. "Why 2,000,000 Americans Are 'Dope' Fiends." *Popular Science Monthly,* June 1930, 42–43, 135–37.

Maas, Peter. "Mafia: The Inside Story." *The Saturday Evening Post,* 10–17 August 1963, 18–25.

McCormack, Randall. "What is Marihuana?" *Hygeia,* October 1937, 898–902.

McGlothlin, William H., and Louis Jolyon West. "The Marihuana Problem: An

Overview." *The American Journal of Psychiatry* 125 (July–September 1968): 370–79.

McLean, Robert N. "Tightening the Mexican Border." *The Survey,* 1 April 1930, 28–29, 54–56.

McNeil, Marshall. "U.S. Starts New War On Traffic in Narcotics." *News Digest,* 27 August 1956, 7.

"Mao's Dope Industry." *America,* 3 April 1954, 310–11.

"Marihuana." *Journal of Home Economics* 17 (September 1938): 477–79.

"Marihuana Addiction." *Social Work Technique* 2 (July 1937): 173–77.

"The Marihuana Bugaboo." *Military Medicine* 93 (July 1943): 94–95.

"Marihuana Found Useful in Certain Mental Ills." *Science News Letter,* 1942, 341–42.

"Marihuana Gives Some A Jag." *Science News Letter,* January 1939, 30.

Marihuana Menaces Youth." *Scientific American,* March 1936, 150–51.

Marihuana More Dangerous Than Heroin or Cocaine." *Scientific American,* May 1938, 293.

"Marihuana: New Federal Tax Hits Dealings in Potent Weed." *Newsweek,* 2 August 1937, 22–23.

"The Marihuana Problem." *Federal Probation* 9–10 (1945–46): 15–22.

"Marihuana Problems." Editorial. *Journal of the American Medical Association* 127 (January–June 1945): 1129.

"Marihuana Smoking Seen As Epidemic Among the Idle." *Science News Letter,* November 1938, 340.

Marihuana Weed Grows Where Rope Factory Failed." *Science News Letter,* January 1938, 38–39.

"Marijuana and Mentality." *Newsweek,* 18 November 1946, 70–71.

"Marijuana May Lurk in Window Boxes." *Science News Letter,* 28 July 1951, 60.

Markovitz, Eli. "Marihuana Problems." Letter to the Editor. *Journal of the American Medical Association* 129 (January–June 1945): 378.

Markovitz, Eli, and Henry J. Myers. "The Marihuana Addict in the Army." *War Medicine* 6 (December 1944): 382–91.

Marshall, Maud A. "Marihuana." *American Scholar* 9 (Winter 1938–39): 95–101.

Meisler, Stanley. "Federal Narcotics Czar." *The Nation,* 20 February 1960, 159–62.

"Menace of Marijuana." *International Medical Digest* 77 (1937): 183–87.

Menke, Frank G. "Hopping Horses." *Esquire,* April 1936, 37, 206–7.

Merrill, Frederick T. "Dangerous Marihuana." *American Journal of Nursing* 38 (July–December 1938): 872–74.

———. "Marihuana Increasing in Use and Terrifying Effects." *Journal of Home Economics* 34 (September 1938): 477–79.

Miller, Donald E. "Narcotic Drug and Marihuana Controls." *Journal of Psychedelic Drugs* 1 & 2 (1967–69): 27–38.

Moore, George H. "The Narcotic Addict Before the Court: A Judge's View-Point." *Federal Probation* 9–10 (1945–46): 3–8.

Moore, Samuel Taylor. "Smashing the Dope Rings." *Forum* 85 (June 1931): 379–84.

"More Dangerous Than Heroin or Cocaine." *Scientific American,* January–June 1938, 293.

Morgan, Patricia A. "The Legislation of Drug Law: Economic Crisis and Social Control." *Journal of Drug Issues* 8 (1978): 53–62.

Musto, David F. "The Marihuana Tax Act of 1937." *Archives of General Psychiatry* 26 (February 1972): 101–8.

"Narcotics: An Ever-Growing Problem." *Newsweek,* 18 May 1951, 20–21.

"New Approach." *Newsweek,* 24 March 1963, 94.

"Old and New Narcotic Perils: World Drug Control in Operation." *United Nations Weekly Bulletin* 3 (July–December 1947): 361–64.

"Our Home Hasheesh Crop." *The Literary Digest,* 3 April 1926, 64–65.

Parks, Carol. "Harry Anslinger: Distinguished Citizen." *Town and Gown,* September 1968, 47.

Parran, Thomas. "The Problem of Drug Addiction." *Public Health Reports* 53 (July–December 1938): 2193–97.

Parry, Albert. "The Menace of Marijuana." *American Mercury,* September–December 1935, 487–89.

Prosser, William L. "The Narcotic Problem." *U.C.L.A. Law Review* 1 (June 1954): 405–546.

"The Race Horse Dope Racket." *Popular Mechanics,* 13 May 1935, 82–83, 122a.

"A Real All-Out War on Drugs." *Family Weekly,* 25 August 1985, 14.

"Reefers on KPFA." *Newsweek,* 1 March 1954, 92.

Reichard, J. D. "The Marihuana Problem." Editorial. *Journal of the American Medical Association* 125 (January–June 1944): 594.

———. "Some Myths About Marihuana." *Federal Probation* 9–10 (1945–1946): 15–22.

Rosenthal, Michael P. "The Legislative Response to Marihuana: When the Shoe Pinches Enough." *Journal of Drug Issues* 7 (1977): 61–77.

"Roundup Time." *Time,* 24 August 1956, 18.

Ryall, G. F. T. "A Year of Racing." *Polo,* July 1934, 13–14.

Schaller, Michael. "The Federal Prohibition of Marihuana." *Journal of Social History* 4 (Fall 1970): 61–74.

Schur, Edwin M. "The Addict and the Law." *Dissent* 7–8 (Winter 1960–Autumn 1961): 43–52.

Skolnick, Jerome H. "Enforcement of Morals." *Southern California Law Review* 41 (Spring–Summer 1968): 588–641.

Smith, Roger. "U.S. Marijuana Legislation and the Creation of A Social Problem." *Journal of Psychedelic Drugs* 1–2 (1967–69): 93–101.

Snider, Arthur J. "The Wicked Weed." *Science Digest,* January–June 1952, 48.

Sondern, Frederick. "Our Global War on Narcotics." *American Mercury,* 7 March 1950, 355–62.

Spencer, R. R. "Marijuana." *Health Officer* 1 (December 1936): 299–305.

Stanley, Eugene. "Marihuana As A Developer of Criminals." *American Journal of Police Science* 2 (1931): 252.

Sterba, James. "The Politics of Pot." *Esquire,* August 1968, 57–64.

Stevens, Alden. "Make Dope Legal." *Harper's Magazine,* 15 October 1952, 40–47.

Stoddart, Dayton. "Race Tracks: A Billion-Dollar Racket With Murder on the Side." *Liberty,* January 1936, 22–26.

Taylor, Arnold H. *American Diplomacy and the Narcotics Traffic, 1900–1939.* Durham, N.C.: Duke University Press, 1969.

Taylor, Paul S. "More Bars Against Mexicans?" *The Survey,* 1 April 1930, 26–27.

"Teen-Age Dope Addicts: New Problem?" *U.S. News & World Report,* 29 June 1951, 18–19.

"Tests Show Marihuana Does Not Help." *Science News Letter,* 29 April 1944, 278.

"Texas Round-up Time." *Time,* 6 August 1955, 18.

"U.S. Narcotics Commr. Rues 'H'wood Hokum' in Dope Film's Happy Ending." *Variety,* 19 October 1955, 38.

Vogel, Victor. H. "Our Youth and Narcotics." *Today's Health,* October 1951, 24–25, 68–71.

Wadden, Thomas A. "We Put the Heat on Washington Dope Peddlers." *Saturday Evening Post,* 3 October 1953, 19–21, 131–34.

Wakefield, Dan. "The Prodigal Powers of Pot." *Playboy,* August 1962, 57–66.

Wallace, George B. "The Marihuana Problem in New York City." *American Journal of Correction* 5–6 (1943–44): 7.

Walton, Robert P. "Marihuana Problems." Letter to the Editor. *Journal of the American Medical Association* 128 (January–June 1945): 283.

Weber, C. M. "Mary Warner." *Health Digest* 3 (1936): 77–80.

"The Weed." *Time,* 19 July 1943, 54–56.

Wells, Bradford. "A Landis for Racing." *Post Time,* July 1935, 6–7, 39.

"What Happens to Marihuana Smokers." *Science Digest,* April 1945, 35–40.

Wilson, Earl. "The Crazy Dreamers." *Collier's,* May–June 1949, 27–32.

Winick, Charles. "The Use of Drugs by Jazz Musicians." *Social Problems* 7 (Winter 1959–60): 240–53.

Winters, S. R. "Marihuana." *Hygeia,* October 1940, 885–87.

Wolf, William. "Uncle Sam Fights a New Drug Menace . . . Marihuana." *Popular Science Monthly,* May 1936, 14–15, 119–20.

Yawger, N. S. "Marihuana: Our New Addiction." *American Journal of the Medical Sciences* 195 (1938): 351–57.

"A Year of the Harrison Narcotic Law." *Survey,* 8 April 1916, 58–61.

Books

Abel, Ernest L. *Marihuana: The First Twelve Thousand Years.* New York: Plenum Press, 1980.

Albini, Joseph L. *The American Mafia: Genesis of A Legend.* New York: Irvington Publisher Inc., 1979.

Allen, Edward J. *Merchants of Menace—The Mafia: A Study of Organized Crime.* Springfield, Ill.: Charles C. Thompson Publisher, 1962.

American Bar Association. Forty-second Annual Conference in Washington, D.C.,

4–10 October 1932. *Uniform Narcotic Drug Act.* Washington, D.C.: Government Printing Office, 1933.

Anderson, Annelise G. *The Business of Organized Crime: A Cosa Nostra Family.* Stanford, Calif.: Hoover Institution Press, 1979.

Anslinger, Harry J., and Dennis Gregory. *The Protectors: Narcotics Agents, Citizens and Officials Against Organized Crime in America.* New York: Farrar, Straus and Company, 1964.

Anslinger, Harry J., and Will Oursler. *The Murderers: The Story of the Narcotics Gangs.* New York: Farrar, Straus and Cudahy, 1961.

Anslinger, Harry J., and William Thompkins. *The Traffic In Narcotics.* New York: Funk & Wagnalls, Inc., 1953.

Becker, Howard S. *Outsiders: Studies in the Sociology of Deviance.* New York: The Free Press, 1963.

Block, Alan. *East Side–West Side: Organizing Crime in New York, 1930–1950.* Swansea, Wales: University College Cardiff Press, 1980.

Bloomquist, Edward R. *Marijuana.* Beverly Hills, Calif.: Glencoe Press, 1968.

———. *Marijuana: The Second Trip.* Beverly Hills, Calif.: Glencoe Press, 1971.

Blum, Richard, H. *Society and Drugs.* San Francisco: Jossey-Bass Inc., 1969.

Bonnie, Richard J. *Marijuana Use and Criminal Sanctions: Essays on the Theory and Practice of Decriminalization.* Charlottesville, Va.: The Michie Company, 1980.

Bonnie, Richard J., and Charles H. Whitebread II. *The Marihuana Conviction: A History of Marihuana Prohibition in the United States.* Charlottesville: University Press of Virginia, 1974.

Brecher, Edward M. *Licit and Illicit Drugs.* Boston: Little, Brown, Company, 1972.

Brown, Anthony Cave. *The Last Hero: Wild Bill Donovan.* New York: Random House, 1982.

Cassidy, William L. *History of the Schools and Training Branch of Secret Services.* San Francisco: Kingfisher Press, 1983.

Chambers, Carl D., and James A. Inciardi. *Drugs and the Criminal Justice System.* Beverly Hills, Calif.: SAGE Publications, 1974.

Chambliss, William J., and Milton Mankoff, eds., *Whose Law, What Order?* New York: John Wiley & Sons, Inc., 1976.

Cole, Jonathan O., and J. R. Wittenborn. *Drug Abuse: Social and Psychopharmacological Aspects.* Springfield, Ill.: Charles C. Thompson, Publisher, 1969.

Cook, Fred J. "Organized Crime: The Strange Reluctance." In *Investigating the FBI.* Edited by Pat Watters and Stephen Gillers. Garden City, New York: Doubleday, Inc., 1979.

———. *The FBI Nobody Knows.* New York: The Macmillan Company, 1964.

Cook, Shirley J. *Variations in Response to Illegal Drug Use: A Comparative Study of Official Narcotic Drug Policies in Canada, Great Britain, and the United States from 1920 to 1979.* Toronto, Ontario: Alcoholism and Drug Addiction Research Foundation, April 1970.

Cooper, Courtney Ryley. *Here's To Crime.* Boston: Little, Brown and Company, 1937.

Cressey, Donald R. *Theft of A Nation: The Structure and Operations of Organized Crime in America.* New York: Harper & Row, Publishers, 1969.

Demaris, Ovid. *The Director: An Oral Biography of J. Edgar Hoover.* New York: Harper's Magazine Press, 1975.

Drug Addiction: Crime or Disease? Interim and Final Reports of the Joint Committee of the American Bar Association and the American Medical Association on Narcotic Drugs. Bloomington: Indiana University Press, 1961.

Duster, Troy. *The Legislation of Morality: Law, Drugs, and Moral Judgment.* New York: The Free Press, 1970.

Eldridge, William Butler. *Narcotics and the Law: A Critique of the American Experiment in Narcotic Drug Control.* New York: New York University Press, 1962.

Epstein, Edward Jay. *Agency of Fear: Opiates and Political Power in America.* New York: G. P. Putnam's Sons, 1977.

Feder, Sid, and Joachim Joesten, *The Luciano Story.* New York: David McKay Company, Inc., 1954.

Feder, Sid, and Burton B. Turkus. *Murder, Inc.* Garden City, New York: Permabooks, 1952.

Fenno, Richard F. *The Power of the Purse: Appropriations Politics in Congress.* Boston: Little, Brown and Company, 1966.

Finlator, John. *The Drugged Nation.* New York: Simon and Schuster, 1973.

Fooner, Michael. *INTERPOL: The Inside Story of the International Crime-Fighting Organization.* Chicago: Henry Regnery Company, 1973.

Forrest, A. J. *INTERPOL.* London: Allan Wingate, 1955.

Fried, Richard M. *Men Against McCarthy.* New York: Columbia University Press, 1976.

Goode, Erich. *Drugs In American Society.* New York: Alfred A. Knopf, 1972.

————, ed., *Marijuana.* New York: Atherton Press, 1970.

Gosch, Martin A., and Richard Hammer. *The Last Testament of Lucky Luciano.* Boston: Little, Brown and Company, 1974.

Griffith, Robert. *The Politics of Fear: Joseph R. McCarthy and the Senate.* Lexington: University Press of Kentucky, 1970.

Grinspoon, Lester. *Marihuana Reconsidered.* Cambridge: Harvard University Press, 1971.

Gusfield, Joseph R. *Symbolic Crusade: Status Politics and the American Temperance Movement.* Urbana: University of Illinois, 1963.

Helbrant, Maurice. *Narcotic Agent.* New York: Vanguard Press, 1941.

Hellman, Arthur D. *Laws Against Marijuana: The Price We Pay.* Urbana: University of Illinois Press, 1975.

Helmer, John. *Drugs and Minority Oppression.* New York: Seabury Press, 1975.

Higgins, Louis L. *Dope-Ology.* Chicago: Chicago Crime Prevention Bureau, 1953.

Hillsman, Roger. *Strategic Intelligence and National Decisions.* Glencoe, Ill: The Free Press, 1956.

Himmelstein, Jerome L. *The Strange Career of Marijuana: Politics and Ideology of Drug Control in America.* Westport, Conn.: Greenwood Press, 1983.

Hinckle, Warren, and William W. Turner. *The Fish Is Red: The Story of the Secret War Against Castro.* New York: Harper & Row, Publishers, 1981.

Hoffman, Abraham. *Unwanted Mexican Americans in the Great Depression:*

Repatriation Pressures, 1929–1939. Tucson: The University of Arizona Press, 1974.

Inciardi, James A. *The War On Drugs: Heroin, Cocaine, Crime, and Public Policy.* Palo Alto, Calif.: Mayfield Publishing Company, 1986.

Inglis, Brian. *The Forbidden Game: A Social History of Drugs.* New York: Charles Scribner's Sons, 1975.

Jenkins, Philip, and Gary Potter. *The City and the Syndicate: Organizing Crime in Philadelphia.* Lexington, Mass.: Ginn Custom Publishing, 1985.

Kaplan, John. *Marihuana: The New Prohibition.* New York: World Publishing Company, 1970.

Kaplan, Susan, and Christy Macy. *Documents.* New York: Penguin Books, 1980.

Katcher, Leo. *The Big Bankroll: The Life and Times of Arnold Rothstein.* New York: Harper & Brothers, 1958.

King, Rufus. "The American System: Legal Sanctions to Repress Drug Abuse," in Carl D. Chambers and James A. Inciardi, *Drugs and the Criminal Justice System.* Beverly Hills, Calif.: SAGE Publications, 1974.

————. *The Drug Hang-up: America's Fifty Year Folly.* New York: Norton & Company, 1972.

Kiplinger, W. M. *Washington Is Like That.* New York: Harper & Brothers, 1942.

Kirkpatrick, Lyman B. *The Real CIA.* New York: Macmillan Company, 1968.

Kittrie, Nicholas N. *The Right to Be Different: Deviance and Enforced Therapy.* Baltimore: Johns Hopkins University Press, 1971.

Kwatny, Jonathan. *The Crimes of Patriots: A True Tale of Dope, Dirty Money, and the CIA.* New York: W. W. Norton & Company, 1987.

Lee, Martin A., and Bruce Schlain. *Acid Dreams: The CIA, LSD and the Sixties Rebellion.* New York: Grove Press, Inc. 1985.

Lindesmith, Alfred R. *The Addict and the Law.* Bloomington: Indiana University Press, 1965.

McClellan, John L. *Crime Without Punishment.* New York: Duell, Sloan and Pearce, 1964.

McCoy, Alfred W. *The Politics of Heroin in Southeast Asia.* New York: Harper & Row, Publishers, 1972.

Marchetti, Victor, and John D. Marks. *The CIA and the Cult of Intelligence.* New York: Alfred A. Knopf, 1974.

Marks, John D. *The Search For the "Manchurian Candidate": The CIA and Mind Control.* New York: Times Books, 1979.

Martin, Raymond V. *Revolt in the Mafia.* New York: Duell, Sloan and Pearce, 1963.

Maurer, David W., and Victor H. Vogel. *Narcotics and Narcotics Addiction.* Springfield, Ill.: Charles C. Thompson, Publisher, 1954.

Mayor's Committee on Marihuana. George B. Wallace, Chairman. *The Marihuana Problem in the City of New York: Sociological, Medical, Psychological, and Pharmacological Studies.* Lancaster, Pa.: Jacques Cattell Press, 1945.

Merrill, Frederick T. *Marihuana, the New Dangerous Drug.* Washington, D.C.: Opium Research Committee, Foreign Policy Association, 1938.

Messick, Hank. *John Edgar Hoover.* New York: David McKay Company, Inc., 1972.

Mezzrow, Milton "Mezz," and Bernard Wolfe. *Really the Blues.* New York: Random House, 1946.

Moore, William H. *The Kefauver Committee and the Politics of Crime.* Columbia: University of Missouri Press, 1974.

Morgan, H. Wayne. *Drugs in America: A Social History, 1800–1980.* Syracuse, N.Y.: Syracuse University Press, 1981.

———. *Yesterday's Addicts: Society and Drug Abuse, 1865–1920.* Norman: University of Oklahoma Press, 1974.

Murtagh, John M., and Sara Harris. *Who Live in Shadow.* New York: McGraw-Hill Book Company, Inc., 1959.

Musto, David F. *The American Disease: Origins of Narcotic Control.* New Haven: Yale University Press, 1973.

Navasky, Victor S. *Kennedy Justice.* New York: Atheneum, 1971.

Nelli, Humbert S. *The Business of Crime: Italians and Syndicate Crime In the United States.* Chicago: University of Chicago Press, 1976.

Oshinsky, David M. *A Conspiracy So Immense: The World of Joe McCarthy.* New York: The Free Press, 1983.

Oteri, Joseph, and Harry Silverglate. "In the Marketplace of Free Ideas: A Look at the Passage of the Marijuana Tax Act." In *Marijuana Myths and Realities.* Edited by J. L. Simmons. North Hollywood, Calif.: Brandon House, 1967.

Oursler, Will. *Marijuana: The Facts The Truth.* New York: Paul Eriksson, Inc., 1968.

Oursler, Will, and Laurence Dwight Smith. *Narcotics: America's Peril.* New York: Doubleday & Company, Inc., 1952.

Powers, Richard Gid. *Secrecy and Power: The Life of J. Edgar Hoover.* New York: The Free Press, 1987.

Powers, Thomas, *The Man Who Kept the Secrets: Richard Helms & the CIA.* New York: Alfred A. Knopf, 1979.

Ranelagh, John. *The Agency: The Rise and Fall of the CIA.* New York: Simon and Schuster, 1986.

Ransom, Harry Howe. *Central Intelligence and National Security.* Cambridge: Harvard University Press, 1959.

Ray, Oakley S. *Drugs, Society, and Human Behavior.* St. Louis: The C. V. Mosby Company, 1972.

Reasons, Charles E. *The Criminologist: Crime and the Criminal.* Pacific Palisades, Calif.: Goodyear Publishing Company, Inc., 1974.

Reeves, Thomas C. *The Life and Times of Joe McCarthy: A Biography.* New York: Stein and Day Publishers, 1982.

Reid, Ed. *Mafia.* New York: Random House, 1952.

Reppetto, Thomas A. *The Blue Parade.* New York: The Free Press, 1978.

Reuter, Peter. *Disorganized Crime: The Economics of the Visible Hand.* Cambridge, Mass.: MIT Press, 1983.

Rice, Jerry N. *Drug Enforcement: The Early Years.* Washington, D.C.: Drug Enforcement Administration, 1986.

Rogin, Michael Paul. *The Intellectuals and McCarthy: The Radical Specter.* Cambridge: MIT Press, 1967.

Ross, Thomas B., and David Wise. *The Invisible Government*. New York: Random House, 1964.

Rowell, Earle Albert, and Robert Rowell. *On the Trail of Marihuana, the Weed of Madness*. Mountain View, Calif.: Pacific Press Publishers Association, 1939.

Rublowsky, John. *The Stoned Age: A History of Drugs in America*. New York: G. P. Putnam's Sons, 1974.

St. Charles, Alwyn J. *The Narcotics Menace*. Los Angeles: Borden Publishing Company, 1952.

Salerno, Ralph, and John S. Tompkins. *The Crime Confederation: Cosa Nostra and Allied Operations in Organized Crime*. New York: Doubleday & Company, Inc., 1969.

Schiavo, Giovanni. *The Truth About the Mafia and Organized Crime in America*. New York: The Vigo Press, 1962.

Schmeckebier, Laurence F. *The Bureau of Prohibition: Its History, Activities and Organization*. Washington, D.C.: The Brookings Institution, 1929.

Schur, Edwin M. *Crimes Without Victims: Deviant Behavior and Public Policy*. Englewood Cliffs, N.J.: Prentice-Hall, Inc., 1965.

Silver, Gary. *The Dope Cronicles, 1850–1950*. San Francisco: Harper & Row, Publishers, 1979.

Siragusa, Charles. *The Trail of the Poppy: Behind the Mask of the Mafia*. Englewood Cliffs, N.J.: Prentice-Hall, Inc., 1966.

Sloman, Larry. *Reefer Madness: Marijuana in America*. New York: The Bobbs-Merrill Company, Inc., 1979.

Smith, David E., ed. *The New Social Drug: Cultural, Medical, and Legal Perspectives on Marijuana*. Englewood Cliffs, N.J.: Prentice-Hall, Inc., 1970.

Smith, Dwight C. *The Mafia Mystique*. New York: Basic Books, Inc., Publishers, 1975.

Smith, Richard Harris. *OSS: The Secret History of America's First Central Intelligence Agency*. Berkeley: University of California Press, 1972.

Soloman, David, ed., *The Marihuana Papers*. New York: The Bobbs-Merrill Company, 1966.

Sondern, Frederick. *Brotherhood of Evil*. New York: Bantam Books, 1960.

Stafford, David. *Camp X*. New York: Dodd, Mead, and Company, 1986.

Sullivan, William C. *The Bureau: My Thirty Years in Hoover's FBI*. New York: W. W. Norton & Company, 1979.

Talese, Gay, *Honor Thy Father*. New York: Dell Publishing Company, 1971.

Taylor, Arnold H. *American Diplomacy and the Narcotic Traffic, 1900–1939*. Durham, N.C.: Duke University Press, 1969.

Tullett, Tom, *Inside Interpol*. New York: Walker and Company, 1965.

Tully, Andrew. *CIA: The Inside Story*. New York: William Morrow and Company, 1962.

———. *Treasury Agent*. New York: Simon and Schuster, 1958.

Tyler, Gus. *Organized Crime in America*. Ann Arbor: University of Michigan Press, 1962.

Ungar, Sanford J. *FBI*. Boston: Little, Brown and Company, 1975.

Vogel, Victor H., and Virginia E. Vogel. *Facts About Narcotics*. Chicago: Science Research Associates, Inc., 1951.

Walker, William O., III. *Drug Control in the Americas.* Albuquerque: University of New Mexico Press, 1981.

Walton, Robert P. *Marihuana: America's New Drug Menace.* Philadelphia: J. B. Lippincott, 1938.

War Report of the OSS. New York: Walker and Company, 1975.

Wilson, James Q. *The Investigators: Managing FBI and Narcotics Agents.* New York: Basic Books, Inc., Publishers, 1978.

Correspondence

Chrysohos, Stanley S. Chief, Freedom of Information Act, Drug Enforcement Administration, Washington, D.C. Letter to author, 16 January 1986.

Laughlin, Jane M., Disclosure Office, Internal Revenue Service, New York City. Letter to author, 14 January 1986.

Murphy, James J., St. Louis attorney. Letter to Jon M. Austin, Press Secretary to U.S. Senator Thomas F. Eagleton, July 1985. Letter forwarded to author 28 August 1985.

Perretta, A. W., Tax Specialist, Internal Revenue Service, Washington, D.C. Letter to author 12 December 1985.

Powers, Dave, former White House aide to President John F. Kennedy. Letter to author, 11 September 1985.

Government Documents

U.S. Congress, House. Congressman Victor Anfuso commenting on H.R. 3490, 21 June 1951. *Congressional Record.* 82nd Cong., 1st sess. Vol. 97.

———. Congressman Loring M. Black introducing H. Res. 98, 9 January 1932. *Congressional Record.* 72d Cong. 1st sess. Vol. 75.

———. Congressman Hale Boggs introducing H.R. 3490, 3 April 1951. *Congressional Record.* 82nd Cong. 1st sess. Vol. 97.

———. Congressman Fred E. Busbey commenting on H. R. 8700, 2 April 1954. *Congressional Record.* 83d Cong. 2d sess. Vol. 100.

———. Remarks of Congressman Gordon Canfield, 8 July 1590. *Congressional Record.* 81st Cong. 2d sess. Vol. 96.

———. Congressman Emanuel Celler Debating H.R. 3490, 16 July 1951. *Congressional Record.* 82d Cong. 1st sess. Vol. 97.

———. Remarks of Congressman John J. Cochran, 10 February 1943. *Congressional Record.* 78th Cong. 1st sess. Vol. 89.

———. Congressman John M. Coffee speaking for a survey of the Narcotic Drug Conditions in the United States by the Public Health Service, 7 April 1938. *Congressional Record.* H. Res. 642, 75th Cong., 3d sess. Vol. 83.

———. Congressman John M. Coffee introducing H. Res. 642, 17 April 1938. *Congressional Record.* 75th Cong. 3d sess. Vol. 83.

———. Extension of Remarks of Congressman John M. Coffee, 14 June 1938. *Congressional Record.* 75th Cong., 3d sess. Vol. 83.

———. Congressman John Dempsey introducing H.R. 6145, 25 February 1935. *Congressional Record.* 74th Cong. 1st sess. Vol. 79.

———. Congressman Robert L. Doughton introducing H.R. 10585, 24 January 1936. *Congressional Record.* 74th Cong. 2d sess. Vol. 80.

———. Congressman Robert L. Doughton introducing H.R. 6385, 14 April 1937. *Congressional Record.* 75th Cong., 1st sess. vol. 81.

———. Congressman Hamilton Fish introducing H.R. 14136. 10 January 1933. *Congressional Record.* 72d Cong. 2d sess. Vol. 76.

———. Congressman Hamilton Fish introducing H.R. 229, 5 January 1937. *Congressional Record.* 75th Cong. 1st sess. Vol. 81.

———. Congressman Thomas C. Hennings introducing H.R. 3873, 9 January 1937. *Congressional Record.* 75th Cong. 1st sess. Vol. 81.

———. Remarks of Congressman Fiorella H. LaGuardia, 5 December 1930. *Congressional Record.* 71st Cong. 3d sess. Vol. 72.

———. Occupation Excise Tax on Marihuana, H.R. 6906, 75th Cong., 1st sess., 10 June 1937. *Congressional Record,* vol. 81.

———. Congressman Stephen G. Porter introducing H.R. 9054, 23 January 1930. *Congressional Record.* 71st Cong. 2d sess. Vol. 72.

———. Congressman Stephen G. Porter introducing H.R. 11143, 26 March 1930. *Congressional Record.* 71st Cong. 2d sess. Vol. 72.

———. Congressman William H. Stafford speaking on H.R. 3394, 2 July 1930. *Congressional Record.* 71st Cong. 1st sess. Vol. 74.

———. Tax on Marihuana, H.R. 6906, 26 July 1937. *Congressional Record.* 75th Cong., 1st sess. Vol. 81.

U.S. Congress. House. Committee on Appropriations. *Treasury Department Appropriations Bill for 1936. Hearings before a subcommittee of the House Committee on Appropriations,* 74th Cong. 1st sess. 1934.

———. *Treasury Department Appropriations Report for 1943. Hearings before the Committee on Appropriations,* 77th Cong., 2d sess., 1943.

———. *Treasury-Post Office Departments and Executive Office Appropriations. Hearings before a subcommittee of the Committee on Appropriations,* 90th Cong., 1st sess., 1967.

———. Committee on the Judiciary. *Establishment of Two Narcotic Farms. Hearings before the Committee on the Judiciary on H.R. 12781 and H.R. 13645,* 70th Cong., 1st sess., 1928.

———. Committee on Ways and Means. *Bureau of Narcotics. Hearings before the Committee on Ways and Means on H.R. 10561,* 71st Cong., 2d sess., 1930.

———. *Control of Narcotics, Marihuana, and Barbiturates. Hearings before a subcommittee of the Committee on Ways and Means on H.R. 3490,* 82nd Cong., 1st sess., 1951.

———. *Secret Service Reorganization Act. Hearings before the Committee on Ways and Means on H.R. 11452,* 74th Cong., 2d sess., 1936.

———. *Taxation of Marihuana. Hearings before the Committee on Ways and Means on H.R. 6385,* 75th Cong., 1st sess., 1937.

———. *Traffic In, and Control of, Narcotics, Barbiturates, and Amphetamines. Hearings before a subcommittee of the Committee on Ways and Means,* 84th Cong., 1st sess., 1955.

U.S. Congress. Senate. Senator John M. Butler speaking on the appointment of Henry L. Giordano, U.S. Commissioner of Narcotics, 23 August 1962. *Congressional Record.* 87th Cong. 2d sess. Vol. 108.

———. Senator Royal S. Copeland's remarks on H.R. 1143, 22 April 1930. *Congressional Record.* 71st Cong. 2d sess. vol. 72.

———. Senator Royal S. Copeland speaking on the confirmation of Harry J. Anslinger, 18 December 1930. *Congressional Record.* 71st Cong. 3d sess., Vol. 74.

———. Senator Price Daniel introducing S. Res. 67, 18 March 1955. *Congressional Record.* 84th Cong. 1st sess. Vol. 101.

———. Senator Carl Hatch introducing S. 1615, 4 February 1935. *Congressional Record.* 74th Cong. 1st sess. Vol. 79.

———. Senator Carl Hatch introducing S. 325, 6 January 1937. *Congressional Record.* 75th Cong. 1st sess. Vol. 81.

———. Senator Frederick G. Payne commenting on the Control of Narcotic Drugs, 25 May 1956. *Congressional Record.* 84th Cong. 2d sess. Vol. 102.

———. The Control of the Illicit Drug Traffic, 30 April 1956. *Congressional Record.* 84th Cong. 2d sess. Vol. 102.

U.S. Congress. Senate. Committee on Foreign Relations. *International Opium Protocol. Hearings before a subcommittee of the Senate Foreign Relations Committee,* 83d Cong., 2d sess., 1954.

———. Committee on Human Resources. *Human Drug Testing By the CIA, 1977. Hearings before a subcommittee on Health and Scientific Research of the Committee on Human Resources on S. 1893,* 95th Cong., 1st sess. 1977.

———. Committee on Immigration. *Deportation of Aliens Convicted of A Violation of Narcotic Law. Hearings before the Committee on Immigration on S. 3394,* 71st Cong. 3d sess., 1931.

———. Committee on the Judiciary. *Communist China and Illicit Narcotic Traffic. Hearings before the subcommittee to Investigate the Administration of the Internal Security Act and Other Internal Security Laws,* 84th Cong., 1st sess., 1955.

———. *Juvenile Delinquency. Hearings before a subcommittee to Investigate Juvenile Delinquency on S. Res. 89,* 83rd Cong., 1st sess., 1953.

———. *Juvenile Delinquency. Hearings before the subcommittee to Investigate Juvenile Delinquency on S. Res. 54,* 86th Cong., 1st sess., 1959.

———. *Illicit Narcotics Traffic. Hearings before the subcommittee on Improvements in the Federal Criminal Code of the Committee of the Judiciary on S. Res. 67,* Part I, 84th Cong., 1st sess., 1955.

———. Select Committee on the Investigation of Improper Activities in the Labor Management Field. *Hearings.* Part 32, 85th Cong., 2d sess. 158.

———. Senate. Special Committee to Investigate Organized Crime in Interstate Commerce. *Hearings on S. Res. 202 and S. Res. 129.* 82d Cong., 1st sess., 1951.

U.S. Department of Health, Education, and Welfare. *Narcotic Drug Addiction Problems: Proceedings of the Symposium on the History of Narcotic Drug Addiction Problems,* 27–28 March 1958, Bethesda, Maryland. Washington, D.C.: Government Printing Office, 1958.

U.S. Department of Justice. National Institute of Justice. *A Guide to Interpol: The International Criminal Police Organization in the United States.* Washington, D.C.: Government Printing Office, 1985.

U.S. Department of the Treasury. *Annual Reports of the Commissioner of Narcotics For the Fiscal Year Ended June 30, 1931* through *June 30, 1960.* Washington, D.C.: Government Printing Office, 1932.

———. *Annual Reports of the Secretary of the Treasury,* 1930–1962. U.S. Department of the Treasury, Washington, D.C.: Government Printing Office.

———. National Commission and Marihuana Drug. Abuse. *Marihuana: A Signal of Misunderstanding.* Washington, D.C.: Government Printing Office, March 1972.

———. *Comments on Narcotic Drugs: Interim Report of the Joint Committee of the American Bar Association and the American Medical Association on Narcotic Drugs.* Washington, D.C.: Government Printing Office, 1959.

———. *Traffic in Opium and Other Dangerous Drugs For the Year Ended December 31, 1932* through *December 31, 1964.* Washington, D.C.: Government Printing Office, 1932.

———. *Uniform Narcotic Drug Act Drafted by the National Conference of Commissioners on Uniform State Laws, 4–12 October 1932.* Washington, D.C.: Government Printing Office, 1933.

Interviews with Author

Angleton, James J. Telephone interviews, 19 December 1986, Falls Church, Va.

Anonymous. 13 January 1985, Hollidaysburg, Pa.

Anslinger, Bea. Telephone interviews, 23 January and 9 October 1985, Hollidaysburg, Pa.

Anslinger, William R. Telephone interviews, 10 January and 21 March 1985, Hollidaysburg, Pa.

Belk, George. 7 January 1987, Washington, D.C.

Chappell, Howard. 17 January 1987, Paso Robles, Calif.

Cobus, Abe. 16 January 1985, Altoona, Pa.

Colantino, Thomas. 26 March 1985, Hollidaysburg, Pa.

Cooper, Glen, Special Agent in Charge, Newark. 13 August 1986, Newark, N.J.

Cusack, John T. 7 January 1987, Washington, D.C.

Emerson, Sylva, Blair County Historical Society. 23 January 1985, Hollidaysburg, Pa.

Gaffney, George H. Telephone interview, 26 January 1987, Missoula, Mont.

Giordano, Henry L. 25 March 1985, Silver Spring, Md.

Lusardi, Cornelius. 26 March 1985, Hollidaysburg, Pa.

Martin, John, the Rev. 23 January 1985, Hollidaysburg, Pa.

Means, John, Freedom of Information Act Officer, Drug Enforcement Administration, Washington, D.C. Telephone interview, 17 October 1985.

Picini, Michael G. 29 July 1987, Alexandria, Va.

Tripodi, Thomas. 30 July 1987, Alexandria, Va.

Van Zandt, Jimmy. Telephone interviews, 30 January and 13 March 1985, Arlington, Va.

Withrow, James, member of law firm of Donovan, Leisure, Newton, and Irvine. Telephone interview, 5 February 1985, New York City.

Newspapers

Anderson, Jack. "Castro Has A New Weapon: Dope." *Washington Post,* 29 July 1962.

"Anslinger Suit Figure Sought in Mafia Probe." *Altoona Mirror,* 4 August 1965.

"Anslinger Suit Trial Shifted to Pittsburgh." *Altoona Mirror,* 14 May 1965.

"Assumes New Duty As Treasury Aide." *New York Times,* 2 October 1940.

"Bar Urges Reform." *New York Times,* 19 February 1955.

"Bill Sinks Teeth In Narcotics Code." *New York Times,* 15 January 1955.

Burnham, David. "Police Shake-up Shifts 3 Top Aides in Narcotics Unit." *New York Times,* 17 January 1968.

"Commissioner Sued For Libel." *Altoona Mirror,* 29 January 1965.

"Congressman Says Federal Men Protected Diamond." *New York Times,* 11 February 1932.

Cormier, Frank. "Narcotics Chief Is Quitting His Post." *DuBois Courier Express,* 9 July 1967.

Crewdson, John M. "Ex-C.I.A. Aide Asks Immunity to Testify." *New York Times,* 7 September 1977.

———. "Files Show Tests For Truth Drugs Began in O.S.S." *New York Times,* 5 September 1977.

"Cuba Puts Luciano in Detention, Seeks End of U.S. Narcotics Ban." *New York Times,* 23 February 1947.

"Cuba Will Deport Luciano to Italy." *New York Times,* 25 February 1947.

"Drug Addict Ban Puzzles Director." *New York Times,* 10 May 1949.

"Ex-Narcotics Commissioner Sued For Libel." *Altoona Mirror,* 30 January 1965.

"Expect Altoonan Will Be Retained." *Altoona Mirror,* 28 March 1933.

"'Fugitive' Label On Addicts Urged." *New York Times,* 20 September 1951.

"Gang Strife Landed to Apalachin Edict Against Narcotics." *New York Times,* 28 February 1960.

"Gene Krupa is Arrested." *New York Times,* 21 January 1943.

"Genovese Given 15 Years in Prison In Narcotics Case." *New York Times,* 18 April 1959.

"Genovese Guilty in Narcotics Plot." *New York Times,* 4 April 1959.

"H. J. Anslinger Honored at Hollidaysburg Picnic." *Altoona Mirror,* 9 August 1963.

"H. J. Anslinger Plaque Placed in Courthouse." *Altoona Mirror,* 16 August 1963.

"Hollidaysburg Community Picnic." *Blair Press,* 7 August 1963.

Horrock, Nicholas M. "Files on C.I.A. Drug-Testing Work Said to List 'Prominent Doctors.'" *New York Times,* 17 July 1977.

Jacobs, John. "The Diaries of A CIA Operative," *Washington Post,* 4 September 1977.

Krupa Gets 1 to 6 Years." *New York Times,* 3 July 1943.

"Krupa Sentenced in Drug Case." *New York Times,* 19 May 1943.

"Luciano to Leave Cuba in 48 Hours." *New York Times,* 24 February 1947.

"Luciano War Aid Called Ordinary." *New York Times,* 27 February 1947.

"Marijuana Camp Sales Fought." *New York Times,* 5 February 1944.

Marro, Anthony. "Drug Tests by C.I.A. Held More Extensive Than Reported in '75." *New York Times,* 16 July 1977.

Meese, Edwin. "Speech delivered before the Knights of Columbus Convention." *New York Times,* 8 August 1985.

Morgenthau Favors Tapping of Wires in Treasury Agents' War on Narcotics." *New York Times, 16 October 1934.*

"Murtagh Scores Narcotics Chief." New York Times, 25 May 1959.

"Murtagh Sees U.S. Lax in Enforcing Narcotic Act Here." *New York Times,* 9 August 1959.

"Narcotic Aide Bars Criticism of Court." *New York Times,* 19 March 1960.

"Narcotics Agent Scores Leniency." *New York Times,* 22 June 1961.

"Narcotics Bureau Head Retiring." *New York Times,* 2 July 1962.

"Narcotics Commissioner Named." *New York Times,* 5 July 1962.

"Narcotics Commissioner Pegged Mafia Years Ago." *Hollidaysburg Blair Press,* 2 October 1963.

"Narcotics-Counterfeit Ring Broken With Seizure of 9 in Federal Trap." *New York Times,* 28, 1951.

"Narcotics Drop Reported." *New York Times,* 21 January 1952.

"Narcotics Policy Divides Officials." *New York Times,* 9 July 1962.

"Narcotics Traffic Is Curbed By War." *New York Times,* 27 September 1942.

"Narcotics Users Are Put at 60,000." *New York Times* 3 June 1955.

"Native Altoonan Handles Big Job Combatting Dope." *Altoona Mirror,* 26 June 1939.

"New York Physician Scores Anslinger." *New York Times,* 8 February 1959.

"Obituary of Harry J. Anslinger." *Altoona Mirror,* 15 November 1975.

"Obituary of Martha Anslinger." *Altoona Mirror,* 10 September 1961.

Pearson, Drew. "Luciano Talked Freely But Revealed Little." *Washington Post,* 15 March 1962.

"Retirement of Robert Anslinger." *Altoona Mirror,* 30 November 1926.

"Roosevelt Opposes Merger Plan." *New York Times,* 20 April 1933.

"Senate Confirms Harry Anslinger." *Altoona Mirror,* 20 December 1930.

"6 Imprisoned by U.S. in Narcotics Ring; Stromberg, Leader Gets 5 Years and Fine." *New York Times,* 24 April 1958.

"Soviet Retorts on Heroin." *New York Times,* 3 May 1952.

"Tax Aide Resigns: Own Returns Eyed." *New York Times,* 27 November 1949.

"Taxpayers Trim U.S. at $116 A Clip." *New York Times,* 5 May 155.

Thomas, Jo. "C.I.A. Says It Found More Secret Papers on Behavior Control." *New York Times,* 3 September 1977.

"Urge Altoonan As Narcotics Chief." *Altoona Mirror,* 20 December 1930.

"U.S. Aide's Attack on Film Assailed." *New York Times,* 25 October 1955.

"U.S. Charges China Spurs Drug Habit." *New York Times,* 5 May 1954.

"U.S. Ends Narcotics Sales to Cuba While Luciano Is Resident There." *New York Times,* 22 February 1947.

Special Collections

Anslinger, Harry J. Official Personnel File, U.S. Office of Personnel Management, Philadelphia.

———. Papers. Thirteen boxes covering the period 1920–70. Pattee Library, Pennsylvania State University, University Park, Pa.

Dewey, Thomas E. Papers. University of Rochester, Rochester, New York.

Donovan, William J. Papers, Army War College, Carlisle, Pa.

Drug Enforcement Administration, Library, Washington, D.C.

Eisenhower, Dwight D. Presidential Library, Abilene, Kansas.

Hoover, Herbert. Presidential Library, West Branch, Iowa.

Kennedy, John F. Presidential Library, Dorchester, Mass.

Manfredi, Henry L. Official Personnel File, U.S. Office of Personnel Management, Philadelphia.

OSS Operational, Administrative, and Support Records, Records Group 226, National Archives and Records Service, Washington, D.C.

Records of the Bureau of Narcotics and Dangerous Drugs. Record Group 170, Civil Archives Division of the National Archives, Suitland, Md.

Roosevelt, Franklin D. Presidential Library, Hyde Park, N.Y.

Siragusa, Charles. Official Personnel File, U.S. Office of Personnel Management, Philadelphia.

Truman, Harry S. Presidential Library, Independence, Mo.

White, George H. Diaries. Perham Electronics Museum, Los Altos, Calif.

———. Official Personnel File. U.S. Office of Personnel Management, Philadelphia.

Index